Nigerian Government and Politics under Military Rule, 1966–79

edited by

OYELEYE OYEDIRAN

St. Martin's Press New York

First published in the United States of America in 1979

ISBN 0–312–57272–7

Library of Congress Cataloging in Publication Data

Main entry under title:

Nigerian Government and politics under
military rule, 1966–1979.

Includes index.
1. Nigeria – Politics and government – 1960 –
Addresses, essays, lectures.
2. Nigeria – Armed Forces – Political activity –
Addresses, essays, lectures.
I. Oyediran, Oyeleye. II. Title.
JQ3083 1979.N54   320.9'669'05   79–15018

ISBN 0–312–57272–7

Printed and bound in Great Britain
at The Pitman Press, Bath

Contents

	Acknowledgements	vi
	Contributors	vii
	Introduction	ix
1	Background to military rule – *Oyeleye Oyediran*	1
2	The civil war – *Turi Muhammadu and Mohammed Haruna*	25
3	The military and the economy – *Akin Iwayemi*	47
4	The civil service: an insider's view – *P. Chiedo Asiodu*	73
5	The civil service: an outsider's view – *Stephen O. Olugbemi*	96
6	The press and military rule – *Lateef Kayode Jakande*	110
7	Foreign policy and military rule – *Ray Ofoegbu*	124
8	Mohammed/Obasanjo foreign policy – *A. Bolaji Akinyemi*	150
9	Local government and administration – *Oyeleye Oyediran and E. Alex Gboyega*	169
10	The military and the politics of revenue allocation – *Oyeleye Oyediran and Olatunji Olagunju*	192
11	Dilemma of military disengagement – *J. 'Bayo Adekson*	212
12	The making of the Nigerian constitution – *E. Alex Gboyega*	235
13	The struggle for power in Nigeria, 1966–79 – *A. D. Yahaya*	259
14	Civilian rule for how long? – *Oyeleye Oyediran*	276
	Notes	288
	Select Bibliography	307
	Appendix	311

Acknowledgements

The idea for this book arose during one of those well known corridor discussions at the Faculty of the Social Sciences, University of Ibadan, shortly after the speech of the head of state, Lieutenant-General Olusegun Obasanjo, to the members of the Constituent Assembly in April 1978 when that body appeared to be deadlocked on the issue of Sharia. I want to thank my colleague 'Bayo Adekson who is a contributor for suggesting to me the need to include this assessment of the impact of military rule on the Nigerian political and governmental processes and institutions among my immediate projects. I also thank him for offering criticisms on my paper in chapter 1.

To Ms Chiu-Yin Wong (together with her colleague in Ibadan, Agbo Areo) goes the credit for persuading me by her frequent letters, cablegrams and visit to suspend work on another project. Without Ms Wong's special interest in this work it probably would not have seen the light of day.

I should like to thank all contributors for meeting my very strict deadline and especially Philip Asiodu for suggesting the inclusion of the chapter on the politics of revenue allocation. I am also grateful to Kofo Popoola and partners for providing some typing assistance. Finally, by tolerating my frequent absences from home, my wife and children (in particular, my son Oyelola) have been helpful in so many ways.

Oyeleye Oyediran

13 January 1979

Contributors

Dr J. 'Bayo Adekson
Lecturer, Department of Political Science, University of Ibadan

Dr A. Bolaji Akinyemi
Director-General, Nigerian Institute of International Affairs

P. Chiedo Asiodu
Former Permanent Secretary, Federal Ministry of Power and President, Nigerian Economic Society

Dr E. Alex Gboyega
Lecturer, Department of Political Science, University of Ibadan

Malam Mohammed Haruna
Associate Editor, New Nigerian Newspapers Limited

Dr Akin Iwayemi
Lecturer, Department of Economics, University of Ibadan

Alhaji Lateef Kayode Jakande
Former President of the International Press Institute, First President of the Newspaper Proprietors Association of Nigeria, and Managing Editor, African Newspapers of Nigeria Limited

Malam Turi Muhammadu
Managing Director, New Nigerian Newspapers Limited

Dr Ray Ofoegbu
Senior Lecturer, Department of Political Science, University of Nigeria, Nsukka

Olatunji Olagunju
Political Division, Federal Cabinet Office

Dr Stephen O. Olugbemi
Lecturer, Department of Political Science, University of Lagos

Dr Oyeleye Oyediran
Senior Lecturer, Department of Political Science, University of Ibadan

Dr A. D. Yahaya
Head, Department of Political Science, Ahmadu Bello University, Zaria

Introduction

With the exception of Panter-Brick's *Soldiers and Oil* the existing literature on the military in Nigeria has concentrated either on the structure of and recruitment into the Nigerian army or the intervention of the military in politics. As the military prepares to return political power to a civilian government it is necessary to examine the impact of its thirteen-year rule on the Nigerian political system. Instead of adopting an institutional approach as used by Mackintosh in his study of the Nigerian political system during the first era of civilian government, it was decided that it would be more fruitful if readers are exposed to an analysis of how Nigerian specialists in different fields see the effect of military rule on the processes and institutions of certain aspects of government and politics. A limiting factor in our choice of topics has been space. We realise that not all aspects of the political system have been included for an in-depth analysis. It is hoped, however, that no critical area has been left out.

Two different views have been included on both the civil service and foreign policy. At least two of the contributors questioned this. On foreign policy in particular, the intention is not to give geo-political views of this issue. Neither is it being claimed that this area (or the civil service) is more important than any other. Nigerian foreign policy, however, has been more controversial among academics during military rule than ever before. Furthermore, it is during military rule that Nigerian academics have been seriously involved in the formulation of Nigerian foreign policy.

While claiming publicly to be an 'outsider' in the formulation of Nigerian foreign policy, the director-general of the Nigerian Institute of International Affairs, Dr Bolaji Akinyemi, has shown in his contribution that he was in a unique position between 1975 and 1979 to give more of an 'insider's' view. One of the critics of Nigerian foreign policy particularly since 1976 has been Dr Ray Ofoegbu, who has presented an 'outsider's' view.

On the civil service two views are presented because of the unusual relationship between 'the practitioners' and 'the academics' who have consistently seen the role of the other in the development of the country as contradictory. Mr Asiodu who presents an insider's view of the civil service was regarded by many, both within and outside the service, as one of the most powerful permanent secretaries during the Gowon days. As late as 1974 a very senior army officer referred to him as one of the six permanent secretaries ruling Nigeria. In his contribution, as in his other writings, he has been a strong defender of the civil service in general and the federal civil service in particular. The 'outsider's' view by Dr Stephen Olugbemi is intended to represent the academic's view of the practitioner and to provide a necessary balance.

Students of civil–military relations have tried to develop theories to explain military intervention in the politics of developing countries. As usual no single theory has been accepted as adequate. Rather than become involved in the debate on the adequacy or otherwise of these explanations, chapter 1 is devoted to an examination of the unfolding of the critical factors which in Nigeria eventually culminated in the takeover of political power by the military. In this chapter attention is focussed on the following: the constitutional background, north–south and ethnic conflicts, minority group politics, the structural dilemmas of the Nigerian army, and the chain of immediate political events preceding the takeover.

In many ways the civil war in Nigeria can be and has been regarded as both a blessing and a curse. Whatever one's view, that event in Nigerian political history is an important landmark which occurred during military rule. What were the causes? To what extent did international financial and diplomatic interest prolong the war? How did the Nigerian economy absorb the financial implications? These and other questions are what Turi Muhammadu and Mohammed Haruna attempt to answer in chapter 2.

The era of military rule witnessed a phenomenal growth in government revenue. According to the Aboyade Commission on Revenue Allocation, federally derived revenue rose from ₦785 million in 1970/71 to ₦6103 million in 1976/7. This resulted in the establishment of a variety of unduly large projects all over the country, many of which were abandoned during the closing years of military rule. Has the growth in financial resources resulted in actual development in Nigeria? How have the various sectors of the economy fared during this period? In chapter 3, Akin Iwayemi examines the effects of military rule on the nation's economy.

As pointed out above, the civil service has been given some emphasis. In chapter 4 the focus is on the impact of military rule on the service while in chapter 5 Stephen Olugbemi concentrates on the role of the senior civil servants on development during military rule. In his view not only are the seemingly commendable contributions of the civil service based on half-truths, but the service has through its advocates and admirers overblown its importance to the Nigerian state. This is indeed a strong indictment which has been answered by Chiedo Asiodu.

What should be the role of the press under military rule in Nigeria? How has the press performed that role? These are the central themes developed in Lateef Jakande's contribution. After a period of benign neglect, the military in 1976 decided to recognise local governments as the third tier of governmental activity in Nigeria. In chapter 9 Oyediran and Gboyega review the debate during the first few years of military rule of whether Nigeria should replace local government with local administration; they analyse the varied policies of state governments on this issue, and summarise the broad features of the nation-wide reforms of 1976.

Revenue-sharing or revenue allocation as a political issue is a permanent feature in most federations. In Nigeria the military, by the nature of its command structure, attempted to depoliticise the issue. Even in its closing days, the military made serious attempts to leave behind for a new civilian government a revenue allocation system devoid of strong political factors. That attempt failed because, as Oyediran and Olagunju point out in chapter 10, the sharing of revenue, like budgeting, is inextricably linked to the political system.

While the problem of civilian succession to political leadership under the military is the concern of Adekson in chapter 11, Gboyega in the following chapter analyses the various attempts to make a constitution for Nigeria during military rule. Much attention is devoted in this chapter to the processes and issues that arose during the making of the 1979 constitution which is to usher in a new civilian government.

Even though the new constitution is scheduled to take effect in 1979, the struggle for power by politicians started much earlier. What group formations have emerged? Which interests are represented in this struggle and what are their chances? Ali Yahaya attempts to decipher these puzzles in chapter 13. The final chapter is speculative. As its title indicates, the aim is to suggest on the basis of available evidence how long civilian rule may last.

1 Background to military rule

Oyeleye Oyediran

Academic interest in direct military intervention in African politics started recently. Until the middle 'sixties, students of African political change directed their attention to the role of political parties, charismatic leaders, institutional transfer, and such other independent political forces. It has been suggested that the lack of interest in the military as a political force is due in large measure to the manner in which the imperial powers granted independence to African countries. Unlike in many Latin American countries, independence in most African countries was granted through constitutional negotiation rather than through military action. This peaceful transfer of power gave considerable advantage to other political forces in the task of nation-building. The failure of these forces helped to prepare the way for the military.[1]

Two major schools of thought have developed in the attempt to explain military intervention in the politics not only of African countries, but also of all developing nations. Janowitz has put forward what is now labelled 'the internal characteristics' model.[2] In this model he suggests that one can explain military intervention in politics mainly by reference to the internal structure of the military. In other words, the social background of the officers, the skill structure and career lines, internal social cohesion and cleavages, professional and political ideology within the military are important factors which help to explain direct military intervention in politics. This is Janowitz's answer to the question, 'What characteristics of the military establishment of a new nation facilitate its involvement in domestic politics?'[3]

The second school of thought regards the first explanation as fallacious. Samuel Huntington's ground for this conclusion is based on the contention that 'military explanations do not explain military interventions' and 'that the most important causes of military intervention in politics are not military but political.'[4] This in Huntington's view is because military intervention in developing countries is only one specific manifestation of general politicisation of social forces and institutions. Societies where most social forces and institutions are highly politicised have political clergy, political universities, political bureaucracies, political labour unions, political corporations, and of course political armed forces. All these specialised groups tend to become involved in political issues which affect their particular interest or groups and also in issues which affect society as a whole. As a result the whole society is out of joint, and no political institution or group of political leaders is recognised or accepted as the legitimate intermediary to moderate conflicts between groups. Furthermore, in such societies, no agreement exists among the groups as to the legitimate and authoritative methods of resolving conflicts.

How useful are these models for analysing the background to military rule in Nigeria? For our purpose, Huntington's model appears more applicable. This, of course, is not to suggest that the internal dynamics model of Janowitz is completely irrelevant. As Adekson has suggested, the two models represent opposite sides of the same coin. Consequently, it is more useful to approach military takeover of political power in African countries not by accepting one and neglecting the other, but by synthesising the two models, thereby combining the advantages in each.[5]

One of the greatest problems facing anyone trying to examine the background to military rule in Nigeria is in determining precisely when the seeds of the takeover and the accompanying tragedy of civil war were sown. For some analysts and *dramatis personae*, the seeds were sown in the 1950s with the formation of political parties on ethnic and regional bases. Some argue that the permanent split of the Nigerian Youth Movement in 1941 which left the group as a Yoruba organisation was the beginning of the plague on Nigerian politics. To others, it is more appropriate to go back even further to the year 1914 when the Southern and Northern Protectorates of Nigeria were amalgamated under one administration.[6] Yet to some, the year 1914 does not go back enough; for if the British government had not formally taken over the administration of Nigeria from the Royal Niger Company in 1900, the trend of events in the following sixty-five years would certainly have been different. One possible way of dealing with this problem is not to approach the subject in terms of dates, or in a chronological order, but rather to concentrate on the unfolding of the critical factors that eventually culminated in military takeover. We will therefore examine the background to military rule in Nigeria from the following perspectives: the constitutional background, north—south and ethnic conflicts, minority group politics (or the politics of state creation), and finally the chain of immediate antecedents and the structural dilemmas of the Nigerian army.

The constitutional background

Modern nationalism began in Nigeria in the 1920s with the formation of Herbert Macaulay's Nigerian National Democratic Party.[7] For various reasons the activities of this political party were restricted to Lagos. It was not until another decade and the formation of the Nigerian Youth Movement that other parts of Nigeria felt the wind of this change in the struggle against colonialism. During this period, and throughout World War II, no serious attempt was made to change the constitution under which Nigeria was being governed. The 1946 constitution of Arthur Richards was promulgated with the least possible consultation with Nigerians. Its key features include the following: (a) division of Nigeria into three administrative regions, each under a chief commissioner; (b) establishment of three regional Houses of Assembly at Enugu, Kaduna and Ibadan with power merely to discuss general legislation and the right to pass their own regional budgets; (c) selection of membership of each regional House from existing native authorities, who in turn selected five of their number as representatives to the central Legislative Council which met successively in Lagos, Ibadan, Kaduna and Enugu; (d) establishment of a House of Chiefs only for Northern Nigeria; (e) selection of membership of the regional

Houses on the ratio 19:20 (north), 14:15 (west), 13:14 (east) and 20:29 (centre) officials to unofficials. Included as unofficials for the regional Houses were five or more Africans or Europeans who were nominated by the governor and at the centre ten of the twenty-nine unofficials who were either chiefs or Europeans nominated by the governor.

The Richards constitution has been described by many nationalists as 'a stratagem of divide and rule'. Coleman has remarked that 'it is unfortunate in many respects that Sir Arthur Richards was governor of Nigeria during the delicate period 1943-1947' since 'he seemed to have a special knack for antagonizing the educated elements'.[8] For Kalu Ezera, even though the constitution achieved the integration of northern and southern Nigeria in a common legislative council, it brought into force the concept of regionalism – the beginning of the process of fragmentation in the country.[9] Awolowo made the most systematic criticism by a single individual soon after the launching of the constitution. To him even though the constitution looked new and pretty, it retained some of the objectionable features of the one it replaced, was marked by unsavoury characteristics of its own and fell short of expectation. In particular he considered the system used to determine the size of regional councils as anomalous, condemned the method of nominating instead of electing members and called for greater decentralisation.[10]

Even though the Richards constitution was to last for nine years, it was expected that limited changes would be made at the end of the third and sixth years. With the arrival of a new governor, Sir John Macpherson, in 1948 and the poor reception which the constitution received,[11] the opportunity was taken between 1949 and 1951 to drastically review the constitution. The process started in 1949 gave Nigerians the first ever opportunity of actively taking part in the formulation of the constitution which came to be known as the Macpherson constitution.[12] The geo-political emotions that were let loose at the Ibadan General Conference in particular and the effects on the development of Nigeria will be discussed below. Here we are mainly concerned with the provisions of the constitution and the extent to which the stage for January 1966 was being set inadvertently by the provisions.

The salient features of the Macpherson constitution were the following. (a) The three regions no longer operated merely as administrative units; each became a political entity vested with executive and legislative powers, but the public service and the judiciary remained unified. (b) A unicamera legislature at the centre – House of Representatives – with 148 members, 136 of whom were elected indirectly from and by the regional legislatures (68, that is 50 per cent from the Northern Region, and 34 each from Eastern and Western Regions). (c) A Council of Ministers, whose advice the governor was to follow on all matters in which he had no discretion, became the organ for formulating policies. It was made up of the governor as chairman, six official members and twelve Nigerian ministers drawn from the House of Representatives (four from each of the three regions). (d) The ministers either in the region or at the centre were responsible for groups of subjects in the council and in the House. (e) The Northern and Western Regions had bicamera legislatures, each with a House of Assembly and a House of Chiefs; the Eastern Region had a unicamera legislature – a House of Assembly. (f) A clear subordination of the regions to the centre. (g) The restriction of the legislative competence of the House of Representatives for bills which related to public revenue and the public service. No bill, motion or petition which involved money could be discussed by the House of Representatives except upon the recommendation or consent of the governor.

The rigid and complicated nature of this constitutional arrangement led to conflicting interpretations of what it actually was. Coleman has referred to it as 'essentially unitary'. Eme Awa sees it as a 'embryonic stage of a federation'. To Awolowo however it is 'a wretched compromise between federalism and unitarianism'.[13] After only two years various crises led to the breakdown of the Macpherson constitution. A new constitution came into force in 1954.

Oliver Lyttleton's name is often attached to this constitution since he was the central figure in its formulation. Kirk-Greene's suggested label, regionalism constitution, is probably more apt, since the constitution provided essentially for 'separate governors, separate premiers and cabinets and legislatures, separate judiciaries, separate public service commissioners, civil services, marketing boards and development plans'. With the introduction of this constitution 'outside the Federal Civil Service and Foreign Service, only the army appeared to be a genuinely national institution'.[14]

As Arikpo has pointed out, 'The 1954 constitution was the kernel of all further constitutional changes which culminated in the establishment of the Federal Republic of Nigeria on 1 October, 1963'. If anything some of the several amendments that were made intensified the strains which existed not only between the centre and the regions, but between the regions, and even communities within each region. In other words not only did the separateness continue beyond independence but, what is worse, it added in its development profoundly serious strains and stresses. These additional elements converged to destroy respect for constitutionalism and the rules of the political game.

The north–south and ethnic conflicts

P. C. Lloyd has observed that 'Nigeria's problems do . . . derive in large measure from the tensions which have arisen between the larger ethnic groups' and that 'the hostility derives . . . not from the ethnic differences, but from competition between peoples for wealth and power'.[15] The basis for this assertion can be seen in the development of the relationship between the various ethnic groups as colonialism gradually ground to a halt in Nigeria.

By the late 1930s, the most important national organisation politically was the Nigerian Youth Movement. Formed in 1934 the organisation by 1938 had successfully challenged Herbert Macaulay's NNDP in the election to the Lagos Town Council. Branches of the Movement were started in many cities in southern Nigeria and in Jos, Kaduna, Zaria and Kano. Some of the leading members included Kofo Abayomi, Nnamdi Azikiwe, H.O. Davies, Obafemi Awolowo, Ernest Ikoli, Samuel Akisanya. In 1941 the NYM ran into trouble over the nomination of a replacement for Kofo Abayomi on the Legislative Council. As a result the organisation was permanently split. As Schwarz noted, 'The NYM was left with an almost entirely Yoruba membership, and thus began the political tension between Ibo and Yoruba that has plagued Nigerian politics ever since.'[16]

Between 1941 and 1950 the unhealthy rivalry between the Ibo and Yoruba was intensified. It was not limited to the political scene; it extended to almost every area in which the two groups met.[17] By 1948 Azikiwe had ceased to be Zik of Africa but Zik of the Ibo nation[18] and soon Awolowo emerged as champion of Yoruba nationalism first through the Egbe Omo Oduduwa and soon after as leader of the Action Group political party.

Until 1950 the ethnic rivalry was primarily limited to the south. The processes of drawing up the Macpherson constitution provided the opportunity for extending it to the north. The starting point was the General Conference at Ibadan in 1950. Of the fifty-three members of this conference called to consider the constitutional recommendations of a drafting committee all but three were Nigerians (thirty-two southerners and eighteen northerners). The major questions that confronted the conference were the size of regional units in the federation, regional representation in the central legislature, revenue allocation, franchise and citizenship, ministerial responsibility and the status of Lagos. Sharp north–south disagreement arose on some of these issues. The Northern delegation demanded (a) 50 per cent representation at the central legislature; (b) per capita division of tax revenue. The Western and Eastern delegates were opposed to both. On the other hand, the Northern delegation was opposed to the demands of the others for cabinet responsibility whether at the centre or at the regional level, or a change in the existing regional boundaries.[19] The Emirs of Katsina and Zaria threatened that unless the north was given half the seats in the proposed House of Representatives, they would seek 'separation from the rest of Nigeria on the arrangements before 1914'. The Northern delegation won on the issue of representation at the centre and the demand to redraw the boundaries between the regions. In the words of Kirk-Greene the decision to allow the north's claim 'was one that was to dominate the shaping of Nigeria's political culture until the First Republic exploded sixteen years later'.[20]

It has been suggested that the defeat of Zik in his bid to enter the House of Representatives in 1951 was motivated by ethnic as well as political party rivalry. What is the background to this episode? When the Macpherson constitution came into force in 1951, there were three principal parties, the National Council of Nigeria and Cameroons (NCNC), the Action Group (AG) and the Northern People's Congress (NPC), each having its basic strength in the East, West and Northern legislature respectively.[21] None of the leaders of the political parties was in the Council of Ministers at the centre. Awolowo led the AG in the Western Region, Ahmadu Bello, the leader of the NPC, led his party in the Northern legislature. Azikiwe who was leader of the NCNC resided in Lagos and became a member of the Western House of Assembly for that constituency.

The procedure for selecting representatives from the regional Houses to the House of Representatives gave the majority party the overall power of choice. The AG had an overall majority in the Western House of Assembly. By its numerical strength, the AG was able to capitalise on the flagrant indiscipline and lack of team spirit in the five-member NCNC team representing Lagos and prevented Zik from becoming a member of the House of Representatives. Some supporters of Zik interpreted his defeat as an attempt to destroy his political influence in the country. The Eastern Regional NCNC representatives in the federal legislature threatened to boycott the House in protest against Zik's defeat. Apart from lust of office by his team mates, Zik regards his defeat as part of the inadequacies of the constitution. To Kalu Ezera, Zik was defeated because he was an Ibo, since his party colleagues who were selected from the Lagos members of the House of Assembly were all Yoruba.[22]

The defeat of Zik was not only part of the ethnic conflict, it was the beginning of the end of the Macpherson constitution. Two other more critical but closely connected issues concern the motion for self-government and the Kano riots. On 31 March 1953, Anthony Enahoro, an Action Group backbencher in the House of Representatives, moved 'that this House accepts as a primary political objective the attainment of self-government for Nigeria in 1956'. This motion was seen by the Northern delegation as directed against them. They believed that it was designed to bring them into public contempt. Nevertheless they were not prepared to 'accept invitation to commit suicide'.[23] During Ahmadu Bello's contribution on his amendment that 'as soon as practicable' be substituted for 'in 1956' he said, 'The mistake of 1914 has come to light and I should like to go no further'. The likelihood that the amendment would be carried led to a walk-out by the members of the AG and NCNC in the House. Furthermore the AG but not the NCNC ministers resigned their ministerial appointments. Booing, both outside the House and on their journey back home in their special train, greeted the Northern members of the House.

The AG and NCNC did not accept the views of the NPC leaders as truly representative of Northern opinion. As a result the AG sent a delegation to the north under the leadership of Chief S. L. Akintola. Akintola's mission caused a riot in Kano on 16 May 1953 in which thirty-six people were killed and over 250 wounded.[24] All this led to the statement credited to the Secretary of State for the Colonies to the effect that 'it is not possible for the Regions to work effectively in a federation so closely knit as that provided by the present constitution' and that there was need to redraw the constitution 'to provide for greater autonomy'.

From the foregoing it is clear that the ethnic bases of the political parties worsened the relationship between the major ethnic groups in the country. Throughout most of the first decade of representative government, there appeared to be an understanding among the politcal parties not to disturb in any serious way each other's influence in each territory. With the approach of independence, the Action Group made very serious efforts to break this understanding especially during the 1959 federal election. It proved most unsuccessful. The result of the election led to an alliance at the federal legislature between the NPC and the NCNC. This election and in particular the 1961 election into the Northern House of Assembly which almost wiped out all opposition in the Northern legislature confirmed the southern fear of the perpetual power domination of the north. How this contributed to the collapse of the First Republic will be discussed later. In the meantime it is necessary to examine the role of minority group politics in the background to military rule.

The politics of state creation

The issue of increasing the number of states in Nigeria was started by political leaders from the south. In 1943 Azikiwe's idea was that Nigeria be split into eight protectorates and Awolowo in 1947 argued for a federal constitution in which each ethnic group is autonomous. In his words, 'Each group however small is entitled to the same treatment as any other group however large'.[25] But creation of more states did not become a strong political issue until each of the three main political parties solidly supported by one of the ethnic majorities had been firmly established in its area of influence – the AG and the Yoruba in the Western Region, the NCNC and the Ibo in the East and the NPC and Hausa-Fulani in the North.

As early as 1950, however, agitation for a Benin Delta Region had started. It gained momentum as the Action Group firmly gained control of the Western Region. In 1954 the Action Group was defeated by the NCNC in the federal election in the West. The support of minority votes in the Benin Delta area contributed largely to this defeat. A year after through the support of the AG government, a private member's motion in the Western House of Assembly for the creation of a Mid-West Region was passed. The support of the AG had strong political motivation. In the first place it conformed with Awolowo's position of ethnic autonomy. More important the support served as a bait to other minority groups in the other two regions.

In the North with the NPC motto of 'One North One People', the United Middle Belt Congress which led the agitation for a Middle Belt State, the Ilorin Talaka Parapo which fought for the transfer of Ilorin province to the Western Region, and the Bornu Youth Movement which sought for the creation of a Bornu State, were all attracted by the stand of the AG on state creation. At different times between 1956 and 1958 each went into alliance with the AG for the achievement of their goal. In the East, the United National Independence Party (UNIP) aimed at the creation of a Calabar-Ogoja-Rivers Region to embrace the Efik-Ibibio from Calabar, the non-Ibo area of Ogoja and the Ijaw from Rivers. Since the NCNC and its leader, Azikiwe, changed their original position and claimed that 'the East can no longer stand dismemberment as a sacrifice either for administrative convenience or for national unity', here again the Action Group became the champion of state creation through its alliance with the UNIP.

At the 1957 constitutional conference in London, one of the most difficult issues to resolve was that of creation of more regions in Nigeria. According to Schwarz, 'claims for no fewer than fifteen were put forward'.[26] This led to the setting up of a Minorities Commission made up of four Englishmen under the chairmanship of Sir Henry Willink. The commission was charged with ascertaining the fears of minorities and proposing adequate means of allaying them. The terms of reference of the commission which in part stated that 'if and only if no other solution is possible to meet the fears of the minority should as a last result detailed recommendations be made for the creation of more regions', showed clearly the reluctance of the British government to create more regions in Nigeria.

The NPC maintained its stand before the commission that the North should not be split. Whatever should happen in the other regions, the party claimed, was none of its business. The AG which had consistently been the champion of minorities also maintained its position even though it played a geo-political game with some ethnic groups. The NCNC was less straightforward. The party supported the creation of more regions in the East (but not the COR whose basis for unity it claimed was 'a negative dislike for the Ibo tribe') only if the same were done in the other regions.

Predictably the commission in its report did not support the creation of more regions most especially because they would not be viable and new regions would create new minority problems. Kirk-Greene has observed that the claim by many Nigerian intellectuals that the seed of the 1966 crisis was sown with the failure of the Willink Commission to recommend the creation of more states in 1958 is unjustified. This he says is because of 'the Commission's precise terms of reference' or 'the probability of violent reaction from the political leaders, the people, and world anti-colonial opinion had any British-inspired move been made to postpone independence in order to set up more states and correct the built-in imbalance of the evolving federal structure'.[27] This is indeed an untenable alibi. As he pointed out above, the British government was opposed to the creation of more regions even before the commission was set up. Furthermore, even though there was disagreement among the leaders at the 1957 conference the fact remains that the regional premiers' conference preceding the London conference agreed that new states might be created and boundaries adjusted on some laid down principles. If the British government had not continued its policy of divide and rule and shown its sympathy in particular to the Northern position on this issue, the terms of reference of the Willink Commission should have been differently worded if the premiers could not be persuaded to honour their earlier agreement.

The ultimatum laid down at the 1958 conference that if the Nigerian leaders wanted independence in 1960 no new states would be created and that if states were to be created the demand for independence should be abandoned was definitely a blackmail. It turned the minority problem into an election issue. As a result the Action Group decided to fight the 1959 federal election on a platform calling for creation of more regions before independence in 1960. This decision and the way the Action Group vigorously championed the cause of the minorities particularly in the Northern Region during the election campaign in 1959 worsened the already bad relationship between the leaders of the party and the NPC leadership in the years immediately after independence in October 1960.

'Signposts to disaster'[28]

Action Group crisis and the treason trial The December 1959 general election which revealed the decisive supremacy of each regional government party in the majority ethnic group of each region was the second federal election in Nigeria – the first was held in 1954. In this election, the NPC emerged with 142 seats, NCNC/NEPU alliance with 89 and the AG with 73 in the 312-member House of Representatives.[29] Even though the two southern political parties had a sufficient number of seats to have formed a coalition government, the NCNC found it more expedient to join the NPC in a coalition with Tafawa Balewa, deputy leader of the NPC as prime minister and Nnamdi Azikiwe, president of the NCNC, as president of the Senate and later, governor-general. (In 1963, with Nigeria becoming a republic, Zik became president.) Awolowo led the opposition in the federal legislature.[30]

Awolowo's failure to become the prime minister can legitimately be regarded as the original source of the Action Group crisis of 1962 and the accompanying treason trial. It should be added, however, that shortly before 1959 the ability of the AG to maintain in public strict discipline within the rank and file of the party was showing signs of weakening. With the decision of Awolowo to move from the West to the federal legislature, there was disagreement within the party over who should succeed him as premier. Against Awolowo's wish, Akintola became premier and soon after began to take control of decision-making in the Western Regional government with the least possible consultation with Awolowo. Within two years of Akintola's takeover of the premiership, dissension within the AG became public knowledge with the newspapers which Awolowo controlled seriously criticising the policies of the Western Regional government. Apart from other personal issues which some writers have raised to the status of ideological differences,[31] the disagreement between Awolowo and Akintola centred primarily on the federal prime minister's idea of strengthening national unity through the formation of a coalition government to be formed by the three major political parties. Akintola strongly supported the proposition while Awolowo was opposed to it.

At the federal legislature, Awolowo as leader of the opposition was very effective in making the government of Tafawa Balewa most uncomfortable through a series of attacks on major and popular issues. These attacks were on colonialism, the economy and corruption. The defence pact signed between Britain and Nigeria formed the central focus of Awolowo's attack on colonialism. He claimed that the pact had been extorted from the Nigerian government by Britain as a condition for granting independence. As a signatory to the original draft, Awolowo alleged that the British used 'barefaced, unabashed and undue influence'. Evidence of strong public opposition to such a pact was effectively played upon by Awolowo to the extent that the students of the University of Ibadan in particular rioted within the premises of the federal legislature and many members of government were maltreated. In January 1962 the pact had to be abrogated.

Nationalisation was Awolowo's answer for radical economic policies which would remove the nation from economic bondage. This as far as the federal government was concerned was unacceptable. Apart from public utilities, shipping, airways, power, railways, communications and marketing boards, the government was not interested in nationalisation. In order to develop the local economy, argued Oktie-Eboh, the federal minister for finance, the country needed capital from outside, and in order to attract capital it was necessary not to frighten foreign investors.

Nigeria's outstanding feature is a dangerous decline in moral values whereby honesty is at a discount and corruption and mediocrity have a high premium. This was Awolowo's assessment of Nigeria's first year of independence. His criticism of the federal government became so dangerously frightening that the federal legislature voted to censure him after his return from London in 1961 where he had lectured Nigerian students in Britain on the incompetence and ineffectiveness of the government. His continued support and that of his party, the AG, for the minority movements added to his popularity all over the country. As a result the NPC/NCNC coalition had no alternative but to go on a counter-attack.

Without the internal rift on policies and of personalities within the AG the chances of success of the counter-attack would have been remote. At the 1962 convention of the AG in Jos, it was openly admitted for the first time by Awolowo, that there existed a rift within the party. The rift got progressively worse to the extent that, at the Western House of Assembly on 25 May 1962, a riot broke out in the legislative chamber. At a reconvened meeting during which the police in anti-riot dress were present, violence broke out and the prime minister instructed the police to clear the chamber and lock it. A state of emergency was declared by the federal government. The governor, premier, ministers, president of the House of Chiefs, speaker of the House of Assembly and the superintendent-general of local government police were relieved of their posts. Dr Majekodunmi was appointed administrator with considerable powers.

Other complementary events followed in quick succession. A commission of enquiry into the financial and investment policies of six Western Regional government statutory corporations including their relations with political parties was set up by the federal government. The commission, headed by Justice Coker, found that the Action Group received ₦4.4 million in cash for National Investment and Properties Corporation in addition to payment of its ₦1.3 million overdraft with the National Bank and that the party benefited from NIPC investment in corporations that published pro-Action Group newspapers. On Awolowo, the commission reported: 'His scheme was to build around him with money, an empire financially formidable both in Nigeria and abroad, an empire in which dominance would be maintained by him, by the power of the money which he had given out'.[32] Akintola was vindicated by the commission. The treason trial in which it was alleged that Awolowo and others planned to overthrow the government also found him and twenty other members of his party excluding the deputy leader, Akintola, guilty and sentenced them to varying terms of imprisonment. Awolowo earned ten years' imprisonment.

Before all this Akintola and Rosiji (general secretary of the AG) had been expelled from the party. With their supporters they formed a new political party, the United Peoples Party, which later merged with a wing of the NCNC in the West to form the Nigerian National Democratic Party (NNDP).[33] With the support of the federal government, both through the administrator of the Western Region and other channels, when the Western House of Assembly reconvened on 8 April 1963 Akintola won a vote of confidence and resumed his leadership of the region till the day of reckoning on 15 January 1966.[34]

The census controversy If the Action Group crisis was the first signpost to the disaster that started in 1966, the census controversy of 1962-4 was not too far from it. As Kirk-Greene graphically put it, from this controversy 'the gunpowder trail was laid, awaiting only the lighting of the fire in October 1965 to result in the final conflagration on 15 January 1966.'[35]

One of the political issues that arise from census figures in Nigeria has always been that they determine the relative numerical strength of each region or state in the federal legislature. (Another issue is the revenue which each region/state collects from the central distributable pool.) The 1952-3 census gave the Northern Region 174 of the 312 seats in the House of Representatives. The Eastern Region had 73, the West 62, and Lagos 3. It was hoped by the southern political leaders that the 1962-3 census would alter the balance in their favour and thus remove the foundation for northern power at the federal level. When in July 1962 (two months after the count) the figures got to Lagos, the population of the Eastern Region rose from 7.2 million to 12.3 million (an increase of 71 per cent) and that of the Western Region increased by 70 per cent from 6.08 million. The Northern figures increased least. An increase of 30 per cent from the 1952-3 figure of 16.8 million was recorded. The British officer in charge, T. Warren, accepted the Northern figures as normal in his report, the Eastern and Western figures he alleged were 'grossly inflated'. As a result checks in selected areas were suggested to the federal authorities. The acceptance of this suggestion and its implementation increased the tension between the governing coalition of NPC and NCNC. While the result of the verification confirmed the Western and Eastern figures, the increase in the Northern figures rose from 30 to 80 per cent. In order to reduce the tension the prime minister announced the cancellation of the whole exercise and ordered a recount. Furthermore he transferred responsibility for the exercise from the minister in charge, Waziri Ibrahim, and took personal control.

The repeat performance produced no better or more acceptable result. When the final figures were announced in February 1964 the North, East, West and Lagos had 29.7 million, 12.3 million, 12.8 million and 6.75 thousand respectively. This meant an overall increase of 74 per cent for the country, 67 per cent for the North, 65 per cent for the East and nearly 100 per cent for the West. By this time Akintola had resumed the premiership of the West. Unlike his southern counterparts, Okpara (East) and Osadebey (who assumed premiership of the Mid-West Region in 1963 – a by-product of the AG crisis) who denounced the final figures, Akintola's government predictably accepted the final result. Osadebey later announced his acceptance 'for the sake of national unity'. The north–south conflict of the 1950s was gradually turning to north–east conflict, with the other governments in the country whose survival depended upon Northern Region support serving as appendages to the north.[36] Thus the hope of the south breaking the predominance of the north at the federal level through the census was dashed.

The 1964-5 federal election If with the help of the Supreme Court the census figures would not be invalidated and thus stop northern domination, there was hope that an appeal to the electorate could be more rewarding in the approaching general election. The 1964-5 election has often been referred to as a classic case of the politics of brinkmanship. It was during this election that the first plot for a military *coup d'état* by some members of the Nigerian army was planned.

What is the story of this 'most perilous display of brinkmanship'?[37] When the NNDP was formed to represent the Yoruba interest, one of its first publications charged Ibo leaders with tribalism in the administration of the Nigerian Railway Corporation and other federal corporations.[38] Even T. O. S. Benson, who was then the first vice-president of the NCNC and federal minister for information, talked of 'unfair and offensive practices against my people', the Yoruba. In London, there was circulation among Western Nigerian students of a publication issued by the office of the agent-general for Western Nigeria in London, listing pages upon pages of critical positions said to be held almost exclusively by Ibos in various federal government corporations. The design was to portray the AG that was planning an alliance with the NCNC for the coming federal elections as a stooge of the Ibos and an enemy of the Yoruba.

Two major alliances were eventually forced to contest the election of 1964. The Nigerian National Alliance (NNA) brought together the NPC, the NNDP apart from other minor political parties such as the Mid-West Democratic Front and Dynamic Party of Dr Chike Obi. The United Peoples Grand Alliance (UPGA) was made up of the NCNC, the AG, NEPU and the United Middlebelt Congress.[39] The UPGA campaign theme was primarily the restructuring of the Nigerian federation in such a way that by the creation of new states the bonds of unity would be strengthened in Nigeria. NNA on the other hand put more emphasis on national unity through the representation of all ethnic groups at the federal level particularly through job opportunities. This theme was more strongly emphasised by the NNDP leaders to attract Yoruba votes. Charges and counter-charges of harassment were made by opposition politicians in all regions. Michael Okpara, leader of the NCNC, was more vociferous on these charges, with discriminate support from the president of the republic, Dr Azikiwe, who accepted the allegations of Okpara but unsuccessfully sought to postpone the election. At one point Okpara threatened that the Eastern Region would secede because the campaign was neither fair nor free most especially in the North.[40] It should be recalled that even if UPGA won all the seats in the south it would still fail to have the majority in the House of Representatives.[41] This made an all-out campaign and the winning of a substantial number of seats in the North more important and necessary.

On election day UPGA leaders asked their supporters to boycott the polling-booth as a protest against the arrest and gaoling of their members who were to contest the election in the North and West. The boycott was totally successful in the East, relatively successful in the West and a complete failure in the North where it was most needed. In practical terms, however, the effect of the boycott in the Western Region was to give the NNDP an advantage since its few supporters in many constituencies voted. This was extremely harmful to the AG in particular, whose leaders had expected that the election would show that they had the support of the majority of the citizens of the Western Region. At the close of election the NPC wing of the NNA had won 162 of the 167 seats in the North. This in effect meant that even without allying with any other political party it could on its own form a government at the federal level. With NNDP winning thirty-six seats, the position of the NNA alliance was most comfortable.

What happened after the election results were announced

underscores the position of Huntington's school of thought that military takeover of government occurs in societies in which there is frequent disagreement among the groups competing for political power as to the legitimate and authoritative methods for resolving conflicts. In Nigeria at this time almost all relevant social forces and institutions became highly politicised to the extent that the country 'tottered perilously on the brink of disintegration and bloodshed'.[42]

By the rules of the game it was the duty of the president to appoint as prime minister the leader of the political party that had the majority in the House of Representatives. Azikiwe threatened that 'I would rather resign than exercise the powers to call on a person to form a government.' There began a stalemate which lasted for almost four days. The prime minister refused the advice of the president to set aside the results of the election. For the first time in Nigerian political history there was no government in Lagos for three full days. Negotiations went on day and night to resolve the crisis. Finally on 4 January 1965 the president announced the re-appointment of Tafawa Balewa as prime minister after the plan drawn up by the chief justice of the federation, Sir Adetokunbo Ademola, and the chief justice of the Eastern Region, Sir Louis Mbanefo, had been accepted by the two warring leaders, Balewa and Azikiwe. By this plan there was to be a broadbased national government, fresh elections were to be conducted in all areas where there had been a total boycott, grievances were to be taken to the law courts and a commission was to be set up to review the constitution. When in March 1965 fresh elections were held, the final results were NPC 162, NNDP 36, NCNC 84, AG 21, NPF 4, Independents 5. As in the boycott of the election, it was the AG that lost most in the negotiations. When the national broadbased government was formed, the AG was not included.

As Anglin has rightly observed, the resolution of this crisis did not resolve any of the fundamental problems facing Nigeria. Instead 'Northern domination, Yoruba disunity and Eastern aggressiveness were all highlighted; as were bitter personal animosities, the ugly scramble for jobs, the resort to force and fraud, the glaring inequalities of opportunities and the growing economic disparities'.[43] But it would take another twelve months before these problems set ablaze the showpiece of democracy at work in Africa.

1965 Western election Mackintosh referred to Western Nigeria as 'the cockpit of Nigerian politics particularly between 1962 and the time of military takeover of politcal power in 1966'.[44] To Dudley, Western Nigeria can be regarded 'not without some justification as the problem area of the Nigerian federation. Even though it is the most homogeneous of the regions (after the creation of the Mid-West region in 1963). It has not been easy for the peoples to unite in the same way that the Ibo of the East or the Hausa of the North have done.' Dudley finds the explanation for this in (a) the long internecine conflicts within the group particularly during the nineteenth century which have been carried over into the present, and (b) the social structure.[45] The following few pages support this position of Mackintosh and Dudley.

The last election to the Western House of Assembly before the crisis of 1962 within the Action Group ruling political party was in August 1960. Since the maximum life of any legislative house under the parliamentary system of government was five years, 1965 gave the people of the region the opportunity to express their will as to which of the contending political groups should govern them - the NNDP which with the support of the federal government had remained in power, or the Action Group which since the 1962 crisis had been in the doldrums both at the federal and regional levels.

In fighting the election, NNDP had the usual advantages of an incumbent. These the party used to the fullest. In order to attract cash crop farmers as supporters, the price of cocoa to be paid to farmers was raised to ₦240 a ton even though the actual selling price was ₦180. In other words, government was paying ₦60 per ton more than the selling price.[46] Various promises of development projects were made daily as the election day drew near. Even NNDP ministers at the federal level promised the setting up of a ₦20 million steel industry in Ondo division and a ₦10 million development project in Ibadan division. Not everything was so sugar-coated, though.

Elected local government councils were dissolved and replaced with management committees made up of NNDP supporters. Obas and other traditional leaders were warned not to oppose government. About a month before election day, the government-owned newspaper *The Nigerian Daily Sketch* warned, 'When an Oba takes it upon himself to oppose the Government, he has shown himself as an enemy of his people.'[47] Finally election speeches emphasised Yoruba solidarity and the need for the Yoruba to realise the fruitlessness of any close relationship with Ibo people. As Akintola put it, 'While the Northerners have a good exchange of commodities in kolanuts and cows with the Yoruba the Ibo have nothing to offer the Yoruba except second-hand clothing.'

The Action Group had other disadvantages apart from being out of power. The organisation of electoral administration was in the hands of the local administrators who were members or supporters of the NNDP even though the overall responsibility of the election was with the chairman of the federal electoral commission, E. E. Esua. Furthermore there was internal conflict between the Action Group/NCNC alliance over nomination of candidates. The original agreement to divide the ninety-four seats equally broke down, particularly in Ekiti and Ijebu areas where the AG and NCNC candidates contested the same seats.

This election produced more violence than had ever been witnessed before. As a result of the disruption – coming from all sides – a ban on all meetings and processions was announced on 19 September. Thousands of Nigerian police were drafted to the region to maintain law and order. In many instances, particularly in the rural areas, the law enforcement officers became the victims of political thuggery and murder. The electoral officers appeared to have suffered even more. This contributed largely to the collapse of the electoral administration. Another contributory factor to this collapse was the manipulation of electoral officers by the politicians. By 30 September, the NNDP was in a position to announce that fifteen of its candidates had been returned unopposed, leaving seventy-nine seats more to be contested on election day. The attempt by the Action Group to use the law courts to stop this rape on democracy failed. The party's request to the High Court for an injunction to prevent electoral officers from declaring candidates unopposed was dismissed.

Serious rioting occurred in various parts of the region on election day. In some constituencies police opened fire and killed civilians. After the election both parties claimed victory and on 12 October, the day following the election, the leader of the Action Group, Alhaji D. S. Adegbenro, announced the formation of an interim government. Two days later he and many of the other leaders of the party were taken into detention. With this, and the formation of a government by Akintola and his party, the NNDP, large scale looting and killing of political opponents followed. The University of Ibadan Students Union appealed unsuccessfully to the prime minister to declare a state of emergency in the region. By November, a few weeks before the Commonwealth prime ministers were due in Lagos, it was clear that open rebellion against governmental power and authority had seriously taken command of the Western Region. The only available force capable of putting it under control if not stopping it completely was the army, which waited for the aeroplanes of the Commonwealth prime ministers to be airborne before striking, and then not as effectively as allegedly planned. Why did the army have to strike without being ordered to do so by its commander-in-chief or, worse still, without the knowledge of its top echelon? The answer can be found in the structural dilemmas of the Nigerian army by 1966.

The structural dilemmas of the army

As an integral part of the body politic, it was difficult for the Nigerian army to be completely immune from all the centrifugal forces in the society, particularly after independence. The intensity of each of these forces varied, but together they were strong enough to disrupt the democratic functioning of the Nigerian political system.

As of 1958, the strength of the Nigerian army was only 7600. When in May 1964 the General Officer Commanding the army announced the plan to increase the size of the army it was by only 2900. Of the 10 500 in April 1965, only a little over 500 belonged to the officer corps (330 of which were of combatant status). This relatively small officer corps was to some students of civil–military relations politically unimportant. As Gutteridge put it in 1964, 'Three to five hundred officers in a country of forty million based mainly on five military stations, the majority of which are far from the capital, cannot for the time being be regarded as a political factor of the greatest importance'.[48] The fact that this numerically small army was able to take control of political power without much difficulty less than two years after this assessment was made goes to show that the whole society at that time was, in the words of Huntington, completely out of joint.

Probably the most important societal cleavage which seriously affected the organisational integrity of the Nigerian army was ethnic and regional conflict. Shortly before independence in 1960 the debate started among the political leaders as to whether courage or educational qualifications should be the basis for recruitment into and promotion within the army. Those who favour courage claim that this is the foundation of army recruitment and to use educational qualifications is to risk the officer corps being dominated by intellectuals who because of their background and training are basically not doers but talkers. This was the position of the leaders of the NPC who often quoted a Hausa saying that 'the warrior is not talkative'.[49]

The supporters of educational qualifications argue that courage alone has become less important in modern warfare. Management of contemporary military technology, they continue, has become very complex. To this group, which included most of the leaders of the NCNC, management of the military, like that of any complex organisation, requires specialised knowledge, acquired not out of mere experience but formally through training. As the *West African Pilot* stated, to emphasise the geography of selection or region of origin rather than educational standard is to produce an officer corps of 'subgrade people'.

Closely tied to this issue was the question of a quota system within the army. As at the Ibadan General Conference of 1950 referred to above, it was argued in 1958 that the Nigerian army should be drawn from each region in the same proportion as the regional population stood in relation to the total population. Since the numerical strength of a political party rather than the strength or merit of its argument determined policy direction, the NPC leaders had their way both on the quota system and the basis for recruitment. As a result it was government policy from 1958 that the Nigerian army would be composed as follows: Northern Region, 50 per cent; Eastern Region, 25 per cent; and Western Region, 25 per cent. When the Mid-West Region was created in 1963 it was allotted 4 per cent while the Western Regional quota was reduced to 21 per cent. During the 1964 general election campaign, UPGA made recruitment and promotion in the army one of its election issues. The party promised that if it won the election, 'recruitment and promotion of members of the armed services will be divorced from tribalism and based strictly on merit and qualification'.[50]

Added to this politicisation of recruitment and promotion in the army was the factor of discipline. As Luckham has observed, discipline was poorly institutionalised due to 'distorted age structure and promotional pattern in turn determined by the rapid indigenization of the officer corps'.[51] Except for eight or nine ex-non-commissioned officers at or near the top, virtually all combatant officers were within the age group 20-35 in 1966. The rate of promotion, which was high, slowed down considerably after 1964. This affected in particular the majors and captains who by 1965 had to wait much longer than their superiors had before moving up.

All these factors – politicisation of the army recruitment and promotion procedure, age differences and promotional opportunities – would on their own probably not have led to the army taking over control of political power. In the words of Luckham, it was the superimposition of unfavourable environmental conditions 'from the civil violence in the Western Region set off by the Regional election of October, 1965 which provided the immediate stimulus for the January 1966 coup'.[52]

2 The civil war

Turi Muhammadu and Mohammed Haruna

Causes and Course

The convening of the Constituent Assembly in September 1977 to work out a presidential constitution for the country presumes a failure of the 1960 independence constitution. And it is often argued that the source of this failure was the earlier constitution's undue emphasis on regional autonomy with the predictable result that at various times the various regions threatened to leave the federation. It was inevitable, the argument continues, that the threat would one day not stop at that.

It is debatable whether the breakdown of politics in 1966 can all be blamed on the 1960 constitution. It is true that the nature of the rules of the political game, is a crucial element in political stability and national integration. However, these two involve not just working out suitable rules but also building a community of economics and above all of values. More than anything else, the problem of unity and stability in this country before the war and even now is of a lack of deep-seated, nationally shared values.

This is relevant to any attempt to identify the causes of the Nigerian civil war, because it is for lack of such deep-seated values, transcending ethnic boundaries, that questions of principle invariably get befogged and become settled along ethnic lines. Corruption, greed and the other such vices which caused the downfall of the First Republic are not ethnic in character, but because 'Nigeria' represented a less concrete concept than that of the ethnic group, the principles of probity and accountability did not seem nationally applicable.

The corrupt politician always invoked the spectre of ethnicism to cover up his guilt, with the predictable result that matters of principle were resolved in an unprincipled manner.

However, 'ethnic groups' are not permanent, unchanging items of history. They have a fluidity which responds to the impact of ideas and to particular historical situations as they arise. In the Nigerian case the role of the 'ethnic factor' has often been misunderstood. Thus the 'Northerners' who are accused of ethnic chauvinism are not an 'ethnic group'. Indeed it is among 'Northerners' that the breakdown of old ethnic barriers has proceeded furthest in historical times.[1] This is because of the conscious effort made by the founders of the Sokoto caliphate, their successors and followers, to build a community that transcended ethnic differences. The British who overthrew the caliphate rulers were interested only in exploiting the economy of the country they had brought together under the name Nigeria.

Unfortunately, the Nigerian elites who took over from the British made no serious effort to evolve any of the nationally shared values essential for national unity. Furthermore, the difficulties of the Nigerian rulers were exacerbated by the persistence of divisive influences operating within and outside the country. As a result of these factors the country at the outbreak of the civil war was, by and large, made up of fairly independent polities as they were put together in 1914 by the British. It is from this failure by both the British and the Nigerian rulers to unify the country in name and spirit that the remote and immediate causes of the civil war can be traced.

Chapter 1 deals with the background to military rule. In that chapter the remote factors which led to the civil war have been analysed. These, according to the author of the chapter, include north-south and ethnic conflicts, minority group politics, the structural dilemmas of the Nigerian army, and a chain of events – like the census controversy, the federal election crisis and so on – which occurred between 1962 and 1965. We do not need to analyse again these factors that resulted in the inability of Nigerian political leaders to evolve minimal nationally shared values. What is necessary is to emphasise that these factors must be taken into consideration when discussing the Nigerian civil war. In this part of our contribution, we shall be concerned with the immediate causes of the war.

The Ibo killings of May and September 1966 in the North, which were probably the point of no return in the march towards the civil war, were in fact merely a culmination of a series of events starting from the coup on 15 January 1966. We do not know the details of the logistics of the coup either from the principal participants who are now dead or the federal military government that set up some investigations into it.[2] We do know, however, that the coup was led and most probably initiated by seven army officers, six of whom were Ibo. These were Majors Nzeogwu, Onwuategu, Ifeajuna, Okafor, Chukukwa, together with Captain Nwobosi and Major Ademoyega, a Yoruba. Nzeogwu led the coup in the North, Ifeajuna in Lagos, and Nwobosi in Western Nigeria. In Kaduna, Sir Ahmadu Bello, the Sardauna of Sokoto and premier of the Northern Region; Brigadier Ademulegun and Colonel Sodeinde, among others, were killed in the revolt. In Lagos, the coup led to the death of the prime minister, Tafawa Balewa; the federal minister for finance, Okotie Eboh; Brigadier Maimalari; Colonel Mohammed; Lieutenant-Colonel Unegbe and Lieutenant-Colonel Pam. The premier of the Western Region, Chief S. L. Akintola, was killed by the coup leaders from the Abeokuta garrison. In essence, therefore, only the Ibo leaders in the East and Mid-West Regions were untouched by the killings.[3]

Even if the coup had been planned with the best of intentions, its outcome looked patently to the other ethnic groups, particularly in the North and West, like an Ibo conspiracy. Firstly, as pointed out above, of the seven ringleaders, six were Ibo. Secondly, but more importantly, the victims were virtually all non-Ibo, even though the Ibo political leaders, as chapter 1 brings out clearly, were as solidly steeped in the vices of the First Republic as any other ethnic group.

However, matters grew even worse when the dust of the January coup settled and General Aguyi-Ironsi eventually took over. Ironsi without doubt initially enjoyed the goodwill of the generality of the public. Even in the North where there was scepticism, the attitude was that of wait-and-see rather than of outright hostility. Unfortunately, Ironsi wasted this goodwill[4] and in this he was not helped by the post-coup actions and words of his fellow Ibos who in public places in Northern towns jeered at and taunted the people of Northern Region for their losses.

Ironsi wasted this goodwill within a period of six months. He refused to bring the January coup leaders to trial even after the Supreme Military Council, over which he presided, had decided in May to do so. Ironsi kept postponing the trial. He surrounded himself with Ibo advisers who irresponsibly urged him to various ill-considered decisions.[5] These included the promotion, against SMC decision, of twenty-one officers to the rank of lieutenant-colonel (eighteen of these were Ibo), and the most politically unwise decision of 'the abolition of federalism as a system of government in Nigeria'.

The effect of all these measures was to heighten fears, especially in the North, of a Machiavellian plot by the Ibos to dominate the country. Protests against the measures which started peacefully degenerated into riots soon after the announcement of a unitary system of government. These led to attacks on Ibos first in Zaria and later in other towns in the North. As Dudley observes, 'The Ibo were attacked not because they were Ibo but because the name Ibo had become more or less synonymous with exploitations and humiliation. It was essentially an attack on a mental stereotype'.[6] The situation was not helped by immediate tales of plans by Ibos to kill off every 'Northerner' of promise right down to primary school age to ensure the success of the plot! Such tales of course were merely rumours; but like all rumours, they were dangerous.

The May attacks led to the exodus of some Ibos from the North and even the West, but the majority remained behind. It was the killings that accompanied the 29 July 1966 countercoup that began the massive migration of Ibos and non-Ibos back to the East. The countercoup, in which Ironsi along with many other Ibo officers was killed, brought Colonel Yakubu Gowon to power. The coup of July was quite evidently aimed at getting even with the Ibos for the January killings and to forestall 'Ibo domination'. However, as with most attempts to settle an eye for an eye, the move to counter Ibo domination went too far and degenerated into the mass killings of Ibos in September 1966.

The massive July-September killing of Ibos was, however, not the only factor that drove the regions even further apart and threatened to break up the country. It was without doubt a very significant factor, but without the leadership crisis which followed in the wake of the July 1966 countercoup it was still possible that the country would have been saved from the horrors of the civil war.

With Ironsi dead, Brigadier Babafemi Ogundipe, as the next in rank, was the rightful successor to the headship of state. However, Ogundipe was unable to assert himself, try as he did, and he briefly disappeared from the scene. Eventually Colonel Yakubu Gowon emerged as the head of state and it was from here that trouble started: for Lieutenant-Colonel Odumegwu Ojukwu, the military governor of the East, would not accept Gowon as his leader. Ostensibly this was because more senior officers were available (Ogundipe was after all still alive). However, it was obvious that firstly, Ojukwu felt superior to Gowon not just in the military scheme of things but in every aspect. Secondly, and perhaps more importantly, Ojukwu as well as his Ibo colleagues felt that Gowon was merely a puppet of the 'Northerners' who were determined to regain the control of political power which they had lost in January.

This unacceptability of Gowon as the head of state of course had its source in the September killings. However, it eventually became a factor in its own right; Gowon was seen as a symbol of 'Northern domination' which in turn was considered a threat to the very existence of Ibos. For the Ibos therefore the solution to this crisis lay not merely in removing Gowon but in breaking up the country and allowing the Ibos a separate existence.

This was unacceptable to the rest of Nigeria and it was the search for a compromise which led to several conferences by 'leaders of thought' in the country and eventually to Aburi in Ghana. All the discussions proved abortive. The Aburi meeting in particular proved to be the thin end of the wedge which split the country into two and threatened to split it into even more bits.

At Aburi it looked as though an accord of sorts was reached. But no sooner were Gowon and Ojukwu back in Lagos and

Enugu than they proceeded to give entirely contradictory interpretations of the accord. For Gowon, Aburi in essence still meant a federation albeit a weak one. For Ojukwu, however, Aburi meant a confederation similar to the East African Community in which the Ibos would be virtually free to run their own lives and thus feel secure. Evidently the two were headed for a collision. With time Ojukwu became increasingly defiant, seizing federal property in the East and generally behaving as a sovereign.

Attempts were made by some groups to prevent the escalation of the crisis. Such groups included the National Conciliation Committee which met Ojukwu in May 1967. Among its members were Sir Adetokunbo Ademola, Chief Mariere and Chief Awolowo. At the meeting in Enugu, it was agreed that if the federal military government lifted the embargo on communications and foreign exchange transactions imposed on the Eastern Regional government, the latter would reciprocate by re-examining the three edicts – the Revenue Collection Edict, the Legal Education Edict and the Court of Appeal Edict – which had been promulgated in March as its interpretation of the Aburi agreement.[8] The federal military government lifted the embargo, but the Eastern Regional government did not reciprocate. Instead a joint meeting was summoned by Ojukwu. In his long address to the meeting, Ojukwu reviewed developments in Nigeria between 1914 and May 1967 with great emphasis on the last ten months of that period. The meeting in obvious awareness of the direction Ojukwu wanted the people to move mandated him 'to declare at the earliest practicable date Eastern Nigeria a free, sovereign and independent state by the name and title of the Republic of Biafra'.[9]

The following day, 27 May 1967, Gowon in an address to the nation accepted that the citizens of Nigeria 'have not given the military regime any mandate to divide up the country into sovereign states and to plunge them into bloody disaster'. But this, he announced, was not to say that he would run away from his duties. In the light of this he declared a state of emergency throughout Nigeria with immediate effect and assumed full powers as commander-in-chief of the armed forces and head of the federal military government for the period of the emergency. Furthermore, he announced the reorganisation of the country into twelve states – three of which were carved out of the Eastern Region.[10]

An outline of the course of the war, including the major battles, is given in the following table.[11]

1967	
6 July	Fighting breaks out between the federal and Biafran troops.
10 July	The First Division of the Nigerian army under Colonel Mohammed Shuwa captures Ogoja. Biafran aircraft bombs Lagos.
15 July	Shuwa captures Nsukka.
25 July	Third Marine Commandos Division of the Nigerian army under Colonel Benjamin Adekunle captures Bonny.
9 August	The rebels invade Mid-West and capture Benin. Later, in a hurried response, a Second Division of the Nigerian army under Colonel Murtala Mohammed is formed.
10 August	Gowon declares total war. Lagos bombed again.
29 August	Murtala recaptures Ore and thus halts Biafran threat to Ibadan and Lagos.
14 September	Murtala recaptures Benin.
4 October	Shuwa captures Enugu.
9 October	Murtala captures Asaba. Subsequent attempts to cross the Niger and capture Onitsha prove abortive.
18 October	Adekunle captures Calabar.
1968	
January	After the abortive attempts to capture Onitsha from Asaba Murtala moves up the Niger, crosses it at Idah and advances down to Awka and Onitsha.
21 March	Murtala captures Onitsha.
5 April	Shuwa captures Abakaliki.
21 April	Shuwa captures Afikpo.

Late April	The entire South Eastern State liberated by Adekunle.
6 May	Adekunle captures Bonny oil field in Rivers State.
19 May	Adekunle captures Port Harcourt and thus completes the sealing off of Biafra from the sea.
26 May	Colonel I. B. M. Haruna replaces Murtala as G.O.C. Second Division.
29 July	Adekunle captures Ahoada, last major town in Rivers State.
4 September	Adekunle captures Aba.
10-11 September	Adekunle captures Oguta and advances on the Uli airstrip which was Biafra's major link with the outside world.
15 September	Biafrans retake Oguta.
16 September	Adekunle captures Owerri.
30 September	Shuwa captures Okigwi.
November/ December	Nigerian air force begins air strikes on Biafran airstrips especially Uli but with little effect.
21-24 December	Biafran offensive to recapture Owerri and Aba foiled.
1969	
22 April	Biafra recaptures Owerri.
12 May	Major reshuffle of Nigeria's army commanders. Obasanjo takes over from Adekunle, Jalo from Haruna and Bisalla from Shuwa.
27 December	Third Division links up with the First at Umuahia.
1970	
7 January	Third Division recaptures Owerri.
11 January	Ojukwu flees Biafra for Ivory Coast.
12 January	Obasanjo captures Uli airstrip. Lieutenant -Colonel Philip Effiong who took over from Ojukwu broadcasts surrender over Radio Biafra.
13 January	Gowon accepts Biafran surrender.[12]

International involvement

That the war lasted for as long as two and a half years, despite the vastly superior federal might, was due to a combination of factors, not the least of which was the succour the rebels got from the international involvement in the conflict. Of course, the will to survive as Biafra was also a very important factor but without the assistance the rebels received from overseas, their determination might well have worn thin quite early in the conflict.

According to Stremlau,[13] at the beginning of the war Ojukwu's government probably had more than twenty million dollars' worth of foreign exchange. This was sufficient to fight a short war. In the event, however, the war dragged on much longer than Ojukwu had initially hoped, and he became faced with foreign exchange problems. Firstly, the ₦20 million reserve was quickly depleted by dubious arms deals in which the Biafrans were duped. Secondly, following the intensification of the war, the oil fields which would have provided him with a vital source of foreign exchange fell into federal hands. Similarly, the ports which would have provided outlets for the palm produce of the region were taken by federal forces. Thirdly, the sudden replacement of the old Nigerian currency by the federal government in January 1968 left the rebels with useless notes.

It is obvious, therefore, that without the financial contributions and credits provided by outside 'humanitarian' organisations as well as sympathetic countries Biafra would have been without much of the wherewithal to sustain itself during a long war.

As Dudley has rightly observed, the role of external influences in the civil war has been the subject of considerable controversy. Furthermore, he said, 'the controversy was conducted on what were essentially partisan lines and was characterised more often by a great deal of emotion rather than reason.'[14] It is necessary to analyse briefly what occurred and its effects on the war.

There were two major areas of international involvement. The first was in the supply of arms to the two warring groups. The second and equally important area was in the supply of relief materials to the starving population.

Unlike the rebels, the federal government purchased its arms directly through various governmental institutions in Britain, France, USSR, Belgium, USA, Czechoslovakia and Holland. Shortly after the start of the war and for reasons not too difficult to see, France (with its interest in oil exploitation in the war-affected area),[15] Holland, and Belgium imposed an embargo on the sale of arms to Nigeria. The rebels bought arms mainly from private suppliers. In August 1968 France became the chief supplier. According to G. Thayer,[16] France also provided the rebels with foreign currency for the purchase of arms and other supplies. Between September and October 1968 the rebels were supplied by France with up to 300 tons of arms weekly. There is a general consensus that the French arms 'began at a time when the secession had all but collapsed and in preventing that collapse, arms delivered by France to the rebels helped to lengthen the period of the war by more than one year, a year within which the agony of malnutrition and starvation reached its peak among the civilian population in the rebel areas.'[17] Other countries which for selfish reasons supplied arms to the rebels included South Africa, Israel and Portugal.

It ought to be pointed out that the support of Britain and the USSR of the federal cause were for different reasons. The USSR was interested in having a solid economic foothold in Nigeria. Britain on the other hand was more interested in influencing the federal war policies. The continued British pressure on the war policies of the federal government made dependence on the USSR for arms greater.[18]

Various relief organisations from the western countries got involved in the war. Their involvement had two major effects. In the first place it provided the rebels with free and effective publicity. According to Kirk-Greene,[19] Oxfam mounted a heavily advertised appeal for £200 000 to stop the starvation, in particular, of children. Secondly, the involvement of relief organisations provided the rebels with foreign currency. This was possible, according to Lindsay,[20] through the buying of locally produced foodstuffs and payment of landing fees for relief aircraft. The relief organisations involved included the International Committee of the Red Cross (which in the words of Kirk-Greene 'prepared an airlift that promised to be on a scale second only to that which saved Berlin in 1948'),[21] Africa Concern, the French Red Cross, and of course Caritas International.[22]

All the internationalisation of the war did not, however, earn 'Biafra' any substantive diplomatic recognition. With the exception of the inconsequential island of Haiti in the West Indies, diplomatic recognition of Biafra came from Africa. These countries were Tanzania, Zambia, Ivory Coast and Gabon. Tanzania was the first African country to recognise Biafra on 13 April 1968. In his defence of this move, Nyerere said:

> For 10 months we have accepted the Federal Government's legal right to our support in a 'police action to defend the integrity of the State'. On that basis we have watched a civil war result in the death of about 100 000 people, and the employment of mercenaries by both sides. We watched the Federal Government reject the advice of Africa to talk instead of demanding surrender before talks could begin. Everything combined gradually to force us to the conclusion that Nigerian unity did not exist.[23]

In May Zambia followed. If the motives of Tanzania and Zambia could be said to be altruistic, those of Ivory Coast and Gabon were most probably ulterior. For like the French (from whom Houphouet-Boigny and Bongo receive their inspiration) Ivory Coast and Gabon entertained morbid fears of the potential a big Nigeria possessed for influencing the politics and economics of the West African sub-region.[24]

The war of words

It is probably impossible to compare the success of the rebel propaganda and that of the Nigerians on the domestic front because they faced essentially different challenges at home. Of course both were concerned to mobilise a solid domestic front. However, whereas for the beleaguered Ibos the war was a real threat, for much of the Nigerian public it was little more than a bad dream. This meant that whereas the first task of Biafran propaganda was to imbue the Ibo with the belief that they were invincible, Nigerian propaganda was concerned with no such thing. As St Jorre has put it, the problem was rather to keep the public sufficiently interested so that the apparently inevitable victory did not elude the country by default.[25] In addition the federal government was also thinking ahead to post-war Nigeria. The ordinary Ibos would have to be reintegrated into federal Nigeria after the war. Federal propaganda could therefore not afford the emotive and insulting words which the Biafran radio was broadcasting night after night.

Because the dice were loaded against them on the battleground, the Biafrans set greater store by propaganda. They knew that their salvation lay in going to the peace table to negotiate a settlement which in the circumstances was likely to guarantee Biafran sovereignty. However, the only way to compel Nigeria into negotiations was to convince the world that the war was genocidal and thus get world opinion to force Nigeria to stop the fighting.

Biafra's propaganda unit was called the Directorate of Propaganda and was headed by Uche Chukwumerije, now the publisher of the Lagos-based *Afriscope* magazine. The directorate had several committees, including the Psychological Warfare Committee responsible for the content of all propaganda, the Political Orientation Committee responsible for organising university students to explain and justify government policies at the village level which was considered the most crucial, and the Overseas Press Service responsible for the external distribution of the directorate's releases.

The approach the directorate adopted was to portray the war as genocidal rather than a war of unity. And in the genocidal campaign itself, the war was deliberately represented as a religious conflict in which the backward Muslims were determined to impose Islam all the way to the sea.[26]

The genocidal campaign appeared credible. The 1966 pogroms in the North were real as were the brutalities of the war as it proceeded. In fact, however, the genocide was a myth. After the initial blood-letting during September 1966, the Ibos were allowed to leave for home completely unmolested. As the war progressed, more Ibos lived safely outside Biafra than inside. And as for the war being a religious conflict with the Muslims on the offensive, Gowon's government was more

Christian in membership than Muslim, as also was the fighting army. However, in wars anything can appear credible. And so it was that the Biafran Directorate of Propaganda was able to generate such extreme phobia for Nigerians among the Ibos that the world was left with little doubt that the only way the Ibo would ever feel secure was outside Nigeria.

This then was the source of the 'success' of Biafran propaganda abroad and not the Geneva-based Markpress, hired by the Biafrans to sell their case, important though its role was. The Markpress headquarters, according to Uche Chukwumerije, served merely as a 'mail-drop' for material that had been written by the Biafrans themselves. According to Stremlau[27] there was hardly any difference in the Radio Biafra transcripts of propaganda material and subsequent Markpress releases.

It can be argued that propaganda success abroad was not a result of the literature produced by the directorate because it was too virulent to be credible to an audience far removed from the theatre of war. What probably helped the propaganda effort most were the first-hand accounts given by foreigners who lived in or visited Biafra. The directorate orchestrated the visits by such foreigners to make sure they left with the unmistakable impression that the Biafrans were prepared to suffer death to be sovereign.

In contrast Nigeria's efforts to put across its point of view met with hardly any spectacular successes. Partly the Nigerian authorities were to blame. Firstly, they were slow off the mark, for while the Ibos started making their case from 1966 when secession looked inevitable, the federal government did nothing. Secondly, for a long time (and perhaps even now) it was never clear which, between the Ministry of Information and that of External Affairs, was responsible for external publicity. The feuding, of course, had an adverse effect on Nigeria's propaganda efforts. Thirdly, there was Gowon's well-intentioned but naive distaste for propaganda. He believed that that the Nigerian case was so self-evident it needed no restating.

However, the Nigerians were also severely handicapped from the beginning. The May-September 1966 killing of Ibos made the Nigerian case difficult to understand not only for the western press but also their readers. Moreover there was a generalised sympathy for the Ibos arising from the belief that they were the Jews of Africa and certainly the most westernised Africans. These and other prejudices probably weighed more against the federal authorities than their own shortcomings. In other words, it is possible that even without the shortcomings, Biafra would still have won the war of words. As John Stremlau pointed out, 'It was simply impossible to match the imagery of genocide with a discourse on the twelve-state federation.'

Peace meetings

Even before the first shot of the war was fired Nigerians and foreign interests made serious attempts to bring the federal and secessionist leaders together to avert hostilities. The most important peace conference of this period was the meeting held at Aburi near Accra, Ghana, on the invitation of Ghana's head of state, General Ankrah, in January 1967. It was attended by all the members of the Supreme Military Council. The two principal characters were, however, Gowon and Ojukwu.

Gowon was concerned at this meeting with evolving a new command structure for the Nigerian army and the reintegration of the Nigerian armed forces. It seems that he felt that once the army was brought together under an accepted leadership then the unity of the country would be preserved and the associated political problems solved. Ojukwu on the other hand saw Aburi as a forum for obtaining legitimacy for confederal arrangements, which would allow each region full control over its internal affairs and a veto over any policy decisions taken by the central government in Lagos. The final communiqué renounced the use of force to settle Nigeria's internal differences. On the central/regional relationships the members of the Supreme Military Council reaffirmed their belief in the workability of 'the existing institutions subject to necessary safeguards'.[28]

But, the Aburi meeting solved nothing. It did not ease tension in the country. A few days after the meeting the two sides began to put different interpretations on the decisions of the military leaders. It is fair to say that most people on reading the communiqué came to the same conclusion as Malcolm Macdonald, a British diplomat in Nigeria, who said in a communication to the incoming British High Commissioner to Nigeria, Sir David Hunt: 'It's simple and that's its merit: the Constitution is to be further amended to give each region almost complete autonomy, and in return the East acknowledges the unity of Nigeria and recognises the Federal Military Government with Gowon as its head.'[29]

If this decision had been implemented, the federal government would have found it impossible to govern and carry out the functions allocated to it. This point was well articulated in a memorandum to Gowon by federal permanent secretaries and the federal attorney-general. Nigeria would have become a confederation. Later Gowon said that the intention was not to have regional armies or to allow any governor to veto any decision by the Supreme Military Council. Ojukwu on the other hand saw Gowon's interpretation as an act of bad faith and a breach of agreement. From January 1967 until the formal declaration of independence in May 1967, Ojukwu and his close advisers were preoccupied with preparations for secession and the civil war.

Four more peace talks were held under the auspices of the Organisation for African Unity and the Commonwealth Secretariat, at Kampala, Addis Ababa, Niamey and Monrovia. At first the OAU intervened under the agency of a Consultative Committee of six heads of state (Mobutu, Tubman, Ankrah, Ahidjo, Diori and Haile Selassie). The decision to appoint this committee was taken at the OAU summit meeting held in Kinshasa in September 1967. Chief Obafemi Awolowo led the Nigerian delegation and was given the firm instruction by Gowon to oppose any attempt to put the Nigerian civil war on the agenda. But a strong pressure group made up of some heads of state from French-speaking Africa and East Africa was determined to discuss the issue. Chief Awolowo distinguished himself in resisting this attempt to internationalise the civil war by adhering to 'the technical point that the OAU had no jurisdiction to interfere in our affairs and if it did so it would open a floodgate of future interferences which few of the others present could afford themselves'.[30] In the end it was decided that an OAU Consultative Committee be set up. Furthermore the heads of state resolved among other things to condemn secession in any member state. They also assured the federal military government of the assembly's desire for the territorial integrity, unity and peace of Nigeria.[31]

The Consultative Committee held several meetings in Lagos, Addis Ababa and Niamey during the war. But throughout they never deviated from their belief in the territorial integrity of Nigeria, due largely to the steadfastness of Haile Selassie, Diori and Ahidjo. At the end of their first visit to Lagos in November, the committee reaffirmed the OAU summit decision condemning all secessionist attempts in Africa and agreed that as a basis for return to peace and normal conditions in Nigeria the rebels should renounce secession and 'accept the present administrative structure of the Federation of Nigeria' – that is, the twelve-state structure.

In spite of this success, the pressure on the federal military government to negotiate with the secessionists continued unabated. Public opinion in most of Europe and America was strongly against the FMG. Governments in these countries were being urged to cut off diplomatic relations with the federal government and to stop selling arms to Nigeria. These governments were in turn insisting that the FMG should show some good faith by going to the conference table with the representatives of the secessionists. Various agencies peddled a series of compromise solutions to the war, insisting that military victory could not bring peace to Nigeria.

On 23 May 1968, under the auspices of the Commonwealth Secretariat, representatives of both parties met in Kampala, Uganda. The secessionist delegation was led by Sir Louis Mbanefo. In his opening address he demanded an immediate ceasefire, removal of economic blockade and withdrawal of federal troops from the three Eastern states. Then discussions of the proposals on both sides could take place. The proposals by the secessionists included a demand for a political arrangement 'which gives Biafra full control of the security of the lives and property of her citizens in and out of Biafra'.[32]

Chief Anthony Enahoro who led the federal government delegation asserted the inalterability of the twelve-state federation. He also reminded the representatives of the secessionists that 'in military terms the concept of Biafra is now dead . . . the rebel regime is now confined to two or three towns and their environs in the interior of what journalists like to describe as the Ibo heartland. In these circumstances I suggest we address ourselves here at this meeting to the need to lay a sound foundation for a political solution at a later stage.'[33]

In the end, after nine days of fruitless discussion, the conference wound up. Nothing of substance was achieved as each side refused to budge. The war continued and the pressure on the federal government to meet again with the secessionists also continued. Some European and American newspapers even blamed the federal government for the failure of the conference. Predictably not much was said about the abduction and subsequent murder of a stenographer in the Nigerian delegation from his hotel in Kampala – an abduction which threatened to abort the conference right from the start.

The major peace conference took place in August 1968. It was an end-product of the two-day meeting of the OAU Consultative Committee in July at Niamey and six days of preliminary talks by the two sides following the meeting of the Consultative Committee. At the preliminary talks it was agreed that the agenda for Addis Ababa would be as follows:

(1) arrangement for a permanent settlement;
(2) terms for a cessation of hostilities, and
(3) concrete proposals for transportation of relief supplies to the civilian victims of the war.

The Ethiopian emperor performed the opening ceremony at Addis Ababa on 5 August 1968 and appealed to both sides to seize 'this last chance' to find a peaceful solution. Chief Enahoro, who again led the federal delegation, spoke briefly, repeating the federal government's principal conditions for a settlement. But Ojukwu, who led the large secessionist delegation, spoke for two hours, contrary to the agreed procedure. There was no trace of compromise in the speech. Rather he hammered upon the secessionist claim that physical survival of the Ibos could only be guaranteed in an independent Biafra. As Gowon did not attend this meeting Ojukwu soon left Addis Ababa and appointed Professor Eni Njoku as leaders of the secessionist delegation.

Nothing was achieved at the conference on the arrangements

for a permanent settlement or the cessation of hostilities. Neither side was prepared to yield ground. The secessionists wanted an immediate ceasefire. The federal side on the other hand insisted on a renunciation of secession. As the conference progressed and its futility became clear the leaders of delegation, Enahoro and Eni Njoku, left Addis Ababa, thus reducing the importance of the meeting. But rather than allow the conference to be a total failure, Haile Selassie prodded what remained of the delegates to negotiate on the third item on the agenda – transportation of relief materials to the civilian population in the war-affected area. This had become a serious matter due largely to the effective secessionist propaganda in Europe and America. The federal government was under pressure to grant free passage to humanitarian organisations seeking to deliver food, medicine and clothing to the victims of the war. The summer of 1968 marked the height of the propaganda war against the federal military government especially on the issue of transportation of relief material. The federal government was largely willing to support land transportation routed through 'land corridors' and daylight flights by relief organisations into Uli airport. But for strategic reasons Ojukwu and his aides preferred unrestricted night flights.

On 14 August, Emperor Haile Selassie proposed to both delegations a plan 'for simultaneously opening land and air relief corridors' into the secessionist enclave, with Lagos as the principal staging area, so as to ensure that Nigeria's sovereignty would not be violated. The plan also included elaborate provisions for international inspections during all phases of the operations. But even while the talks were going on in Addis Ababa, von Rosen, leading five of his Swedish collaborators, defied the federal government ban on night flights and undertook well publicised night missions into Uli airport to deliver relief material. Thus the talks at Addis Ababa made no progress. A solution was sought between the emperor, Gowon and the International Committee of the Red Cross, the major relief agency which had suspended night flights on the federal government's orders. On 3 September, under the aegis of Emperor Haile Selassie, the FMG and ICRC announced an agreement permitting ten days of unrestricted daylight flights to Uli airstrip. The Addis Ababa talks wound up on 9 September without achieving any success. The other peace talks – in Monrovia, April 1969 (under the auspices of the OAU Consultative Committee) and Kampala, August 1969 (promoted by Pope Paul) – achieved nothing. They merely served as a forum for both sides to restate their well known and irreconcilable conditions for a settlement. The editorial by the *New Nigerian* on the moves to convene more peace talks following the failure of the second Kampala conference reflects the thinking at the time of the federal military government. According to the paper:

> The Federal Government has reiterated its willingness to hold peace talks with the rebels, without preconditions, according to a statement in Lagos.
>
> In any preparations for a peace conference there should be one overriding precondition: any talks must be on the basis of one Nigeria. The unity and territorial integrity of this country are not negotiable. Any peace talks would be meaningless if the rebels are allowed to talk about the possibilities of secession while the Federal Government talk about the unity of Nigeria. Not only would such talks be meaningless but they would be bound to end in failure. . . .
>
> So far as we can see from rebel pronouncements the differences between the two sides are still fundamental and total. One side stands for the existence of the nation; the other stands for its destruction and disappearance. Any peace talks under these circumstances will be just another nonsense exercise.
>
> Meanwhile the Federal Government should intensify the operations to capture the remaining areas under rebel control. Above all capture Uli, which Dr. Azikiwe reminded everybody this week is the vital entry point of rebel wherewithal necessary to fight the war, and sustain the rebellion.[34]

The war economy

An important aspect of the war was the management of the economy during the war period. There is still some dispute as to the exact cost of the war. It is estimated on the federal side by Chief Obafemi Awolowo who was the federal commissioner for finance during the war that the federal government spent £230.8 million (or ₦460.15 million) in local currency and £70.8 million (or ₦140.16 million) in foreign exchange to finance the war. On the secessionist side there is some uncertainty. To get a true account one has to add up all the foreign exchange reserves of the former Eastern Nigeria government that were used initially by Ojukwu to purchase arms at the beginning of hostilities, and all the expenditures by the relief agencies who kept the secessionists afloat during most of the war. One estimate suggests that 250 million American dollars were expended by these agencies in the last fifteen months of the war to keep Biafra alive.[35]

A more relevant aspect of this is how both sides reorientated their economies after the hostilities. Chief Obafemi Awolowo's account of this issue, in a lecture at the University of Ibadan five months after the war, is one of the most exhaustive in detail and perceptive in judgement. On the one hand Nigeria lost the income to be derived from the war-affected areas. On the other hand the army had to be expanded twenty times and more arms and ammunition purchased than envisaged in the 1962/8 development plan in order to prosecute the war.

To finance the purchase of military hardware and to feed the troops the federal military government adopted some monetary and fiscal measures. For example, there were cuts in the approved estimates of all the ministries throughout the country except Defence and Internal Affairs in the budget of 1967/8, and for the duration of the war additional expenditures were not readily allowed except in respect of the following, in the order arranged below:

(1) the conduct of the war including war publicity;
(2) assistance to states;
(3) agriculture;
(4) roads.

In addition a 5 per cent surcharge on duties was imposed on a number of consumer goods, a 5 per cent compulsory savings by all salary and wage earners in the pay as you earn system, and a one naira flat rate charge on all community and poll taxpayers. In 1968 the import duty surcharge was raised from 5 to 7½ per cent, excise duties were imposed on a number of domestic manufacturers and a once-for-all levy made on all pioneer companies with an annual profit of at least £5000 (or ₦10 000).

A number of other measures were introduced. In 1968 the Central Bank was directed to finance the state marketing boards in place of the commercial banks. The commercial banks for unknown reasons refused that year, contrary to the practice, to finance the purchase of produce. Yet in the absence of oil the agricultural products, especially cocoa and groundnuts, became the principal foreign exchange earners for the federal government. In the *Annual Abstract of Statistics, 1970* (a publication of the Federal Office of Statistics, Lagos) it is shown that between 1966 and 1968 revenues from petroleum dropped from $257 million to $104 million, and in 1968 accounted for only 7 per cent of Nigeria's export earnings. Earnings from palm oil products fell even more sharply, from $93 million to $29 million. Income from cocoa, on the other hand, jumped from $79 million to $145 million, while the sale of groundnut products remained relatively steady, fetching $155 million in 1966 and $146 million in 1968. With the liberation of oil-producing areas in 1968 petroleum did provide a large amount of foreign exchange for the federal government in the concluding months of the war.

On the secessionist side, the war was started with more than $20 million in foreign exchange belonging to the former Eastern Nigeria. This was used to purchase arms for the new recruits taken on after the declaration of secession in May 1967. In addition some of £30 million in Nigerian currency in circulation in the secessionist enclave at the beginning of hostilities was unloaded in the black market abroad. But the federal government blockade of the enclave effectively prevented the secessionist regime from exporting oil abroad. And in January 1968 the federal government introduced a new currency which rendered valueless the Nigerian currency the agents of the secessionist regime were illegally exchanging abroad in the black market to earn foreign exchange.

The net effect of these measures led many observers to speculate that the secession would come to an end in August 1968: the regime was short of foreign exchange and not sufficient arms were coming in. But at this time the secessionists were winning the war of propaganda in Europe and America. Voluntary organisations, in addition to putting pressure on their governments to deny arms to the federal government and thus force it to negotiate with Ojukwu, were also giving donations in money and in kind to the so-called 'starving population of Biafra'. This became the main source of both the relief material for the civilian population and the arms for Ojukwu's army. According to John Stremlau:

> Any person or organisation wishing to transfer money to Biafra in order to pay for local goods and services would make a deposit into the London branch of the Ibo-owned African Continental Bank, and an equivalent sum would be released in local currency that was valueless outside Biafra. The sum paid to the Bank immediately became available to the Biafra government as external revenue, and could be invested in military equipment, used to pay Markpress for its propaganda services, or allocated for other foreign purchases.[36]

As observed earlier, the relief organisations kept the secession alive most probably inadvertently. When the war ended in January 1970 the federal military government proved wrong all the predictions that the end of the war would be marked by the deaths of many people. Not even mass trials of war criminals took place, much less the genocide predicted by the western press. There was also no recrimination among the general public. With adequate preparation post-war rehabilitation and reconstruction in the war-affected areas and the reintegration of the Ibos into Nigerian society were a comparatively easy exercise.[37]

3 The military and the economy

Akin Iwayemi

As in the body politic, the military phase of Nigeria's development spanning the period 1966 to 1979 also brought about some fundamental changes in the economic system. It is pertinent at this stage of the military rule to undertake an assessment of these changes.

The critical importance of political stability as a prerequisite to rapid economic development in any society cannot be overemphasised. Political disorder not only distracts the economy from performing its normal functions but also disrupts and even paralyses economic activies.[1] The military has contributed significantly to maintaining a commendable level of political stability in the country particularly since the end of the civil war in 1970.[2] This is a credit to the military.

The political order created by the military facilitated rapid economic growth during this period. Since 1970 Nigeria has experienced the most rapid economic growth in its history. Thanks are also due to oil. The considerable internalisation of the benefits of the exploitation of our oil resources during the military regime is an additional credit to the regime.[3] Finally there are two important decrees which may change the orientation of industry and agriculture in the future. These are the indigenisation decrees and the Land Use Decree. While the indigenisation decrees attempt to foster national economic independence and self-reliance, the Land Use Decree attempts to remove obstacles (such as the land tenure system) to large-scale agriculture in the rural areas and minimise land speculation in the urban areas. The implementation of these decrees has, however, left much to be desired. The indigenisation decrees have created a few Nigerian 'merchant capitalists' and worsened the distortion in income distribution. Also the foot-dragging that has so far accompanied the effective implementation of the Land Use Decree may eventually frustrate the decree.

The military was unable to resolve two major issues, namely rocketing defence expenditure and persistently serious inflation. Throughout most of this period the military was an ever increasing and largely unsatiated consumer of scarce economic resources and it contributed little of it in return to the economy in terms of productive services. In fact it had little perceptible modernising role.[4]

The huge size of the military during peace time (which by 1977 stood at approximately 250 000 men, a twenty-four-fold increase over the 1966 level) has had serious implications for the allocation of public resources. While it is true that we cannot place any specific monetary value on defence, the unproductiveness of the huge military force in peace time in the economic sense, and the huge chunk of the 'national cake' it consumes every year since 1970 without any significant productive return has continually given concern to analysts.[5]

The highest inflation rates ever witnessed by the Nigerian economy also occurred during the military era. Policy makers during the period found the solutions to the inflationary situation to be very elusive. The major contributing factors were rapid demand growth (based on oil wealth) in the face of supply and infrastructural bottlenecks, imported inflation and deficit financing by the government. Although inflation is reducing it is still in double figures.

The analysis that follows considers the performance of the economy during the military era vis-à-vis the post-independence civilian regime. The military era is divided into two periods, namely the 'war economy era' between 1966 and 1969 and the 'post-civil war era', 1970 to 1977, for which data exist. The post-civil war phase will be considered as one, although politically it covers two distinct regimes – Gowon, up to 1975 and Mohammed Obasanjo since 1975. The main reason for this is the lack of any significant economic difference between the two regimes.

Economic growth in post-independent Nigeria – an overview

The aggregate indices of economic growth used in the following analyses are based extensively on national accounting data and other statistics published by the Federal Office of Statistics and the Central Bank of Nigeria. The statistical and conceptual problems associated with the use of national accounts figures in developing countries must be kept in mind in interpreting the results. However, in the circumstances they give the best approximate indicators of what is happening in the economy and in what direction the economy is moving.

Table 3.1 (at the end of the chapter) gives a comparative picture of the growth performance of the Nigerian economy since 1960. The real rate of economic growth during the 1950s was 4 per cent per annum.[6] The post-independence civilian era between 1960 and 1965 witnessed a greater expansion in the level of economic activity over the previous period. The annual real rate of growth was an impressive 5 per cent. The period during which the military was in power experienced the fastest growth rate in Nigerian economic history. For example, the economy grew at a very high rate of 8 per cent per annum between 1966 and 1975.

At the aggregative level the military era was far better than any other in the nation's economic history. The single most important contributory factor to the fast pace of economic growth during the military era was oil wealth which rapidly accumulated between 1970 and 1973 and then rocketed in 1974 due to the rise in oil prices brought about by OPEC of which Nigeria is a member. The performance of the economy was not consistently impressive during the military era. In fact during the civil war years (1966-9) there was a downturn in economic activity and the growth rate of the economy plunged to 2 per cent per annum. The end of the civil war witnessed a resurgence of the economy and since 1970 the country has never looked back. The growth rate of the economy has averaged 8 per cent since then. Investment, exports, imports, money supply, prices and government fiscal operations vastly expanded during the military era.

Other key indicators of economic performance which will be elaborated upon later in the chapter are contained in tables 3.2 and 3.3.

Economic performance during the civilian era, 1960-65
The first five years after independence exhibited a fairly impressive growth rate compared with the colonial period. The real national output increased annually at the rate of 5 per cent (see table 3.1). However, the real *per capita* income was less impressive, rising from the very low level of ₦48.1 in 1960 to ₦53.8 implying an annual growth rate of 2 per cent.[7]

The performance of the economy during this period was uneven. The first half of the period witnessed little growth. In the years 1963 to 1965 investment grew at the rate of 13 per cent annually in real terms and the investment ratio increased from 13 to 19. The very high investment activity was an important contributing factor to the moderately encouraging economic performance.

Economic development is not simply growth in the level of economic activity and investment but also involves structural transformation occurring in the various sectors during the process of economic growth. The rates of growth of different sectors during the First Republic are shown in table 3.2. The rate of growth of the agricultural sector barely kept pace with population growth. It grew at 2 per cent per annum. Oil and mining expanded at the explosive rate of 38 per cent. This was mainly due to the rapid development in the oil sector from a relatively low base. Real value added in manufacturing increased by approximately 16 per cent while that of building and construction was 10 per cent annually. Electricity and water supply more than doubled their output within the same period. The growing sectors during this period were oil and industry.

The varying sectoral growth rates had impact on the sectoral composition of national output (see table 3.3). Although agriculture was still the mainstay of the economy, between 1960 and 1963 its share declined below 60 per cent for the first time. Oil and mining quadrupled its share and the manufacturing sector also increased its share of national output by nearly 150 per cent. The service sector also marginally improved its share.

Money supply increased at an annual rate of 6 per cent (table 3.5) but this did not inflict any serious inflationary problems on the economy. The general price level based upon the available urban consumer price index (which will be used to measure the rate of inflation in the economy) only showed a small increase of 3 per cent per annum.[8] The food component of the consumer price index (nearly half the weight) rose by only ten percentage points during the whole period, reflecting the resilient nature of the agricultural sector in providing the bulk of the food consumed in the country. For example, while the food production index with 1965 as base rose by twenty points, food imports were relatively stable (see table 3.6). Deficit financing by the federal and state governments was a key explanatory variable in the expansion of money supply. Table 3.7 gives the extent of government deficit during this period.

The economy was faced with balance of payments problems during this period. The main trends in the balance of payments statistics are shown. Merchandise trade was in deficit although the deficit declined for most of the period except for 1964. The balance on current account (goods and services) showed a fluctuating but fairly large deficit. The balance of payments deficit declined from ₦84.4 million in 1960 to ₦25.4 million in 1964.[9] By 1965 there was a marginal balance of payments surplus of ₦4.6 million. Oil was an important factor in generating this surplus. The country's foreign exchange reserves were run down from ₦370 million in 1960 to ₦197 million in 1965 to partially finance the deficits (see table 3.10). Foreign capital inflow supplemented the foreign reserve drawings above. The serious foreign exchange situation necessitated stiff tariff measures on imported goods. Declining traditional exports coupled with import requirements of rapid economic growth were mainly responsible for the deteriorating balance of payments situation. Oil was just becoming a very important export item.

The main objective of economic policy during this period was economic growth and fiscal, monetary and development policies were geared to fostering this objective.[10] Industrial policy was geared towards the encouragement of import-substituting industrialisation under a free enterprise system. Fiscal incentives including high tariff protection were designed to encourage private, domestic and foreign investment. Agriculture was consistently neglected and the rural sector based on agriculture was deprived of development funds in favour of the urban areas.[11] This encouraged the rising incidence of urban drift. Rural income worsened vis-à-vis urban income and this trend was to continue in the future.

There was no discernible price and income policy during this period. This was essentially due to little or no inflationary tendency. There was only one wage rise for civil servants in 1964 following the Morgan Commission Report. Monetary reforms to strengthen the Central Bank's control over the economy were introduced and institutional reforms to modernise the capital market were undertaken. However, there was no major tax reform and tax incentives were designed primarily to encourage manufacturing activities. Exchange rate policy was geared towards maintaining the stability of the Nigerian currency, and improvement of the external reserves.

Overall economic policy during this period was relatively effective in ensuring moderately rapid industrial growth but also contributed to the rural-urban drift and worsening income distribution. The stagnation of agriculture had begun.

Economic performance and policy under the military, 1966-77

The military era will be divided into two periods, namely the 'war economy era' spanning 1966 to 1969 and the 'post-civil war era', 1970-77. The latter phase will cover both the reconstruction period and euphoria period of oil boom.

The political and military crises of 1966 to 1969 had devastating effects on economic performance during this period. National output in 1967 and 1968 fell below the 1962 value. However, by 1969 the worst was over and the economy had recovered. Read GDP in 1969 was ₦3234.5 million, surpassing the pre-war output level (table 3.2). This is a remarkable recovery considering that in the previous year output was at the low level of ₦2544.2 million. The overall rate of economic growth during this early phase of the Gowon military regime was 2 per cent.

The genesis of the economic crisis during the war economy era can be traced to the political crisis of 1964 and 1965 and the civil and military crisis of early and mid-1966. These disorders created uncertainty, which dampened and discouraged the investment activities of private, domestic and foreign investors. From 1967 the national effort was geared towards maintaining the unity of the country and the economy suffered considerably from the war effort. Investment fell from ₦550 million in 1966 to ₦465 million in 1969, an annual decline of 3 per cent. The exclusion of the eastern states from national accounting data in 1967 to 1969 also accounts for the low figure.

Agricultural output declined by an average of 1 per cent annually. Unfavourable weather, poor transportation facilities and declining prices contributed to the decline. The food production index fell for most of the period. The food import index rose to 132 in 1966 and then declined considerably for the next two years, reaching seventy-four in 1968 – the height of the civil war. Stringent fiscal measures as regards imports during the war also contributed to the decline in food imports. By 1969 the food import index had risen to 115. Agricultural exports were also seriously affected.

The annual increase in value added in oil and mining fell from an all time high of 38 per cent in the previous five years to an all time low of 8 per cent during this period. The civil war paralysed activities in oil-producing areas of the country. Industrial activities were also affected. The rate of growth of industrial output was 4 per cent during the whole period.

Money supply grew at a higher rate than during the civilian regime: for example, between 1966 and 1969 money supply grew at the rate of 7 per cent per annum. The increased money supply was generated by the need to finance government war effort and increasing budget deficits. However, in spite of the increased money supply, prices were not seriously affected. Consumer prices rose by only 2 per cent annually. This was an improvement over the pre-civil war period. In fact the consumer price index fell in 1967 and 1968. By 1969 prices were shooting up, reflecting the increasing supply shortages and pent-up demand suppressed by the civil war. The fall in prices in 1967 and 1968 was due largely to a fall in food prices. In 1966 the food price index was 133.1. This high level was due to the disruption in distribution activities and transportation facilities following the civil disturbances in the northern part of the country and also the resulting mass movement of people. By 1968 it had fallen to 112.6 implying that agriculture was able to supply enough food for local consumption in spite of the war effort. The absence of demand by the eastern states for food from other parts of the country was also a contributing factor to the food situation. The non-food price index rose gradually throughout the period.

The trade balance improved and a trade surplus of ₦62 million was generated in 1966. This trade surplus fell in 1967 and 1968 to ₦41 million and ₦35 million respectively. By 1969 the trade surplus had risen to ₦167 million. The trade surplus was due largely to oil, for there was a trade deficit in the non-oil account. The oil surplus in 1969 was ₦236 million higher than the pre-civil war era. Oil had now become one of the most important export items. The deficit on current account continued and rose from ₦151 million in 1966 to ₦203 million in 1968. This deficit fell to ₦129 million in 1969. The balance of payments was in deficit throughout the period in spite of a rapidly rising surplus on the oil account.

In 1969 the economy had partially adjusted to the civil war, especially in those areas outside the war zones, and an upturn in the economy had started. High tariffs on imported goods and rising domestic demand gave added markets to import-substituting industry. By 1969 the index of industrial production had surpassed the pre-civil war level.

Overall the civil war had uneven effects on the various sectors in the economy. It was more devastating on building and construction and transport. Industry and agriculture responded to increased demand, withstood the rigours of war and increased their output. The civil war era witnessed the first discernible step towards an oil policy. The government wanted the local retention of benefits from oil production to increase. Capital allowances that oil companies could claim were reduced. Posted prices were also established and were henceforth to be negotiated with the government. Posted prices also became the basis for revenue calculation. Royalties and other payments which were formerly deducted from the 50 per cent government share of oil profits were now to be treated as part of the expenses that go into oil production costs. Concession agreements were also reviewed, shortening the length of the concession periods. Nigerianisation of employment in the oil companies was to be actively pursued by the government.

The post-war economy, 1970-77

The overall performance of the economy since the end of the civil war has been remarkable. The economy not only recovered quickly from the devastation of the civil war but settled down to an impressive growth performance. Real national output increased by 8 per cent annually between 1970 and 1975. The rate of growth of real investment was an incredible 35 per cent during the same period, nearly triple that for the civilian regime. Such performance had never before been witnessed in the nation's economic history. The major contributing factors to this vast expansion in output and investment were rapid growth in the oil sector and the huge government investment activities in the Second and Third National Development Plans based largely on the enormous financial resources from oil at the disposal of the government.

The post-civil war era was not a period of consistently rapid economic growth. The immediate post-war momentum of 1970 and 1971 slackened in 1972 and 1973. This was due mostly to the exhaustion of pent-up demand suppressed by the civil war, the Sahelian drought, and the moderation in oil output. By late 1973 and early 1974 the short-lived oil boom had started due to oil prices which quadrupled in less than a year. For example, Nigerian oil (light crude) rose from $3.8 per barrel in October 1973 to $14.7 per barrel on 1 January 1974. Oil revenue rose tremendously and jumped from ₦1 billion in 1973 to ₦4 billion in 1974. However, by the fiscal year 1975/6 the oil boom had started to evaporate due to the slump in world demand for oil and deliberate government efforts to limit production. By 1976 the oil euphoria was virtually gone.

Sectoral performance during the period varied. The performance by building and construction, manufacturing and the oil sector was impressive (see table 3.2). Agriculture continued to do badly and further declined by 1 per cent yearly. The share of agriculture in national output dropped below 30 per cent for the first time. Oil and manufacturing marginally improved their share.

Agriculture has consistently stagnated during the military era. The main factors responsible for the poor performance of this agricultural sector, which still employs more than 70 per cent of the labour force, include low productivity, the low level of technology in use, inadequate modern inputs, devastating weather conditions (the Sahelian drought which hit most of the north in 1972 and 1973), inadequate and unco-ordinated government policy in agriculture, and poor extension services.

The food production index continued its downward trend, declining from ninety-four in 1970 to an all time low of sixty-three in 1972. By 1974 it had risen to eighty-two but was still below the pre-civil war level. The rate of food demand outstripped food supply throughout the period. In other words the nation increasingly could not feed itself during the military era. The food imbalance had to be increasingly supplemented by food imports which have been rising very rapidly in the last few years. Between 1970 and 1975 the food import index nearly doubled. In fact an increasing proportion of the population, particularly those in the urban areas, depend largely on imported food (mainly rice, meat, fish, milk, wheat and sugar). Food imports increased at an annual rate of 25 per cent between 1970 and 1977,[12] nearly five times those of the pre-military era. The food deficit had a serious impact on the domestic price level as well as on the balance of payments. Export crop production also suffered serious setbacks, that arose largely from neglect due to the oil bonanza. In fact by 1977 the export of groundnuts, oil palm and cotton had almost ceased.[13]

The food shortage embarrassed the military as well as policy makers. The government embarked on a group of measures to accelerate food production. These measures included supplying farm inputs and technology to farmers at highly subsidised prices, the introduction of price guarantees to farmers for their food crops, reform of the marketing board system and the creation of seven commodity boards[14] to replace the old marketing boards. Two nation-wide food campaigns were also launched during this period, namely the 'National Accelerated Food Production Programme' in 1972 and the 'Operation Feed the Nation' campaigns which started in 1976. These two campaigns have so far had an insignificant impact on marketable food surplus and food prices and inflation in general.

Other long-term government actions to improve the food picture include the establishment of River Basin Development Authorities throughout the country with the grandiose objectives of establishing food plantation, irrigation facilities, flood control and water reservoirs. These river basin projects have yet to take off except for the Chad and Sokoto River Basins.

The Land Use Decree of 1978 was a laudable attempt to reform the agricultural sector. The essence of the decree in the rural areas was basically to facilitate large-scale farming.[15] The lack of effective law enforcement to back up the decree and the foot-dragging that is accompanying its implementation has left the decree rather ineffective so far. Although the decree vests all undeveloped land in the state, people are still selling land.

In the export crop sector some reforms were also carried out. The pricing policy of the marketing boards which, for several decades, has had devastating impact on farmers' income, and the decline in investment and output were reviewed. The double tax system (export duty plus produce sales tax) was abolished. The new commodity boards were now primarily to be concerned with the interest of the farmers. So far this has not yielded any significant result, but it is still early days.

Import substitution behind high tariff protection was an important factor responsible for the impressive growth performance of the manufacturing sector. However, the manufacturing sector before 1972 was largely dominated by foreign enterprises. For example in 1970 foreigners owned 63 per cent of paid up capital while private Nigerians owned about 10 per cent, and the remainder was owned by the state.[16]

In 1972 the Nigerian Enterprises Promotion Decree, also known as the 'indigenisation decree', was promulgated. The decree embodied the new government policy orientation as regards foreign investment. The essence of the decree was to retain a substantial fraction of the benefit of industrial development in Nigeria. This decree was reviewed substantially in 1977, resulting in phase 2 of the decree which was designed to correct problems that had arisen with the 1972 decree. During phase 1 several small businesses became the exclusive domain of Nigerians and several other categories of business were to have 40 per cent equity participation by Nigerians through sale of shares. During phase 2 some sectors were to have 100 per cent Nigerian ownership and several large-scale commercial and industrial enterprises were to increase Nigerian equity participation to 60 per cent. Several companies complied.

The main objective of the decree was to increase effective domestic participation in and control of industrial enterprises. This was laudable but the way the decree has worked out in practice has been the subject of heated debates.[17] It has merely replaced foreign exploiters with a small group of local 'nouveau riche' merchant capitalists.

In most enterprises, Nigerians soon found out that ownership or majority shareholding does not automatically imply control of such enterprises. It seems that even seven years after the first indigenisation decree control is still elusive. The indigenisation decree was also manipulated by local capitalists to widen further the income gap between the rich and the poor.

The manufacturing sector is still largely characterised by high-tariff, high-cost industrial structure dominated by a few consumer goods, geographical concentration in a few cities, and low technology and low labour absorption. The basic engineering, iron and steel industries are yet to be established. However, the government is making efforts to fill the vacuum. In fact in pursuit of its objective of controlling key sectors of the economy, it has embarked upon gigantic capital projects during the current Third National Development Plan (1975-80). These projects include three steel mills, at least two refineries (with one already completed), petrochemical plants, cement factories, pulp and paper and fertiliser projects. Only a fraction of these projects will be completed before the military relinquish power to the politicians in October 1979.

The efficiency with which the infrastructural system responds to the demand of the economy determines the ease with which economic growth proceeds. An inadequate infrastructure has resulted in serious disruption of economic activities, lower economic growth, and high social costs. To ease the infrastructural bottlenecks huge investments have been devoted in the current development plan to both the transport and power sectors.[18] However, four years after the beginning of the Third Development Plan and in spite of the huge investments committed to these sectors, there is still no really reliable and efficient infrastructure. Several of the proposed projects will definitely overlap into the next plan. Reliable electricity or telephone services are still elusive.[19] It must be pointed out that these infrastructural problems have both a demand and supply dimension. The demand problem is exponential growth in demand (due to oil wealth) in the face of inadequate supply that results from the long investment gestation lag. These problems will remain with us for a long time.

Oil has so dominated the Nigerian economic scene, particularly since late 1973, that the ripple effects of any short fall in the oil sector are soon felt throughout the economy. Oil has become the leading sector of the Nigerian economy in terms of growth of output, but its employment effect is small.

Oil production in commercial quantity is a recent phenomenon. By January 1970, we were producing 0.6 million barrels a day. Output increased rapidly to an average of 2.2 million barrels a day in January 1974. The slump in world demand coupled with the deliberate government policy of restricting output (a joint OPEC decision) led to a fall in output to 1.5 million barrels a day in 1975. However, there was an improvement in 1977 with output increasing to 2 million barrels a day.

Two factors were mainly responsible for the importance of oil in the 1970s, namely rapidly rising oil prices and the increased participation of the government in oil exploitation (through the then Nigerian National Oil Corporation, NNOC, now called the Nigerian National Petroleum Corporation). The state has now acquired 55 per cent of equity in oil-producing companies in the country. National oil policy during that period has been an offshoot of decisions made at OPEC meetings. Production and price decisions are often based on joint decisions by members of the organisation. The development of domestic refineries, pipeline networks and petrochemical industries are part of the Third National Plan. In fact Nigeria's oil is currently overpriced in the world market compared to our North African competitors. Nigeria is now actively participating in crude oil exploitation, refining and marketing activities through the NNPC.

Oil has dominated government finances particularly since 1971 when it constituted about half of total government revenue, double the previous year's share. In 1974 this proportion had risen to 81 per cent. The critical dependence of government revenue on oil is shown in table 3.8. In 1977 oil revenue was ₦5.8 billion out of a total government revenue of ₦8.2 billion. The fall in production in recent years largely accounts for the declining government revenue from oil. The oil bonanza resulted in vastly increased government fiscal operations (see table 3.7). There were increasing budget surpluses between 1970 and 1973 except from 1972 when the surplus dropped to ₦62 million. By 1974 the budget surplus had reached ₦1.3 billion. The situation has changed since 1975 with increasing annual deficits which have reached an unprecedented ₦3.3 billion. The main reasons for the rising deficits have been the fall in oil revenue below the projections of policy makers and the heavy commitments of government in the Third National Development Plan (₦30 billion) and the financial requirements of the new states that have been created. While federal government expenditure increased by 47 per cent annually, retained revenue only grew by 27 per cent between 1970 and 1977. However, an encouraging phenomenon is the rising share of capital expenditure as a proportion of total expenditure. Since 1974 it has averaged slightly more than 60 per cent, reflecting the development orientation of government expenditure.

Oil has also dominated exports in the post-civil war period. In 1970 it constituted 58 per cent of total Nigerian exports; by 1976 it was 94 per cent of total export proceeds. Oil has enhanced the balance of payments position. In 1974 there was a huge balance of payments surplus of ₦3 billion due to the oil bonanza. However, the ever worsening oil market coupled with rapidly rising imports has led to a return to deficits which by 1977 had reached ₦422 million.

External assets rose from ₦180 million in 1970 to ₦3.7 billion in 1975, due largely to the contribution of oil. The reserve position was such that Nigeria could finance two years' imports in 1974. However, the foreign exchange reserves started to decline in 1976 when they fell by nearly ₦300 million and by August 1978 they had fallen to ₦1 billion due largely to the decline in demand for oil, rapidly rising import requirements of economic growth and the insatiable tastes of people for imported luxuries.

The government has resorted to foreign borrowings from the World Bank and the Euro-dollar market because the financial requirements of rapid economic growth have far outstripped locally available resources. In 1978 $1 billion was borrowed from the Euro-dollar market and about the same amount will be borrowed in 1979 from the same source. Oil euphoria has vanished fast! The gap between expected and realised oil output has had a devastating impact on government financial and investment activities. Several projects have been abandoned or cut down in size.

The vastly increased government fiscal operations and the monetisation of the huge foreign exchange earnings of oil were the main factors responsible for the rapid increase in domestic money supply. Money supply rose from ₦608 million in 1970 to ₦4.8 billion in 1977 – an annual increase of 34 per cent which is nearly five times the pre-1970 increase. In fact in 1975 alone money supply increased by 74 per cent, dropping to 46 per cent in 1977. The increased money supply coupled with supply shortages, the Udoji salaries award of 1975 and imported inflation combined to create serious inflationary problems which have proved intractable. The consumer price index rose from 150 in 1970 to a whopping 423 in 1977. The situation has worsened since 1975 although a slight improvement occurred in 1979.

Inflation has become virtually the nation's number one problem. Food prices have increased rapidly each year (see table 3.5). An anti-inflation task force has been established, but although an income and productivity board was created thereafter to lay down prices and incomes guidelines, there have been few positive results. Strikes for higher pay are illegal under the military regime but wild cat strikes for higher wages still take place.

In the last few years of the military regime there has been a downturn in economic activity. The oil boom has burst. The civilian regime will inherit an economy that is sluggish and faces serious balance of payments problems.

Defence and the economy

Military expenditure has vastly expanded since the military overthrew the civilian government in 1966. The annual trend in defence expenditures between 1960 and 1975 is shown in table 3.11. In 1961 total military expenditure was ₦4 million, rising to ₦25 million on the eve of the civil war in 1966. The size of the military during this period was just under 11 000 men. The war effort tremendously increased the size of the army and the defence budget started to grow rapidly. By 1969 it stood at approximately ₦360 million. There was a marginal decline in the immediate post-war years (1970 and 1971) but it started to rise again in 1972. The ₦1 billion mark was attained in 1975. Defence expenditures actually doubled between 1974 and 1975 although the civil war had ended almost six years before. Military expenditure nearly quadrupled during peace time (1970-75).

The impact of military expenditure is highly significant in the allocation of national and public resources.[20] During the pre-military era defence constituted only 6 per cent of government expenditure. This rose to an average of 33 per cent between 1967 and 1970. From this peak it has been declining, reaching 12 per cent in 1975, but that is still about double that of peace time era. The dramatic increase in the size of the military to 250 000 by 1975 and the slow implementation of the demobilisation of the army (a very sensitive issue for the military) has been responsible for the increased defence budgets.

In 1975 7.6 per cent of real GDP was taken by defence. This is higher than that for Canada, France, West Germany, Brazil, India and South Korea, to mention a few countries which are richer and more developed than Nigeria.[21] Usually there is some correlation between the level of wealth, degree of external aggression and level of defence expenditure. It seems that there is no such correlation in the current Nigerian situation. Being in power, the military has tended to 'modernise' itself. Military expenditures have become a heavy burden on the economy. It is paradoxical that a poor country like Nigeria can continue to devote such a substantial fraction of her resources to unproductive military expenditures in peace time. Other socio-economic demands of the people have to be sacrificed.

Conclusions

The military contributed significantly to the development of the Nigerian economy during its regime. The economy not only witnessed the highest growth in its history but it was also during the military rule that the indigenisation decrees and the Land Use Decree came into existence. Although serious problems have risen as regards these two decrees, in principle they were laudable efforts that politicians could have hesitated to execute for selfish interests. Also the political stability maintained by the military since 1970 must also be recognised.

The military regime could not solve three major problems in spite of various attempts to provide remedies. These were inflation, stagnating agriculture and heavy defence expenditure. The incoming civilian regime will have to find solutions to these very serious problems or they will have very grave consequences for the country's economic development.

Table 3.1

Annual real growth rates of the Nigerian economy, 1960-75
(in percentage)

Period	*GDP*	*Investment*
1960-65	5	13
1966-9	2	–3
1970-75	8	35
1966-75	8	22

Note: The GDP and Investment growth rates are in constant 1962/3 prices. Figures are for fiscal years April to March.

Source: Computed from Federal Office of Statistics *National Accounts of Nigeria 1960/61 to 1975/76* (1978).

Table 3.2

Sectoral growth rates in the Nigerian economy for selected periods 1960-75 in constant prices
(in percentage)

Period	*Agriculture*	*Oil & Mining*	*Manufacturing*	*Building & Construction*
1960-65	2	38	15	10
1966-9	–1	8	6	1
1970-75	–1	12	14.5	21

Source: F. O. S., *National Accounts of Nigeria 1960/61 to 1975/76*, Lagos.

Table 3.3

Sectoral composition of national output in Nigeria for selected years, 1960-75
(in percentage)

	1960	*1963*	*1970*	*1975*
Agriculture	64.1	55.4	43.8	28.1
Oil & Mining	1.2	4.8	12.2	14.2
Manufacturing	4.8	7.0	7.6	10.2
Building & Construction	4.0	5.2	6.4	11.3
Others	25.9	27.6	30.0	36.2
	100.0	100.0	100.0	100.0

Source: F. O. S., *National Accounts of Nigeria 1960/61 to 1975/76.*

Table 3.4

National income, investment, exports and imports series in Nigeria, 1960-77

(₦ million)

Year	*Real GDP*[a]	*Real Investment*[a]	*Exports*[b]	*Imports*[c]
1960	2483.4	321	330	432
1961	2492.2	370	347	445
1962	2597.6	352	334	407
1963	2825.6	389	372	414
1964	2948.0	501	429	508
1965	3146.8	585	537	551
1966	3044.8	550	568	513
1967	2572.2	462	484	447
1968	2544.2	405	422	385
1969	3234.5	466	363	497
1970	4187.6	748	885	756
1971	4654.0	1065	1293	1079
1972	4933.4	1144	1434	990
1973	5236.0	1094	2277	1225
1974	5854.5	1858	5795	1737
1975	6100.5	3319	4926	3722
1976	n.a.	n.a.	6751	5149
1977	n.a.	n.a.	8674	7297

Notes:

n.a. = not available
a = in constant 1962/3 prices
b = in current prices (f.o.b.)
c = in current prices (c.i.f.)

Source: (1) GDP and Investment Series from F. O. S. (1978).
(2) Exports and imports from S. B. Falegan, 'Trends in Nigeria's Balance of Payments and Policy Measures for Self-Reliance' presented at the NISER Workshop on Trade towards Self-Sufficiency and Self-Reliance in the Nigerian Economy, Ibadan (1978).

Table 3.5

Money supply and consumer price index
1960-77

	Money supply (₦Million)	Consumer price index (1960=100) *All Items*	*Food*
1960	240.7	100	100
1961	243.0	106.4	109.8
1962	252.4	112.0	118.0
1963	268.6	108.9	106.7
1964	305.2	110.1	105.7
1965	316.9	114.4	110.5
1966	344.9	125.5	133.1
1967	313.4	120.8	119.3
1968	328.1	120.3	112.6
1969	426.8	132.3	133.9
1970	608.4	150.6	164.4
1971	628.9	174.1	211.4
1972	700.2	179.6	216.6
1973	827.2	189.3	223.6
1974	1178.4	214.7	258.7
1975	2044.1	287.4	367.2
1976	3293.0	348.2	465.7
1977	4794.6	423.1	592.2

Source: Central Bank of Nigeria, *Economic and Financial Review*: 4, 1 (1966); 10, 1 (1972); 16, 1 (1978).

Table 3.6

Index number of food production and imports in Nigeria 1960-75

Year	*Food Production Index* (1964/65 = 100)	*Food Import Index* (1965 = 100)
1960	82	105
1961	92	106
1962	92	108
1963	103	98
1964	100	118
1965	102	100
1966	89	132
1967	89	99
1968	80	74
1969	90	115
1970	94	150
1971	87	214
1972	63	204
1973	72	234
1974	82	199
1975	–	271

Source: Ojo M. O. (1977) 'Food Supply in Nigeria 1960-1975' in Central Bank of Nigeria, *Economic and Financial Review* 15, 1 (1977).

Table 3.7

Federal government retained reveneue and expenditure
1961/62 to 1977/8
(₦ million)

Years	*Retained revenue*	*Current expenditure*	*Capital expenditure*	*Total expenditure*	*Surplus/ Deficit*
1961/2	156.8	96.8	76.0	172.8	–16
1962/3	166.8	103.6	98.6	202.2	–35
1963/4	173.4	119.6	81.8	201.4	–28
1964/5	164.6	142.6	86.0	228.6	–64
1965/6	190.2	156.6	100.0	256.6	–66
1966/7	185.0	188.4	104.8	293.2	–108
1967/8	159.4	185.0	123.0	308.0	–149
1968/9	185.9	255.0	115.0	370.0	–184
1969/70	356.5	513.0	157.0	670.0	–59
1970/71	755.8	488.0	119.0	607.0	149
1971/2	1084.3	529.0	212.0	741.0	343
1972/3	1067.6	689.0	317.0	1006.0	62
1973/4	1733.8	784.0	529.0	1319.0	415
1974/5	4077.0	1076.0	1684.0	2762.0	1315
1975/6	4026.2	1920.0	3823.0	5804.0	–1778
1976/7	5040.9	2562.0	4342.0	6904.0	–1863
1977/8	5574.1	3091.0	5784.0	8875.0	–3301

Sources: (1) World Bank, *Nigeria: Options for Long-Term Development*, p.227 for data from 1961 to 1966 (1974).

(2) Federal Ministry of Finance, 'Declining Government Revenue and Measures for Mobilisation of Internal Resources for Economic Development and Self-Reliance' (1978).

Table 3.8

Oil contribution to federal government revenue, 1961-77

	Oil revenue	*Total revenue*	*Oil Revenue* / *Total revenue %*
1961	17.1	223.6	7.6
1962	16.9	238.8	7.1
1963	10.1	249.0	4.1
1964	16.4	277.6	5.9
1965	27.1	321.0	8.4
1966	37.7	339.2	11.1
1967	41.2	300.0	13.7
1968	23.3	299.9	7.8
1969	72.5	435.9	16.6
1970	196.4	758.1	25.9
1971	740.1	1410.9	52.5
1972	576.2	1389.9	41.5
1973	1461.6	2171.3	67.3
1974	4183.8	5177.1	80.8
1975	4611.7	5861.6	78.7
1976	5548.5	7070.3	78.5
1977	5821.5	8251.3	70.6

Source: As in Table 3.7 above

Table 3.9

The balance of payments in summary, 1960-77
(₦ million)

	Trade balance	Balance on goods and services	Balance on current account	Balance on capital account	B/P deficit (–) or surplus (+)
1960	–88.6	–135.2	–138.6	54.2	–84.4
1961	–87.4	–115.8	–123.4	64.0	–59.4
1962	–67.2	–97.2	–97.6	29.8	–67.8
1963	–29.2	–103.6	–109.0	69.2	–39.8
1964	–68.6	–173.4	–173.4	147.6	–25.4
1965	–5.6	–132.8	127.4	132.0	4.6
1966	62.0	–120.8	–118.4	96.8	–21.6
1967	40.8	–181.4	–116.0	122.8	–43.2
1968	34.6	–202.6	–168.2	160.0	–8.2
1969	166.8	–129.4	–108.6	80.6	–28.0
1970	173.0	–95.0	–50.0	49.2	–0.8
1971	285.0	–231.2	–229.4	293.4	64.0
1972	477.5	–295.2	–309.5	259.2	–50.3
1973	1024.1	–136.8	107.7	59.2	166.9
1974	4439.3	3124.6	3062.5	–5.9	3056.6
1975	1487.1	119.4	42.6	141.1	183.7
1976	1293.5	–161.5	–259.3	–50.6	–309.9
1977*	639.6	–537.8	–656.5	234.4	–422.1

*Provisional.

Source: S. B. Falegan, 'Trends in Nigeria's Balance of Payments and Policy Measures for Self-Reliance' presented at the NISER Workshop on Trend towards Self-Sufficiency and Self-Reliance in the Nigerian Economy, Ibadan (1978).

Table 3.10

Foreign exchange assets of Nigeria, 1960-77

(₦ million)	
1960	372.7
1961	348.5
1962	285.9
1963	192.4
1964	193.5
1965	197.1
1966	184.6
1967	102.1
1968	105.3
1969	114.6
1970	180.4
1971	302.7
1972	273.3
1973	438.6
1974	3266.6
1975	3702.6
1976	3481.6
1977	3034.0
1978*	1045.8

*1978 figure is for January to August 1978 and is provisional.

Sources: (1) Central Bank of Nigeria, *Economic and Financial Review*: 9, 1 (1971); 14, 1 (1976).
(2) Falegan S. B. (1978).

Table 3.11

Defence expenditure and national income, 1961-75

Year	*Defence expenditure (₦ million)*	*Defence/GDP*
1961	4.05	0.2
1962	8.82	0.4
1963	9.69	0.4
1964	24.7	0.9
1965	29.19	0.9
1966	25.10	0.7
1967	107.50	3.9
1968	162.62	6.1
1969	359.91	10.1
1970	314.85	6.0
1971	285.90	4.4
1972	370.25	5.0
1973	420.16	3.8
1974	532.92	3.8
1975	1116.70	7.6

Sources: (1) Adesanoye F. I. (1977) 'Nigerian Defence Policy' for data on defence expenditure.
(2) GDP data from Table 3.4.

4 The civil service: an insider's view

P. Chiedo. Asiodu

In discussing the position and role of the civil service, received opinion has tended to view the whole period of military rule as one unbroken period with no differences at various stages of its development. This is not really accurate. Rather, it is useful to break up the period into three:

(i) January 1966 to May 1967 – the Ironsi and early Gowon administrations.
(ii) June 1967 to July 1975 – the years of the civil war and the later Gowon period.
(iii) July 1975 to the present under Murtala Mohammed and later Olusegun Obasanjo.

It is true, thanks to the press in particular, and frequently articulated views amongst other sectors of the Nigerian 'élite', for example academic and business leaders, that the popular image of the civil service during the period of military rule has been one in which the civil service is seen as being very powerful (more powerful than is traditional and proper), inefficient, overpaid, self-seeking and corrupt. According to this view the bureaucracy exploited the 'innocence' of the military in government and assumed new powers. Almost as a corollary their perquisites and privileges increased and they grew more corrupt. The impression is almost given in some circles of a bureaucratic conspiracy against the country's true interests.

On the other hand the internal view during this period and now increasingly articulated (with the drastic alteration of the ground rules since 1975, as civil servants appear to have been held politically responsible for government decisions by the manner of the Purge of 1975) has been one of the civil service being misunderstood and abused, underpaid, undefended against libel and slander, unpraised for much dedicated and useful work during the several critical years of the immediate past but rather used as scapegoats by the rulers and their critics and would-be dispossessors alike.

As a matter of fact the structures, powers and functions of the civil service have remained substantially the same during the period under review and so have the motivations of the members of the public services. The altered public view will be analysed to separate myth from reality and genuine misunderstandings from calculated misrepresentations of the civil service as a strategy for attacking the 'oppressors' by proxy and for securing power.

Structure and role of the civil service before military rule

The structure of the civil service inherited at independence divided the service into four main groups. (This structure was formally established after the adoption of the Gorsuch Report of 1954 and was essentially the same in all of Commonwealth Africa patterned as it was on the British model.) At the apex was the administrative and professional class, below it the executive class with its general and technical and specialised cadres. Then the clerical and technical grades, and at the bottom the sub-clerical and sub-technical grades. The entire system was managed by the most senior officers of the administrative and professional class. Professional and technical departments were integrated into ministries together with other departments – administrative and personnel, financial, and so on – as necessary. Each ministry was under a permanent secretary who was expected to co-ordinate all the work of the ministry and tender the 'final' official advice of the ministry to the minister on policy matters. The selection and role of the permanent secretary were the source of much bitter resentment on the part of 'professional' officers which we shall examine later.

This then was the structure under the civilians. The entry qualifications for the various posts had been fixed years before. These, briefly, included a second class honours degree (or a masters degree where the educational system was the American type) for appointment to the administrative class, an honours degree and/or equivalent professional qualifications for appointment to the professional and scientific posts; a degree, or prescribed technical or professional qualifications, or equivalent training and experience for appointment to the executive class – general or technical as appropriate, School Certificate or GCE (Ordinary) for the clerical grades and Primary VI for the sub-clerical and sub-technical jobs.

These were the formal provisions. In practice, however, some flexibility was allowed for, given the educational disparities in the country and the paramount need 'to reflect the federal character' in the civil service . . . for amongst other things, issues of loyalty which we shall discuss below.

The role of the higher civil service under the civilians

As is often the case in these matters many of those who have sought to comment on the 'altered role' of the higher civil service during military rule have not paid adequate attention to studying what was indeed the position under the civilians.

The higher civil service may here be defined as the most senior corps of administrative and professional officers. These would include permanent secretaries, deputy permanent secretaries and administrative officers of equivalent grade then (that is, pre–Udoji Salary Group 6 and above); directors of professional departments and their deputies and in matters concerning the statutory bodies and corporations, the chief executives, general managers and assistant general managers of such bodies.

The main role of the higher civil service was to advise the ministers on matters of policy on functions allocated to the ministries. Once policy was decided by the ministers collectively in cabinet, or individually where the minister was competent to do so, it was the duty of the higher civil service to ensure that such policy was faithfully carried out as efficiently as was possible given the resources available and the circumstances prevailing.

Work on policy formulation might include gathering the necessary data, carrying out extensive inter-ministerial consultations, occasionally consulting external interests, and at the end of the process the permanent secretary would marshall all the information available and indicate the possible options and the consequences and repercussions of pursuing alternative courses of action. He would also, if he was worth his salt, firmly indicate the option preferred in order to facilitate the decision-making process for his minister. The minister might agree or disagree. In the latter case it was right and it was expected that there would be further discussions between the minister and his chief adviser, the permanent secretary, to clarify issues before a final position was taken by the minister. Once the minister took his final decision that was usually the end of the matter as far as the official was concerned.

There were, however, occasions when it did not end there. Where the permanent secretary felt very strongly that a wrong decision was about to be taken and that the cabinet through the prime minister should have the whole story, the permanent secretary had the right, and occasionally exercised it, to see the secretary to the prime minister and, if necessary, the prime minister himself to brief him. It was not mere fiction that federal permanent secretaries were appointed by the prime minister and were sworn in before the president, and that there was the doctrine of collective responsibility of the cabinet as a whole for the decisions of the government. Similar provisions applied in the regions.

Moreover, on matters submitted to the cabinet the complete files on the issues had to be forwarded to the Cabinet Office. This was to enable the secretary to the prime minister and his staff to see all the advice tendered on contentious and important issues and to be sure that all necessary inter-ministerial consultations had been held. The word of the minister alone on such subjects and such occasions was not always considered a sufficient basis for committing the government to a major course of action for which the government would be held collectively responsible. Quite a few issues might have been decided otherwise but for these time-tested procedures.

Of course, it was always open to a minister who felt overruled on a matter which he considered one of principle or of political faith to resign.

Once a decision was taken by the government, notwithstanding the arguments behind the scenes, it became the minister's duty to take responsibility for it publicly, defend it in parliament, and reject any criticisms of officials supposedly giving the advice on which the decision was based, or executing such policy.

The question remains: what were the various sources of policy ideas under the civilians? In theory governments could be elected on the basis of fully worked out party programmes on all important issues of government policy for the duration of their mandate, usually four to five years. In practice except for one or two issues – for instance, free primary education in the Western and later Eastern Regions in the late 1950s – this was not the case, for the simple reason that the parties were not long enough established nor rich enough to assemble party bureaucracies of the right quality and size to do such detailed policy planning and detailed programme formulation. Responsible government was introduced in the regions only in 1951 and in the federal set-up in 1957. Independence came in October 1960 and by January 1966 the civilian era came to an abrupt end.

Pressure groups such as chambers of commerce, trade unions, professional associations, market women, had their special interests. However, they were as yet not organised and equipped to offer well articulated comprehensive policy options – even on matters dear to them.

It was of the nature of a developing country like Nigeria that manpower of the right calibre was scarce and was thinly spread over the various sectors.

Therefore, nowhere outside the civil service was there an adequate concentration of the right type of talent which could begin to rival it in the relative competence and authority with which the higher civil service offered policy advice to ministers, informed by their share as citizens in the general patriotic feeling and the yearnings to improve the standard of living of the people as a whole, and modernise the economy in the prevailing context of a mixed economy which relied heavily on foreigners for technology and capital. (The Oil Boom had not yet arrived!)

Even under the civilians, therefore, the primacy of the higher civil service as the source of policy advice was clearly established. The 'masters' and the formal, publicly visible decision-makers were, however, the ministers individually and collectively.

This then was the picture under the civilians – the formal theory and structure and the practice. The problems discussed below remained, however, and were to loom large in the public view in the circumstances of military rule.

Continuing problems of the civil service

Problem areas remained. Public contact with the government was often with the junior civil servants. They often gave offence to the public through slowness, inefficiency and rudeness. Petty corruption also flourished. Those in higher civil service were often distrusted by the politicians, particularly by those not in office and therefore interacting with the civil service from a distance. There was also an important question – how to be sure that the permanent secretary and his team were loyal to the minister, particularly if the higher official was from a region and tribe different from that of the minister. In the regions (which were in any case one-party states) the problem was solved drastically by Northernisation, Easternisation and Westernisation and minority fears were often inflamed in the process.

Rivalries between administrative and professional officers

The professional officers bitterly resented what they considered to be their subordination to the administrative class after the implementation of the unpublished Newns Report on Ministerial Integration. The main complaint was that permanent secretaries, who were the heads of ministries, were 'always' chosen from the administrative class. Again, in matters of remuneration, except for one or two cases, such as the chief medical adviser, and solicitor-general, the highest salaries of professional officers were lower than that of the permanent secretary. The Udoji Report concept of a chief executive to whom a number of directorates or departmental heads would report, would even appear to 'worsen' the position for them even though the report clearly confirmed that the top position was open to them and also set out procedures for training and selection to make this easier than before.

Other grounds for resentment included the fact that because of the rapid withdrawal of expatriate political/ administrative officers after independence and their replacement by Nigerian administrative officers, the latter were often younger than their professional colleagues whose work they had to co-ordinate in the ministry.

There were also suggestions of interference with 'professional' advice by administrative officers, hence the demand that so-called professional ministries, for example, Ministries of Works and Housing, Health, Agriculture, should be headed by professional officers. In this connection nostalgic reference was often made to the 'colonial golden days' when such departments in Nigeria were under professional officers who often had guidance on professional matters from a superior in the Colonial Office in London and not in Nigeria.

Indeed, as is often the case in Nigeria, the debate was informed neither by logic, nor by an historical view, nor by charity. Logically, no one should expect that the structure of a service appropriate to a colony and protectorate should suffice and remain unchanged after the transition to independence. In the colonial situation final policy decisions were taken in London. There the highest policy-formulating officials were to be found. In a sovereign Nigeria all such functions had to be performed in Lagos. Final official advice had to be given by people trained to co-ordinate all the inputs in the ministry – including those from professional and specialised departments. Therefore, a new cadre of top administrators or managers had to be created. But even in the colonial setting, the governor-general, chief secretary, governors, and the very senior co-ordinating officers assisting the chief secretary were administrative officers, though before independence in the federal government all but three were expatriate and white. In the field, the resident, a political/administrative officer, was supreme.

The head of a large firm of architects or engineers is busy soliciting for new business, then planning its execution, finding and recruiting the men to do the job, negotiating financing, and ensuring all other logistical support to execute the contract successfully, and in the end ensuring that he is paid for the work done, and that the 'profit' is properly accounted for. He is not engaged himself in preparing architectural and engineering designs. He is engaged in managing a business. How should it be different in government with vastly more complex ministerial organisations and responsibilities and problems of liaison and joint responsibilities with many other ministries? How often in real life in developed countries is an engineering company manufacturing high technology products or selling complex technology not owned and managed by a non-engineer but an effective entrepreneur?

There is no gainsaying the fact that running a ministry calls for the highest managerial skills. Such skills can be acquired by any intelligent and talented official – administrative or professional. The important thing in managing the system is to optimise methods for discovering and motivating officials of promise from either group and training them to attain their highest potential.

Indeed it is illuminating to examine the backgrounds and careers of the federal permanent secretaries in 1974. Of the head of the service and seventeen permanent secretaries, only five started their careers in the government as administrative officers. The head-of-service himself started as a statistician and rose to the post of acting chief statistician before transferring to the administrative service. The others represent diverse professions and callings including engineering, agriculture, law, archaeology, journalism, trade unionism, industrial relations and trade promotion. One may also add that in two states medical doctors were the permanent secretaries in Ministries of Health.

It also did not require too much of an historical view to discover the reason for the relative youth of the senior indigenous administrative officers in the federal government. (Because of earlier Nigerianisation in the Western and Eastern Regions some of the older administrative officials had gravitated there in the middle 'fifties.) It was only a matter of time, not beyond the working life of the then incumbents, before the promotion prospects of administrative officials would revert to normal, and both professional and administrative officers would run the same course.

Again, it does not require much research to discover that careers and promotion prospects moved even faster in the newer departments. For example, an engineer or science graduate converting to petroleum engineering would be on superscale salary within seven years of joining the service.

A rational understanding of the functions to be performed, appreciation of the temporary dislocations of the career patterns of different classes of officials, greater charity towards one another in discounting personality clashes, would have kept the Administrative *vs* Professional rivalries in proper perspective. This did not happen. The internal dissensions inspired often colourful stories about civil service machinations which gave the service a bad image to the public, and more important to the officer corps of the military, that they contributed in no small way to the *debâcle* of 1975.

The structure and role of the civil service under the military

The structures of the civil service in particular and the public services generally have remained the same under the military as they were under the civilians. There is the same division into administrative and professional class, the executive class and the clerical grade and the sub-clerical group. The formal entry qualifications remain the same. The functions of the civil service have remained unaltered. There has also been no radical change in the functions assigned to the ministries and their departments. What then has accounted for the radically changed public image of the civil service during military rule, particularly between 1966 and 1975?

The role of the civil service under the military has remained basically the same but with several important qualifications regarding the context of their operations which account for the radical change in the public perception of their role.

First, with the suspension of parliamentary institutions and the ban on party political activity there has been no place for party bureaucracies in policy formulation and the highly visible public manoeuvres which often characterise such party activities.

Second, during the very dramatic first period of military rule, from January 1966 to May 1967, there were no politicians associated with the government. The position of ministers had been abolished and no appointees took their place. This was because the permanent secretaries successfully resisted the initial idea to appoint them to the political headship of their ministries. They preferred to remain civil servants as before. So, instead of tendering their advice to ministers who then took papers to council, the permanent secretaries now initialled council memoranda and in effect tendered their advice to the cabinet collective as a whole. In the circumstances such advice was not qualified by any party political considerations and could not appear to proceed from the mandate of any elected representatives of the people. Decisions flowing from them could be characterised as being imposed on the people.

Third, this was the period of deepening crisis and of the gathering storm of secession. The dilemma was real. It was easy to see the advantages, economic and political, of remaining one country, federal but united, but the federal argument was going by default. This was therefore a period which required public defence of the federal unifying ideal, with promises of reform and greater justice. In the absence of ministers (or, later, commissioners) on both sides, and in a situation where the protagonists were the military leaders themselves, it fell to the leaders of the federal civil service to undertake the task of defending the federal ideal. The consequences for their public image were predictable and were permanent. They were now seen as 'political masters' and no longer civil servants.

Fourth, although civil commissioners were appointed in June 1967, several of them well known political leaders, their appointment by nomination did not confer on them the authority normally derived from a popular mandate. Some of them felt their position anomalous and while willing to do their best to salvage the Nigerian state from anarchy and collapse, they looked forward to the earliest possible end to the civil war and military rule. This was a situation which naturally led to mutual mistrust between the new 'political masters' the military, and the former and 'future' rulers, the politicians. The civil servants' role, as always, was patriotically to serve the government-of-day to the best of their abilities. It is easy to see that such conduct also make their leaders suspect before the politicians, who would naturally resent what appeared to them to be bolstering up a 'usurpation'.

Fifth, it must be conceded that in matters relating to the management of the nation's finances and the economy some civil servants showed great distrust of the business sector. They appeared to claim a monopoly of patriotism, were sometimes rigid and impractical and occasioned much offence thereby.

Sixth, there was no parliament and no formal public forum for public advocacy of particular government policies which would necessarily have been undertaken by the political heads of the ministries, that is, the commissioners. This made clandestine manoeuvres inevitable and secret denials of particular government policies which proved unpopular easy. Less scrupulous people would spread false stories and half-truths about the genesis of particular government decisions. Nor was Gowon willing to impose greater discipline and public coherence amongst members of his government.

The impression was given that government decisions were formulated in great secrecy by a few officials and imposed without anyone – even those in formal positions of authority – being aware of them. This was quite false but no one tried to dissipate it. And the human being everywhere dreads and resents being governed in secrecy and by 'cabals'.

Notwithstanding these built-in difficulties of the situation there is no gainsaying the magnitude of the challenge and problems of Nigerian survival which were faced and overcome in the period 1966-75. The civil service contribution in the period was impressive. It proved resilient enough. Its claims to loyalty and objectivity were accepted by the army and the public, hence its success in helping to arrest total disintegration at the very critical points in the history of that period. The negotiations leading to a restoration of a government immediately after the July 1966 coup have been adequately described elsewhere.

The conduct of the civil war was far from efficient in many ways, but the political purposes were canvassed internally on the federal side so well that it was relatively easy to achieve an unprecedented reconciliation and re-integration after the war.

On the economic front there were impressive achievements. The financing of the war was managed and inflation kept in check while a good rate of economic growth, particularly industrial growth was sustained, with the 1970-74 plan heralding more impressive development than ever before. Fifty-five per cent control of the nation's oil resources and more than competitive prices, as well as relatively larger per barrel revenues than several other oil producers when all non-comparable factors are discounted, were achieved and this transformation in the oil sector was made without public acrimony or disruption in oil production and exports as sometimes occurred elsewhere. Moreover, there was a steady development in the country's standing in world diplomacy, particularly amongst African countries.

The Adebo and Udoji Commissions

The role of the Nigerian government necessarily expanded after the achievement of independence. An indigenous government would naturally desire to move faster to develop the economy, social services (particularly education and health) and the infrastructure. In addition there would be new dimensions in managing the external relations of a sovereign country. The final determination of policy which in the colonial context was done in London now must be done in Lagos. These developments literally exploded on the Nigerian politician and official alike because the transition period from colony to independent nation happened very fast once it began, and in any case the British had neither a tidy blueprint for such a process nor a large number of officials able and willing enough to direct such a transition.

It was soon obvious, therefore, that the civil service would need reforms to adapt its structure and orientation to its new developmental and management role in the face of a rapidly expanding public sector. It would also need new salary structures and incentives to attract and retain people of the right calibre in a new context of a rapidly growing private industrial and commercial sector offering attractive and prestigious enough careers.

It was to this end that the Adebo Commission of 1970 and the larger Udoji Commission of 1973 were set up. The former largely confined itself to an interim salary award in 1971 to ease the erosion of real incomes in the civil service. The award was a 30 per cent increase for the lower paid and about 10 per cent for superscale officers, that is, officers then earning above £2292 per annum. It should be remembered that superscale salaries had remained static since 1957 while the lower grade salaries had not been revised since the Morgan Commission Report of 1964.

The Udoji Commission recommendations were more far reaching. They abolished the multiplicity of salary scales in the public service with numerous prefixes from the alphabet (scales A, B, C, D, etc.) and grouped all salaries in the public services (defined to include not only the civil service, but university staff, the judiciary, and the public corporations and other parastatal organisations) into Grade Levels 1-17. The report also recommended considerable salary increases in an attempt to harmonise salaries in the public sector with salaries of people with 'equivalent' training and responsibilities in the private sector. Moreover, since salaries and wages had been frozen, and strikes banned for several years, it recommended some arrears although in its decisions the government went beyond the arrears recommended by Udoji.

Further, the Udoji Report sought to unify the service. It tackled the age-long dispute between professionals and administrators by making more explicit the policy that the executive leadership of a ministry (Udoji recommended the title of chief executive but the government retained the title of permanent secretary presumably largely because of the provision in the constitution and the fact that the substance was more important than the name) was open to any officer with the right talents. The report in effect re-emphasised the leadership position of the official head of a ministry or extra-ministerial organisation. To make equal access to the highest positions demonstrably visible the report recommended unified cadres and the same management training at the more senior levels.

The report also contained recommendations for improving and systematising training in the service, for setting targets and measuring results, and for improving morale – all these things hopefully designed to increase productivity and justify the large increases in salaries.

A little time has been spent in describing the Udoji Report because of the way its implementation by the government came to dominate the public view of the civil service. Large arrears were paid in one fell swoop. The large increases in salaries – in some cases near 100 per cent though on the average nearer 30 per cent – were announced with screaming and inflammatory headlines in the press all characterising the increases in a phrase very popular with the Nigerian press, 'Bonanza for Civil Servants'. The inflationary consequences in the market place were immediate and disastrous.

More unfortunately, since the government lacked the means to control the situation, the private sector successfully manoeuvred and where necessary staged strikes to restore its differentials which had been largely historically acquired through government neglect of its employees and not for economically determined reasons of productivity, scarcity, or risk.

Internally, the report rather than resolving seemed to exacerbate the Administrative *vs* Professional tension. The upper echelons of the administrative service were portrayed as self-seeking mandarins who had benefited the most. But the truth was otherwise. No one dared to criticise the upper ranks of the armed forces whose hierarchical positions within the public sector either in comparison to Nigerian structures before the civil war, or to existing situations in Britain, Europe or America, had appreciated the most.

No attention seemed to be paid to the reforms for greater productivity and efficiency. It became a convenient scapegoat for the economic ills of the country and the upper civil servants, who were considered to have offered selfish advice, were held responsible.

Relations between the federal and state civil services

One area in which military rule has meant a radical change

has been in relations between federal and regional/state civil services. The colonial unitary service was broken up in 1954 into federal and regional civil services in the wake of the adoption of the Macpherson constitution and in the quest of making Nigeria a 'true federation'.

The federal and regional, later state, governments were co-ordinate and sovereign in their respective spheres and it was considered necessary that each region should have its own civil service loyal to it and answerable to no other authority. The regional and state civil services considered themselves equal to the federal civil service and resented any leadership role from the latter notwithstanding the needs of national integration.

The historical fact that the regions attained self-government before independence was granted to the centre, and the political pressure to indigenise was manifest much earlier in the regions, meant that with higher pay and more rapid advancement the regional services were able to entice a number of senior indigenous people from the chief secretary's office and the departmental headquarters in Lagos. Two or three years later independence came, and the Nigerians they left behind began to assume the highest positions with the rapid exodus of the expatriates.

Such 'senior' men who had gone to the regions could not forget their seniority and resented any moves towards enhancing the leadership role of the federal civil service. Pay and perquisites were equal. The myth was also created that responsiblities were equal. Thus the permanent secretary of the Ministry of Finance of a region felt he was doing equally responsible work as the federal permanent secretary of finance who besides supervising the Treasury had to manage Nigeria's monetary policy in an international setting. It was also not considered relevant that there were some very important posts and responsibilities with no regional counterparts – for example, in the Ministries of Defence, External Affairs, or Mines and Power.

The political context encouraged this. The regions were the basis of power in the civilian days and federal ministers and parliamentarians were only 'delegates' from the regions. The regional governments were powerful enough to stifle the development of the federal government despite its formal responsibilities.

All those dramatically changed with the advent of military rule which also coincided after 1971 with the dramatic rise in oil revenues, the bulk of which is retained by the federal government. The splitting up of the four large regions into twelve smaller states in May 1967 was also very important.

The unified military command meant that in the final analysis regional, and later state, military governors would take instructions from the head of the federal military government and commander-in-chief of the armed forces. Larger federal revenues meant increasing dependence by the states on the federal government to finance their services. They also meant that the federal government could take on additional responsibilities. This happened particularly in education and agriculture (which is discussed more fully in chapter 10, on the politics of revenue allocation).

Such a radical change in the relative status of the federal and state governments could not but be reflected in the relative status of the federal and state civil services. The Udoji Report also made this new situation explicit and salaries at the highest levels were adjusted to reflect the primacy of the federal civil service.

Attitudes, however, die hard. The attitudes of suspicion, antagonism and resentment were still strong in 1975. It is instructive to recall that even with the politicians absent, the bulk of official advice from the regions in 1966 until the eve of the civil war was in support of a so-called confederal solution. It was easy for them to characterise the role of the federal permanent secretaries who sought to preserve an effective workable federal arrangement as one of 'power-seeking'.

These attitudes seemed to provide evidence from within the civil service in support of those criticising the upper civil service for growing powerful and political during the military regime.

The grave failure in public relations

The altered context in which the civil service endeavoured to carry out its traditional functions has been described above and consequently the altered public perception of the role of the civil servants who now looked like political 'masters'. However, there seemed to be an insufficient appreciation of the altered circumstances on the part of the leaders of the civil service. They carried on as before except for a few politically wise ones. There was no special public relations effort to tell their own story to counter the reckless allegations being rumoured about their power, and their usurpation of the functions of commissioners and the posts of corporation chairmen which in civilian times were part of the patronage system. New pushful businessmen lamented the great fortunes they might have made but for the alleged obstruction of 'powerful civil servants'.

A good public relations effort would have set the record straight – that often, particularly on the economic front, civil service advice was frequently ignored in preference to that of some external wise men, that on the political front detailed programmes for the return to participatory democracy and full civilian rule had been submitted in 1970 and again in 1971, that leading civil servants had no part in the decision to postpone the promised return of civilian rule in 1976, certainly not the much discussed 'super-permanent secretaries'.

It is true that such a campaign would have been against the rules but in retrospect far graver harm has been done to the country in not breaking such rules in order to afford some degree of open government in the absence of the public forum of parliamentary debate on government measures. The fury of the 'Purge' with its wholesale onslaught on the public services might have been alleviated if accurate and less prejudiced information had been made available in wider circles before the 'change of administration' in 1975.

The post-July 1975 situation: the Purge

The overthrow of Gowon at the end of July 1975 was immediately accompanied by a massive and unprecedented purge of the public services. It was argued that the civil service was politically responsible for the 'drift and indecision' of the later Gowon years and that its machinery must be overhauled to make progress. Accordingly over 11000 people were retired or dismissed, some in disgrace. In any country this would be a very large number of people to lose. In a developing country with endemic problems of manpower shortage the consequences would very soon be felt.

To accomplish the Purge in a matter of weeks and 'with immediate effect' – a highly popular phrase at the time – no due process was observed. The Civil Service Regulations, requiring the making of a formal charge or statement of the grounds on which disciplinary action is to be taken and inviting a defence even with only a delay of twenty-four hours or less, were set aside. There was no attempt to observe simple procedures of natural justice. Inspired complaints not brought to the attention of the alleged culprit would within hours lead to announcements dismissal or retirement on the radio.

The results were predictable. While a few genuine malefactors may have been disciplined, many more thousands of innocent, patriotic, hardworking and dedicated civil servants who had incurred the anger of some unknown and secret complainants lost their jobs.

It must be said that at first the Purge with its assumed promise of clearing the field for a more efficient, responsive and polite public service appeared popular. So also was the government posture of putting civil servants in their place – for instance, in publicly announcing 'that Permanent Secretaries were no longer to attend meetings of the Federal Executive Council'. Of course in the past they were there in attendance and would soon again be required in attendance in order to facilitate council business by supplying necessary details and information.

The Purge did not affect the formal structure of the public services. Some individuals were simply removed and others took their places in the circumstances already described. The consequences, as internal and other evaluations have shown, were on the whole counter-productive as regards productivity, initiative and risk-taking, innovation, morale and loyalty to the government of the day. Those who had taken risks to expedite government business, or had been loyal enough not to disclose their disagreements with the government behind the backs of their commissioners, had been amongst those purged. Their successors would not normally wish to be so caught out. The Purge also led to the early voluntary retirement of a number of experienced and useful officials. Security of tenure in the civil service had been seen to be drastically and irreversibly broken. Only an unwise man would wish to stay on longer than necessary not knowing what would happen after a future change of government, however peaceful.

The public service on the eve of civilian rule

As civilian rule approaches, the grave consequences of the Purge are only just beginning to assume their full dimensions. There are serious shortages of manpower and recruitment is poor. Amongst the depleted service experienced staff are very few. Since the Udoji Report training has become more systematised, but with poor recruitment and the exodus from the service the benefits are not too manifest yet. Morale is very poor and *esprit de corps* not satisfactory.

Unfortunately these manpower shortages and poor morale exist in a situation of the massive extension of the public sector since 1966 and even more so since 1975 with the creation of new regulatory and industrial and commercial organisations, and the increase of state administrations from four to twelve and finally to nineteen. Morever, the functioning of a presidential system would create additional workload for the civil service which must provide the means for the political rulers to explain their policies and organise consent for their government measures. This is the measure of the crisis.

The civil service and the future

It should be quite clear that where the civil service was not efficient enough and adequate for its tasks before 1975, it is now in a worse position. The country is expected to embark on a new phase of industrial and agricultural development involving more sophisticated technology, larger public-sector led joint ventures, more complicated international financial negotiations. A priority, therefore, must be to recreate a dynamic and efficient civil service. This task will not be easy even if successive governments accept the need.

There are a number of problems which need to be solved arising from:

(i) Heterogeneity of Nigerian society.
(ii) Nigeria being largely a pre-scientific society.
(iii) The nature and extent of competition in a developing country.

The heterogeneous nature of Nigerian society and the wide disparities in educational development of the various states have made it impossible to maintain uniform standards for everyone as regards recruitment, the measurement of performance and advancement within the civil service. Standards have been varied in the pursuit of the desirable goal of federal balance of ethnic groups and states. But such variations have meant some deserving officers being unjustly superseded, and this has depressed morale. It is also arguable that the beneficiaries, denied the stimulus of competition, do not strive to attain their full potential. Where the 'will to excellence' is absent in the civil service or is not regarded as a laudable motive, the country is bound to suffer. Nor will good recruits agree to enter such a service if they have attractive alternatives. The solution in the Nigerian case must be a compromise in which great discretion is adopted in the variation of standards and it is also made clear to all that it is a temporary expedient. Not enough care seems to have been shown in this regard in the last few years.

The public image of the higher civil service is largely what other members of the élite say it is. These are academic leaders, business leaders and independent professionals. True, the upper civil service in the years 1966 to 1975 may have exhibited a poor appreciation of the need for good public relations but the public debate amongst the other members of the élite about government policies and the role of the civil service in their formulation and execution was often not conducted on logical or scientific principles. Evidence often was neither offered nor sought for statements confidently made – especially where such statements were about wrong decisions or improper conduct. For example, I have referred to the widely diffused falsehood that 'super-permanent secretaries' advised that the 1976 civilian rule date should be postponed. Again, with regard to corruption, wild assertions were often made of people gaining tens of millions of naira from kickbacks without relating such figures to the value of the contract itself, or the possible profit margin the contractor had and from which the alleged kickbacks would be paid. Even less considered is the simple question as to how one can obtain such precise information. Is it from the accountants to the projects or accomplices? Or is it, perhaps, planted information?

Even more disconcerting are very wild statements by 'scholars' on easily verifiable comparative situations. For example: 'Oil is dearer in Nigeria than any OPEC country', or, 'There are empty ports in North Africa waiting for trans-Saharan routes which presumably can handle millions of tons of additional cargo for Nigeria, the question of costs apart'.

Some of these negative indications are perhaps due to the nature of competition in a situation of acute poverty where everybody is starting literally from scratch. All means are used to overtake the opponent or rival. Painful comparisons are continuously being made of the material rewards achieved by people in different sectors of activity, with no attention paid to the element of personal choice or vocational commitment.

While understandable, all these factors create a negative environment for healthy striving. Such a context adversely affects effort and output in the public services more than the private sector because traditionally everyone feels he is entitled to criticise publicly the civil servant who is paid from the taxpayers' money. Beyond a certain limit it becomes counter-productive.

If a successful effort is to be made to rebuild the civil service, then all members of the élite must co-operate to create a better environment. The current anti-élitist slogans must, by so called progressives, be discounted. The communist party in a communist country is an èlitist organisation *par excellence* and rightly so. So is the officer corps of a well trained army!

Conclusion

The following conclusions emerge from our survey of the civil service during military rule in Nigeria from 1966 to 1979. The structure inherited from the British has remained intact under the military as under the civilians before them. The role of the upper civil service in advising on policy and carrying out agreed policy remained the same. However, the suspension of parliament and political activity under the military and the inability or unwillingness of the key military leaders to function in the style of politicians by constantly explaining their policies and *organising consent* for them, and the presumed innocence of the military leaders, exposed the upper civil service to the full glare of publicity. Further, the easy fortunes made by a few persons, as is usual in the conditions of war, coupled with the vast economic opportunities made possible by the oil boom, expanded the prize of success and heightened the resentment of those who felt left out. Civil servants were now seen, however unfairly, as wielders of political power and dispensers of vast economic patronage. Unused to this sort of exposure the civil service gravely failed in its public relations and its image was severely damaged.

The achievements during the period of keeping the country whole, sustaining the economy and greatly accelerating its development after the war, taking over many more sectors for public sector and indigenous control – including the vital oil sector – were considerable by any standards and the civil service contribution was impressive.

Yet when the change of government came in 1975, the pent-up resentments resulted in the massive Purge which, conducted without due observance of the rules of the civil service or of natural justice, gravely demoralised and weakened the civil service. Contrary to the publicly stated goals, productivity, initiative, innovation, discipline and morale have suffered. Although the structure and role remain the same, authority is gravely dented.

It is ironical that the military regime under which civil servants are thought to have enjoyed unprecedented power and prestige has, in its closing stages, reduced the civil service capacity and will for effectiveness.

This is particularly serious since the public sector responsibilities have vastly expanded in the period 1966-78; nineteen state administrations and more complex local government organisations have also been established, and the return to democratic rule involves additional workload and pressure on the civil service.

For the future, it is imperative to rebuild the civil service. A totally new approach is needed in which the intellectual, social and economic environment is created to enable the country to recruit, train, and pay the civil service it requires for its next more sophisticated stage of economic development and modernisation.

5 The civil service: an outsider's view

Stephen O. Olugbemi

A technically competent, efficient and effective civil service is a *sine qua non* for a modern state. The consequences of continued technological and social development for the role of government in society tend to indicate that such a civil service would remain an indispensable component of governments in the future. Indeed, as the Adebo Salary Review Commission has rightly pointed out, 'the effectiveness of the government is to a large extent determined by the efficiency and competence of the civil service'.[1] What is in dispute, however, are the proper limit of the role of the civil service in the affairs of the state, and the conditions under which the institution can more effectively serve the larger interests of its society rather than its narrow corporate interests.

In conventional administrative thought, the civil service is an instrument both for policy advice and for the implementation of the will of the state as determined by legitimate political institutions to which the service must be both subordinate and subservient. Indeed, Max Weber warned that the subjection of the civil service to political control is necessary to prevent the institution from becoming a master rather than the servant of society as well as for ensuring the effective discharge of its functions.[2] Fred Riggs' (1969) 'strong constitutive' system has the same supervisory and control jurisdiction over civil service functioning as Weber's political authority.[3] The *modus operandi* of the civil service in such a system is such that would insulate it from blame when government policies misfire while allowing it a share of the credit for successful public policies.

Against this conventional wisdom is the Development Administration perspective[4] which, in addition to the traditional role of the civil service, seeks a wider and more prominent role for it in the goal-setting processes. Identifying economic development as the goal of emergent states and attributing to their bureaucracies a capacity for initiating and managing development that is unmatched by any other group of élites, development administration makes the effectiveness of the civil service contingent not upon extra-civil service control but upon unfettered opportunities to apply its creative talents and capabilities. In the words of Milton J. Esman,

> The emphasis on control of bureaucracy in the context of most of the developing countries is a misplaced priority, *one that might seriously retard their rate of progress. We ought to be much more concerned with increasing the capacity of the bureaucracy to perform, and this we see as a function of greatly enhanced professional capability and operational autonomy rather than further controls.*[5]

The emphases are important as they underscore the true intention of development administration which is increased state and bureaucratic control over individual human beings. Brian Loveman was right then in describing development administration as a 'euphemism for autocratic . . . rule'.[6] But since the civil service would not act by itself to take control of governments, it had had to rely on military regimes such as Nigeria's for the opportunity for 'creative activity' and leadership in the management of development. The point of interest, however, is how and for what purposes the civil service would direct its 'creative' talents in such a sytem. Answers to this and similar questions are better sought within the framework and perceived social consequences of declared public policies. Such answers, we submit, must define the public – that is, non-civil service – image of the institution. Accordingly, the thesis is submitted that in so far as the interests of the Nigerian state are distinguishable from the collective and/or sectional interests of the members of the civil service, Nigeria's higher civil service had exploited its partnership with the military to further and protect its corporate interests or those of its principals.

A military-civil service coalition government

On taking over the government of Nigeria on 15 January 1966, the military proscribed the political institutions of state power and disbanded the politicians. The leadership vacuum thus created was filled by members of the higher civil service, first by incorporation, and latterly by accretion as of right. Illustrative examples of the former include the establishment of an executive council comprising top civil servants for the Northern Region by Major C. K. Nzeogwu on 16 January 1966; subsequent similar developments in the three regions; the predominance of civil servants in the working parties established by General Ironsi; and the 'Delegation of Statutory Functions Order' of 1 September 1966 by which the statutory functions of individual members of the pre-1966 Federal Executive Council (FEC) were delegated to appropriate permanent secretaries and other heads of extra-ministerial departments.

What began initially as incorporation by the ruling military seemed to have been transformed into participation as of right in the immediate post-civil war period when, unannounced and without required constitutional amendments, top federal bureaucrats became members of the FEC alongside their commissioners. Indeed, Mr C. O. Lawson, a former secretary to the federal military government and head-of-service, had justified this unusually high level of political involvement on the ground that the higher civil service has, on account of its career, a great stake in the life of the 'nation' than the civil commissioners. According to Mr Lawson,

> Although the basic role of the civil servant is the same under both regimes (i.e. civilian and military), two factors have entered into the situation under the military regime and these have affected the public image of the civil servant. Firstly . . . it would seem that the minister today (that is the commissioner) is less deeply involved in governmental affairs than his predecessor for reasons which are not unconnected with the fact that all the main participants

> in the work of government today, with the exception of the commissioner, have their careers to think about . . . The effect of this is that part of the special glamour with which the minister was clothed in the civilian regime has been transferred unintentionally and imperceptibly to the Permanent Secretary. The other important factor is that because of the welcome pre-occupation of the military leadership with social and economic development rather than political activities, the civil servants now find an unprecedented opportunity for creative activity.[7]

That was 1973 but not even the partial reforms following the purges of the service undertaken by the Mohammed/Obasanjo administration in 1975 had any substantial moderating influence on the pre-eminence of the civil service in state affairs.

The close partnership between the civil service and the military in government has been explained from three standpoints. First is what may be termed the 'commonality of characteristics and interests' argument, the kernel of which is that people and institutions which subscribe to identical ethos tend to pull together for mutual advantage. It has thus been suggested that the military and the civil service tend to pull together because of their identical organisational, behavioural and ideological characteristics as bureaucratic institutions.[8] As a bureaucracy, the civil service shares with its military opposite number such attributes as functional specialisation, role specificity, a hierarchical organisation that is characterised by centralisation, upward and downward communication flows, and superior-subordinate relationships; order, discipline, internal cohesion and *esprit de corps*; secular rationality; and a commitment to goal achievement and to national service. These commonalities serve both to pull the two institutions together and to distinguish them from other social and occupational groupings. According to Milton J. Esman they constitute separately and collectively a 'relatively small, energetic and cohesive group of political entrepreneurs'.[9]

Second, there is the 'power of knowledge' explanation – a sort of social Darwinism – which postulates that only the technically competent should lead. Where he is not leading, it is the duty of those in leadership structure. Surely, the Nigerian civil service was cast in this image for much of these twelve years of military rule: with Major Nzeogwu's self-assuring declaration that 'after all, we have now got experts to do the job for us'[10] or the incessant pontification by insiders on the expertise and managerial capability of the civil service?[11]

Finally, there is the 'deficiency of the military' explanation, the thrust of which is that the military in most systems is, organisationally and in terms of managerial skills, incapable of ruling even the simplest of modern societies alone.[12] Enlightened self-interest would therefore push it in the direction of alliance with other groups, particularly the civil bureaucracy with which it shares many characteristics.

Each of these explanations has some validity for the emergent military-civil service coalition in Nigeria. That coalition and the sequestration of partisan politics which it initiated transformed Nigeria from a 'political' into an 'administered' society. The goal of that coalition was given as national development which has been variously defined to include the securing of:

(i) national unity and political stability;
(ii) a bountiful and self-sustaining economy;
(iii) social justice;
(iv) a democratic state.

The national unity objective

The most important single policy issue in the military administration of Nigeria is the unity and stability of the country. The military came into power, it will be recalled, because these attributes of a vigorous state were imperilled. The initial efforts of the military at national integration provoked the crisis of May–July 1966 which culminated in the thirty-month-long civil war. The heavy costs of the post-civil war reconstruction and rehabilitation programmes were borne to create the psychological satisfaction upon which lasting peace and harmony could grow and flourish. The public image of the civil service is, in part, a function of its role in all of these episodes.

Some commentators on Nigeria's problem of unity and stability had commended the civil service for its invaluable contributions in this area. The service is commended, for instance, for providing the semblance of government, order and continuity when everything seemed lost; for cosseting the military administration through its shaky early days; for being undaunted in its advocacy of and support for 'one Nigeria' when all other groups caved in to centrifugal forces; for providing the organisational and technical resources for the administration of the post-civil war reconstruction programmes; and for inspiring and directing further socio-economic development of the country.[13]

It would seem, in retrospect, that these seemingly commendable contributions are based on half-truths. Conspicuously omitted or underplayed are the contributions of a section of the higher civil service to the ill-conceived and ill-fated integration policies of General Ironsi;[14] the contributions of sections of the Northern Region civil service to the massacre of southern Nigerians, particularly Ibos, resident in that region in May and September-October 1966;[15] the encouragement which Ibo civil servants gave the secession inclination of Odumegwu Ojukwu;[16] the role which some civil servants played in the 1973 census controversy;[17] the overt centralisation tendencies of the federal civil service for sectional group interests; and the overt support of the regional civil services for a confederal rather than a federal Nigeria in 1966-7 – a support which according to Mr P. C. Asiodu, a former federal permanent secretary, derived from the parochial orientations of the regional services and their determination to resist any suggestion of federal civil service pre-eminence. In the judgement of Mr Asiodu,

> In place of one civil service which before 1954 had posted officers from one corner of Nigeria to another regardless of ethnic origins, we now had five civil services increasingly parochial and resentful of any suggestion of federal civil service pre-eminence, or of the need for federal directives or leadership in the national interest . . . The flow of official advice in the regions in support of a confederal

solution to the 1966 crisis owes much to the regionalistic and separatist developments from 1954 onwards.[18]

The above extract helps to reveal some of the veiled motives which inspired the actions for which the civil service, particularly the federal one, had been commended. If the civil service had cosseted the military administration through its initial shaky days and if it had secured order and provided continuity in government when everything seemed lost, it was because such actions were advantageous to its corporate interest bearing in mind the silent though perceptible feud that was developing between this crop of 'well-informed, well-educated technocrats' and the assemblage of 'poorly educated, uninventive, and largely rural political class' which controlled the pre-military government and administration of Nigeria.[19] Similar consideration for class and sectional interests could be inferred from this extract in respect of the overt centralisation of the Nigerian federal system under Gowon, as well as the repudiation of state civil services to a second order of importance which issued from the report of the federally commissioned Udoji Public Services Review Commission. Indeed, what we saw and are still witnessing in military-led Nigeria is the dilemma of equating the interests of the ruling class with those of the political community at large.

Besides, it is contestable whether an internally incohesive group such as the Nigerian civil service, operating within an equally poorly integrated political community, has any abiding lessons in unity to impart.

The import of the foregoing is that the structural and ideological weaknesses of the Nigerian civil service vitiated its capacity to contribute positively to the attainment of national unity and stability. Whenever it was associated with an integration effort, its actions were dictated more by veiled sectional interests than considerations for the common good.

The economic development objective

To development administrationists, the great attraction of bureaucratic leadership in the modernisation of new states is its greater capacity, relative to other groups, to induce and manage economic growth in fulfilment of the aspirations of their peoples.[20] This greater capacity derives, it is said, from the organisational characteristics and derivative attitudinal dispositions of bureaucratic institutions. It includes an abundant supply of technical skills; a capacity for large scale management; a disposition to accept and try new ideas; a time sense that makes men more interested in the present and the future than in the past; a better sense of punctuality; a greater concern for planning, and organisation, and efficiency; a tendency to see the world as calculable; a faith in science and technology; and a belief in distributive justice as the ultimate goal of the state.[21] Imbued with these traits, a bureaucracy would, the contention runs, transform a poor state into a prosperous one provided it is not subjected to controls from without itself.[22] It would seem that the experience of Nigeria with bureaucratic leadership in economic development is a mixed bag of successes and disappointments.

The success story is that comparative summary indices of growth record impressive achievements since the military came into power. For instance, the GDP rose from ₦4928.2 million in 1971 to ₦14.411 billion in 1974/5, showing an average annual rate of growth of about 10 per cent at 1962/3 factor cost. The contribution of the manufacturing sector to GDP rose by 1.2 per cent in 1971 while employment in that sector rose by 13.2 per cent in the same year. The share of wages and salaries as a proportion of the value of gross output in manufacturing rose from 8.1 per cent in 1970 to 9.4 per cent in 1971 while gross outputs and industrial costs grew at 12.5 per cent and 12.8 per cent in 1970 and 1971 respectively. Gross federal government revenue grew from ₦758 million in 1970 to ₦5700 million in 1976. Similar increases were recorded in the volume of government-funded social services and in the magnitude of public expenditures.[23]

The disappointments of our development efforts can be put thus: the average Nigerian has never had it so bad, with galloping double-digit inflation of the order of 20-25 per cent in some areas; a low per capita income of about ₦205; scarcity of essential commodities; mounting unemployment; inadequate and grossly inefficient public utilities; pauperisation of the rural sector by uncontrolled rural-urban migration and the relative neglect of agriculture and other rural sector occupations; increasing but dangerous dependence on oil as the main source of public revenue; a food import bill of unprecedented and ridiculous magnitude; and a sharp reversal of the nation's status from being a net lender to becoming a net borrower in the international money market.[24] The civil service cannot, in our judgement, escape responsibility for our economic failures for three reasons.

First, our economic failures are a sad commentary on the much-vaunted competence of a service which apparently lacks the capacity to (1) objectively establish and forecast input resources and relate them to needs; (2) establish the forward and backward linkages which make integrated development possible; (3) establish meaningful and co-operative rapport with all planning agencies; (4) distinguish the practicable from the desirable; and (5) stimulate in the mass of Nigerians the mental outlook that is supportive of self-propelled progress.[25] This is why attempts by top civil servants to explain and rationalise the nation's economic failures in terms of organisational and resource inadequacies tend more to evoke anger than sympathy from those who know where the nail is pinching.[26]

The second reason is the poor prioritisation of our development objects. Rather than be guided by intensely felt social needs, our development planners seem to have allowed their own interests to determine development decisions. The relative neglect of agriculture and other related services which touch upon the widest spectrum of the society derives from this weakness in the planning process.[27]

Lastly, the poor civil service leadership in development may be explained by the concept 'bureaucratisation', defined as the premature and/or unwarranted expansion of the role of government into areas of economic life which, in an open, non-socialist society like Nigeria, are normally reserved for private initiative. Three variants of this phenomenon were manifest in Nigeria at this period.

The first is the expansion of the role of government in certain areas of initiative from regulation and general control to overt participation, ostensibly to protect the country against exploitation, particularly by foreign private capital. Examples are in the industrial and agro-industrial sectors where such undertakings as the iron and steel basic complex, petrochemicals, fertiliser production, and the production of petroleum for local consumption are reserved exclusively for the federal government while others, such as plantation production of traditional cash crops and basic industrial raw materials, food industries, forest product industries, building materials and construction industries, and passenger motor vehicle assembly and related undertakings, are allowed only for joint government-private sector participation in which the proportion of government equity participation may not be less than 35 per cent.[28] While a measure of control and restriction is, admittedly, necessary for reasons of national interest, our contention is that these full-blown measures were premature, given, particularly, the well known shortage of skilled manpower and the disappointing performance of public enterprises in Nigeria.[29]

The second is the involvement of senior civil servants in the management of public enterprises either as chairmen or as board members. According to Mr Allison Ayida, he was a member of over fifty boards in his capacity as permanent secretary, federal Ministry of Finance.[30] Many senior civil servants were known to be chairmen of three to five boards and members of several others in addition to their normal jobs. A number of dangers followed from this role multiplication. First, public enterprises tended to be denied the service of outside, non-civil service, expertise which otherwise could have benefited their operations. Second, a senior civil servant serving on several boards at the same time might never have enough time for any of them, let alone his scheduled job, whatever his ability might be. Decline in efficiency and productivity were the inevitable results. Third, the possible extension of civil service rigidities to supposedly business enterprises might hamper efficient and productive performance.

The third manifestation of bureaucratisation in Nigerian administration is in the unbridled proliferation of administrative and executive agencies even where the facilities to make them work are known to be non-existent or slender. Apart from the new ministries established to cope with expansion in government functions, twenty-three new agencies were established during the Second National Development Plan period, 1970-74.[31] In 1976, eight new River Basin Development Authorities were established simultaneously. Similarly, the number of universities was increased from six to thirteen within one year. The point is not that these institutions were not necessary, but that too many of them were created too soon and apparently without sufficient forward planning. There seems then to be considerable wisdom in the assertion by Fred Riggs that in a system in which the bureaucracy is a self-serving mechanism uncontrolled by independent political forces, policies irrational for the country's economic development but rational in terms of the administrators' own self-interest tend to be developed.[32]

The objective of social justice

According to development administrationists, the ulitmate goal of bureaucratic leadership is social justice or, if you like, distributive justice. The justification for bureaucratic leadership in the economic sphere, they argue further, is its greater capacity to produce that which must be distributed. What they fail to say is that (1) those who have are often reluctant to part with their possessions for any reason whatsoever; (2) even when and where redistribution is compelled, it is the privileged who determine who gets what, how and when; and (3) in the event of a redistribution, the net gain still remains with the privileged whose new share is an addition to their previous accumulations. The implication is that, short of a revolution, social equity is impossible to achieve in a situation where, as in a bureaucratic regime, power resources are skewed in favour of a group, particularly the ruling group. Four examples from the Nigerian experience may help to illustrate this contention.

First, the salary raises made to public servants following the recommendations of the Public Services Review Commission (the Udoji Commission) had the effect of undermining an important component of the incomes policy of the government whose objective is to minimise existing inequities in wealth, income and consumption standards which may tend to undermine production efficiency, offend a sense of social justice, and endanger political stability. Although by the new salary grants the lowest paid civil servant has an absolute increase of about 130 per cent over his previous minimum wage as compared to about a 70 per cent increase for his head of department, the gap between their absolute earnings closed by only 2 per cent, that is, from the 4 per cent of pre-Udoji to 6 per cent post-Udoji. Besides, while it takes the lowest paid employee ten years to attain the maximum of ₦870 per annum on his scale, his topmost boss attains his of ₦13 959 per annum in only four years.[33] Within the service, salary disparities between occupational groups and career levels on the one hand and between federal and state civil services on the other are no less offending to a sense of social justice, and were in consequence the source of intra-service upheavals over pay in 1974/5. Against the larger Nigerian society, income inequity between civil servants and the ordinary folk was exacerbated by the Udoji grants and the fringe benefits which accompanied them. It is an act of unpardonable injustice that senior civil servants earn, in addition to their high salaries, between ₦600 and ₦960 per annum as basic allowance on cars they purchased with government loans in a country where the per capita income is about ₦205 per annum.

Second, any talk about social justice is, in our view, no more than a mere declaration of intent where power resources are not evenly, or nearly so, distributed among groups and institutions in the society, or where certain bodies can wilfully expropriate the jurisdiction of others for whatever reason. The phenomenon of bureaucratic imperialism, defined as the expropriation by the civil service of the powers and the jurisdictions of other social institutions, has been a significant feature of the behaviour of the Nigerian civil service since 1966. The result is that there is hardly any of the several extra-civil service public institutions (parastatals), including the universities, whose daily operations are not subject to directives and controls from one civil service department or another. Visible adverse consequences of this development have been a disinclination to innovativeness, use of initiative and experimentation with consequent decline in productivity and effectiveness.

Third, the incomes redistribution effect of publicly funded mass-oriented social services was undermined by the comparatively small investments made in them. Of the eight high priority service sectors slated for development under the Second National Development Plan, 1970-74, for instance, agriculture and related services which employ over 70 per cent of Nigeria's total labour force ran fourth in the allocation of investable funds; health care with its equally wide import seventh, while water supply and sewerage came eighth, as opposed to Transport, Defence and Security, and General Administration which came first, third and fifth respectively.[34] The pattern of resource allocation is not very different under the current plan. Denied of the government support necessary to upgrade his fortunes, the average Nigerian became worse off than his civil service peer.

Lastly, nothing reflects the social Darwinistic predisposition of the ruling civil service élite better than the indigenisation exercise – a public policy measure ostensibly designed to diffuse the means of power and influence by allowing indigenous people to participate in and control the commanding heights of the national economy. But with the mass of Nigerians living below or close to subsistence level and in the countryside with few, if any, banking facilities, it follows that only the urban rich and powerful could muster the resources required for the indigenisation scheme. Indeed, the success of the Nigerian Enterprises Promotion Decree (NEPD) is in creating a new class of indigenous mandarins who now combine political with economic power and influence, and could, therefore, be much more vicious in the exploitation of the country and the common man than the foreigners they displaced. As Professor Aboyade rightly observed, 'Indigenisation of the local economy cannot by itself ensure that the benefits of industrialisation will accrue to the community at large.'[35] Surely, the NEPD was more an instrument for the promotion and preservation of the interests of the ruling class and its urban peers.

The objective of a democratic state

Although the pursuit of democracy as a principle of social organisation and government is inconsistent with military rule, one would expect conscious and determined pursuit of that objective once a military regime commits itself to it. The failure of the Gowon administration to honour its pledge in this regard was a colossal disappointment – one reason, perhaps, for its displacement. And although the extent of civil service support for the 'anti-democracy' stance of that administration (suppression and repression of dissent, unlawful detention of persons without trial, press censorship, restriction of basic citizens' rights, and so on) cannot yet be established (although it certainly acquiesced in it), two current developments tend to suggest the tacit support of the civil service for Gowon's shifting of ground over 1976. One is the loud apprehensions over 1979 in sections of the civil service not, incidentally, out of concern for Nigeria after 1979 but in consideration for entrenched class interests. The other is the widely publicised attempts by many retired civil servants closely associated with the Gowon administration for elective offices in 1979. One of them, it is reported, is seeking the presidency of Nigeria. Once in a position of power and influence, only very few may want to get out permanently. The lesson for post-military civilian administration of Nigeria is obvious: if it must survive and ensure stability for the country, the higher civil service must be debriefed of its assumed intrinsic right to political leadership.

Conclusion

The image of the Nigerian civil service which emerges from this chapter is not that of an angel. It is not one of an outright villain either. Nor is it one of indolence and inaction. It is, indeed, one that is full of intensive and extensive activities determined by and directed towards the satisfaction of the sectional and/or corporate interests of the civil service in the erroneous belief that what is good for the civil service, its top members, or groups of them, is equally good for Nigeria. And if we have shown that the civil service has overblown its importance to the Nigerian state, that lapse in the service should be understood and excused as the inescapable logic of the order in which the service has been enmeshed these twelve years – an order which by its very nature, tends to concede the pride of place to the civil servant.

6 The press and military rule

L. K. Jakande

What should be the role of the press under a military regime? It is often forgotten, particularly by critics of the press, that the press is part and parcel of the society or community it serves. It is the mirror of that society. If, therefore, the society consents to a particular system of government, the press can do no more than work within that system.

If, for example, a society is content to live under a state of emergency for a period of ten years and accepts the necessity for so doing, the press can only try to do its best in the circumstances. Again, if a society's moral standards are such as to place premium on all forms of corruption the extent to which the press can fight against this evil is, for that reason, limited.

All too often, the press is blamed for almost anything that goes wrong in the state and eloquent speeches are made on what the press should have done. In 1974, for instance, a distinguished Nigerian suggested that the press should black-list all corrupt persons and refuse to give them publicity. But this is a mistaken notion of the function of the press. The press is anything but an arm of the police force and it is in any case against journalistic ethics to suppress news of public interest, whoever may be involved. It is for the law enforcement agencies to arrest and prosecute corrupt persons; it is for society at large to disapprove of them rather than share in their ill-gotten gains. It is for the press to report what they do or say.

Therefore, given a military regime and given the existence of emergency regulations, the role of the press must be reconciled to these realities. In the first place, nearly all military regimes proclaim that their intervention in politics is temporary and was brought about by the need to save the nation from collapse or disintegration. When a country is in a state of emergency, it is akin to being in a state of war. In such circumstances, the press should co-operate with the regime accepted by society by deliberately restraining its freedom of action in two vital areas. These are security and defence.

The press should, as a rule, steer clear of these two matters under a military regime. It would be a gross disservice to the nation amounting to disloyalty, for instance, to publish a detailed description of the military disposition of any nation. This is not done even in the most democratic countries in peace or war times. Apart from these two areas, there is a vast territory in which the press can exercise its freedom within the law, and it has a duty to do so without fear or favour. This is the area which challenges the initiative and enterprise and courage of the mass media.

All governments, whether civil or military, royal or republican, autocratic or democratic, prefer being praised to being censured. They like to read in their newspapers and hear on their radio and see on their television sets reports that everything is going on well under their administration. It is a natural and human desire. But it is well known that it is only in Utopia that such a perfect order exists. In the practical world with which we are concerned, things do go wrong (much to our regret) and it is the duty of the press (whoever may be its proprietor) to report and comment upon both the good and the bad.

It is not the function of the press to suppress the bad and thus create the false impression that everything is good. To do so is to endanger its own credibility and to lose public confidence. For be it noted that the failure of the press to report unpalatable events will not automatically obliterate their existence. They will remain there – to the knowledge of at least a section of the community – and perhaps get worse until they assume catastrophic proportions. Better, therefore, that those facts should be exposed and dealt with than that they should be allowed to fester like a bad and untreated sore. In any case, the journalist, in his role as historian, has no choice but to report the truth. For, as the immortals of the profession have said, facts are sacred, comments free.

The vital importance of the freedom of the press to the citizen is not often fully appreciated. Many educated persons assume that the freedom of the press is the business of editors and publishers. But the truth is that the freedom of the press is not the private property of journalists and proprietors. It is no more and no less than the liberty of the citizen to be informed.

On 14 December 1946, the General Assembly of the United Nations declared that 'freedom of information is a fundamental human right, and is the touchstone of all freedoms to which the United Nations is consecrated'. In 1965, a sub-committee headed by Lord Shawcross, was appointed by the Commonwealth Press Union to define the freedom of the press. At its Quinquennial Conference, held in that year, the union adopted the following definition:

> The freedom of the press is not a special privilege of newspapers but derives from the fundamental right of every person to have full and free access to the facts in all matters that directly or indirectly concern him, and from his equal right to express and publish his opinion thereon; and to hear and read opinions of others. In protection of these fundamental human rights, it is essential that the press should be free to gather news without obstruction, to publish the news and to comment thereon.

In our submission, therefore, any restriction on press freedom is not merely an attack on the press, it is a direct encroachment on the fundamental right of the citizen to have knowledge and information. One simple illustration will suffice to drive this point home. We all now know from practical experience that whenever there is to be a *coup d'état* one of the first targets is the national radio, the objective being to control the medium through which information is imparted to the public. That precisely is what happens whenever the freedom of the press is subjected to attack in any shape or form.

It may sound paradoxical, but it is true that a military regime needs a free press more than a civilian one. Under a military regime most of the normal channels of communication between government and people are necessarily in abeyance: parliaments, political parties, constituency organisations, elected local governments, to mention only four. A gap, therefore, tends to exist between the government and the governed. It is the press which fills that gap and which enables the governed to know what their governments are doing and the latter to have the feedback from the former.

This matter of feedback is very, very crucial. However well-intentioned a regime may be, it cannot take for granted the acceptability of its proposals or actions to the people it governs. It must constantly seek to know their reactions. A democratic government would do so through parliamentary debates, discussions at political party meetings, ministerial visits to constituencies or consultations with elected local governments. A military regime can best be served in this regard by a press which freely and faithfully reports public feelings towards government measures. If that press is not free, what the regime gets will not be the genuine article but a distortion.

A free press under a military regime must, however, take into consideration certain fundamentals. An enlightened military governor in this country once summarised the position very ably. He said that by training, soldiers were not used to having their orders questioned, much less disobeyed. When an officer asks a soldier to jump up so as to find out from which direction an enemy shot is coming, the latter has to obey, knowing that he might get killed in the process. There is no room for questioning the wisdom or morality of the order. Therefore, when soldiers in government found their actions being queried on the pages of newspapers or on radio or television their instinctive reaction was to order the critic to be brought to them. The governor added that it was the duty of the press to explain its own role to the soldiers and to stretch its right hand of fellowship to them. He was sure that they would take it.

One needs only add, by way of elaboration, that the ABC of journalism is that a journalist must satisfy himself on five questions about every matter: Why? When? How? Where? and Who? In other words, the training of a journalist is directly antithetic to that of a soldier, yet they are both servants in the master's vineyard, the master being the people, the vineyard the country.

Knowing this, the press has to do its duty of criticising the regime (when occasions call for it) in measured tone and in language that would be considered too mild for seasoned, hard-boiled and thick-skinned politicians. But it must never fail to criticise.

The foregoing paragraphs are the main points made in a public lecture which this writer delivered at the Nigerian Institute of International Affairs in December 1974 under the auspices of the Captain Dare Memorial Committee. It enunciates the philosophy and the principles which guided the role played by the Nigerian press during the era of military government from 15 January 1966 to 30 September 1979.

It was not a role which the military readily conceded. Nor were all the newspapers always united in the pursuit of that role. For example, in 1969 the *Nigerian Tribune* carried an editorial which called for a return to civilian rule. The editorial, captioned 'The way forward' argued:

> The present mood of the country which has been reflected in all spheres of our national life, calls for much more than a realistic reassessment of our situation. It demands certain immediate actions which alone can give this country the necessary change of direction. We offer no apologies to anyone for saying that in our view the time has come for a civilian government. This is a suggestion which will not be well received in certain quarters and will be greeted with suspicion in others. But we are convinced that if we are to steer ourselves out of the present morass, a civilian government is not only desirable but imperative. The most important reason in support of this suggestion is that at present the Nigerian Army is saddled with the onerous task of administering the country in addition to fighting a

> Civil War . . . The Nigerian Army needs to concentrate all its human and other material resources on winning the War. A civilian government will leave the army free to do just that.[1]

The following edition of the *Sunday Times* countered this editorial with another which virtually called for my arrest. It said:

> The demand of the *Nigerian Tribune* for an immediate transfer of power from the Armed Forces to civilians is irresponsible and unpatriotic . . . Its argument is specious and mischievous. The Military Government has to remain until the rebellion is either completely crushed or reduced to manageable size . . . side by side with fighting the war, the soldiers have, with the co-operation of their civilian commissioners, maintained economic stability for the country. They are making great plans for the future economic prosperity of the country. *Nevertheless it is true that there is a growing disenchantment with the military rulers. The reaons are not far to see* . . . But the situation in our country is not normal. To surrender power to civilians now is to invite chaos and anarchy.[2]

Not unexpectedly, as the author of the editorial in the *Nigerian Tribune* I was arrested on 2 April 1969 at 4.45 a.m. and detained in Ikoyi Prison in Lagos and later transferred to the Nigerian prison in Benin City. This arrest was widely publicised in the world press and I was released on 18 April 1969. In spite of such incidents, however, it can be said with complete justification that the Nigerian press as a whole succeeded, as no other press in similar circumstances had done, in maintaining its freedom, its integrity, its right to existence, and its indispensability.

It was, on the face of it, an impossible situation for a free press. After assuming power on 15 January 1966, the military proclaimed a state of emergency. Under this proclamation, any citizen could be arrested without warrant and detained for no stated reason. In addition, there was a decree which empowered the inspector-general of police or the chief of staff, armed forces, to detain persons indefinitely for security reasons and without trial or explanation to the detainee. Under the Armed Forces and Police (Special Duties) Decree of 1967, 'if the inspector-general of police or, as the case may be, the chief of staff of the armed forces is satisfied that any person is or recently has been concerned in acts prejudicial to public order or in the preparation or instigation of such acts, and that by reason thereof it is necessary to exercise control over him, he may by order in writing direct that that person be detained in a civil prison or at a police station; and it shall be the duty of the superintendent or other person in charge of any civil prison or the police officer in charge of any police station, as the case may be, if an order made in respect of any person under this section is delivered to him, to keep that person in custody until the order is revoked.' These two laws were used more against the press than any other section of society.

There was also in existence a Press Law enacted in 1964 which made it a criminal offence to publish any false statement. In other words, an editor could go to gaol for merely reporting innocently that an event took place in the Lagos City Hall whereas it actually occurred at the National Stadium. At one time the military regime enacted a decree which made it a criminal offence to report strikes, lock-outs, and the declaration of trade disputes. If the Nigerian press had taken cognizance of all this legislation and acted accordingly it would have become the most docile press in the world. But fortunately for the nation, the Nigerian press, as a whole, largely ignored the frightening legal position and carried on its duty as it saw it as if the legislation did not exist. This was not without a price.

Journalists and newspaper publishers were arrested in the process and some slept in police and prison cells for offences which quite often were not disclosed to them. But in my addresses to journalists on various platforms, I made a point of stressing that arrests and imprisonment were the occupational hazard of every journalist; and that every newspaper editor had the duty to publish the truth as he saw it regardless of this hazard. At a press briefing in Dodan Barracks shortly after one of these speeches had been reported in the press, the then head of state, Yakubu Gowon, shook his head threateningly at me in disapproval of the speech but later conceded that it was honourable to suffer for one's convictions.

There were, inevitably, several confrontations between the press and the government. One such confrontation came in the heat of a press campaign against corruption in high places. It was a reflection of the public mood at the time. A Nigerian businessman, Mr Godwin Daboh, swore an affidavit on 19 July 1974 alleging several acts of corruption against a federal commissioner, Mr Joseph Tarka. The press reported the allegations and in a concerted crusade for public morality succeeded in forcing the head of state to call for Mr Tarka's resignation.

Following this brilliant performance, another Nigerian businessman, Mr Aper Aku, swore an affidavit making several allegations of improprieties and abuse of office against the military governor of Benue-Plateau State, Police Commissioner Joseph Deshi Gomwalk. This time, Gowon summarily acquitted the governor of the charges against him and, for good measure, accused the press of gunning for the head of state himself. Subsequently, the Nigerian police force issued stern warnings to the Nigerian press.

In a press conference attended by most newspapers on 27 August 1974, at police-force headquarters in Lagos, the then inspector-general of police, Alhaji Kam Selem, said, among other things, that the federal military government might be compelled to take drastic and unpleasant measures to curb the excesses of the press and some cranks who profess to be journalists. He referred to what he called 'misleading and mischievous publications' by a section of the press and declared that the government would no longer 'tolerate Press indiscipline and calculated attempts to undermine the Government's authority'. He said, 'The Government will not allow itself to be blackmailed by the Press or stampeded into taking any action in any matter of public interest.' He reiterated an earlier statement by the chief of staff, Nigerian army, that 'a certain section of the Nigerian Press had overstepped its bounds and deliberately refused to observe the tenets of its profession'. In a direct reply to this statement, the *Nigerian*

Tribune, in an editorial the following day, said *inter alia*:

> There has been no malicious press attack on the Federal Government and certainly the Nigerian Press has no interest whatsoever in making mischief for this or any other government. We think it is most unfair for the Inspector-General to declare that 'some actions of the press are clearly designed to cause unrest in the country'. May we remind the Inspector-General that all Nigerian Newspapers are owned, managed and edited by full-blooded Nigerians all of whom have a stake in this country? What will any or all of them gain from causing unrest? Why should any or all of them want another crisis? For whose benefit? The truth we must face is that the Nigerian Press have a clear and inescapable duty to reflect public opinion and to seek to influence the government of the day. To deter them from that sacred duty is harmful to the Government itself – particularly a military government which does not have the various avenues of direct communication with the people, which are part of parliamentary government. A servile, docile and fawning press is the greatest danger to the Government and the country it pretends to serve. But a responsible press – and the Nigerian Press is most certainly a very responsible press – is an indispensable part of any civilized society. Far from undermining the authority of the Federal Military Government, the Nigerian Press has gone to great lengths to suggest how that authority and the credibility of the Government can be preserved. These suggestions may be unpalatable to some persons in authority but they have been made within the bounds of Nigerian Law. A wise Government would consider these suggestions, weigh them carefully, and take its own decisions on them. A foolish Government would angrily dismiss the suggestions and embark on repressive measures against the press.[3]

But by far the most dramatic and the most exciting of the confrontations was what became known as 'the Amakiri Affair'. Minere Amakiri was the correspondent in Port Harcourt (Rivers State) of the *Nigerian Observer*, based in Benin City (Bendel State). He attended a press conference of the Nigerian Union of Teachers, Rivers State branch, on 27 July 1973. In the conference the union listed a number of grievances against the state government and ended with an ultimatum to stage industrial action if their demands were not met by a certain date. The *Nigerian Observer* published Amakiri's report on 30 July 1973.

By one of those accidents in history which lead to great events, the publication coincided with the celebration of the thirty-first birthday of the military governor of the Rivers State, Commander Alfred Diete-Spiff. This annoyed the governor and his close lieutenants. The report was said to be embarrassing to the governor. The author was sent for by the military governor's office. Amakiri was collected from his house, taken to the governor's office and tortured. His head was shaved with 'an old rusty razor blade'; he was stripped naked and given twenty-four strokes of the cane on his bare back. The *Observer* reported the incident on 2 August 1973, and subsequently published fuller details of the incident. On the basis of this report, I sent, as the President of the Newspaper Proprietors' Association, the following telegram to the military governor:

> I cannot believe that the barbaric act of shaving the correspondent's head, caning him and inflicting bodily injuries on him because his newspaper had published a particular report on your birthday was perpetuated with the knowledge and consent of your Excellency. I urge you in the name of God and in the name of our dear country to condemn publicly, unequivocally and without any reservations whatsoever this primitive assault on the freedom of the press and the dignity of man.

No reply came to that telegram. I therefore summoned a representative meeting of the professional associations in the mass media – the Newspaper Proprietors Association (Nigeria), the Nigerian Guild of Editors and the Nigeria Union of Journalists – to consider how best the Nigerian press could meet the challenge of the new situation. Many suggestions were made: to black out the offending military governor from the press; to withdraw all newspaper correspondents from Rivers State; to demand a public apology from the military governor. In the end the meeting resolved as follows:

(1) To send a strongly worded memorandum to the head of state, Yakubu Gowon, condemning the maltreatment of Mr Amakiri and urging that appropriate punishment be meted out to the wrongdoers.
(2) To publish the memorandum in the press if after four weeks there is no reply from the head of state or appropriate action had not been taken on the matter.
(3) To publish in every newspaper every day for one month the question: 'What Did Amakiri Do?'
(4) To institute legal action against the perpetrators of the deed, if after the said period of four weeks, no satisfactory action was taken by the federal military government.

The letter to the head of state was signed by the presidents of the three organisations. The letter sought to bring to the notice of the head of state 'the brutal assault inflicted on Mr Amakiri by the authorities of the Rivers State Government' and urged that necessary directives be issued to 'all functionaries of the government at all levels so that the uncivilized type of behaviour exhibited in the Amakiri affair might not be repeated in our great country'. When no reply was received after four weeks, the letter was published in the press. Acknowledgement of the letter was received from Dodan Barracks by the press organisations, after the publication; no action was promised. The press, therefore, subscribed ₦3000 and briefed Mr Gani Fawehinmi, a Lagos legal practitioner, to take legal action.

Two writs of summons were issued against the governor's aide de camp, Mr Ralph Iwowari, in which Mr Amakiri sought a declaration that the detention of the plaintiff by the defendant from 4.00 p.m. on 30 July 1973 to 31 July 1973 at the Rivers State Government House was illegal and unconstitutional in that the detention was contrary to Section 21 of the 1963 Constitution of the Federal Republic of Nigeria. He also sought ₦50 000 general and special damages against the defendant, for false imprisonment of the plaintiff by the defendant, and ₦60 000 general and special damages for assault and battery on the plaintiff by the defendant and his agents.

This legal action was successful. It also gave the presiding judge, Mr Justice Ambrose Allagoa, an opportunity to make pronouncements of a far-reaching nature which undoubtedly will for ever be quoted in matters relating to the press and the government. In a judgement delivered on 20 March 1974, before a crowded court in Port Harcourt, Mr Justice Allagoa said:

> The Plaintiff should never have been flogged because whipping as a mode of punishment was abolished by section 385 of the Criminal Procedure Law, as far back as 1970. It is only juveniles that can now be punished by whipping. In the circumstances of this case, and having regard to the prevailing atmosphere of arbitrariness in Port-Harcourt which I believe was responsible for this uncivilized conduct of the Defendant, it might serve as a reminder to all concerned that although there is a military government in power and some democratic provisions of the Constitution were consequently suspended the fundamental rights touching personal liberty, freedom of movement, right to property, freedom of conscience are still provided in the Constitution.

He continued:

> The false picture given about Nigeria by the wide publicity this case got in the outside world was nowhere worse felt than in Abidjan during a meeting of judges from all over the world from the week 26th to 31st August 1973 of which there were about 5 judges from Nigeria led by the Chief Justice of Nigeria including my humble self from the *locus in quo*, Port-Harcourt. It was topical along the corridors of the August Assembly where amongst the most important resolutions passed was the very pertinent question of equality before the law and freedom from arbitrary arrest. It was therefore excruciating for those of us coming from Nigeria. I mentioned this because I sincerely hope that the report of the attitude of the court to

> this blot on our escutcheon will restore the confidence and respect we have hitherto enjoyed as a country that subscribes to the Rule of Law and not a Police State. The Rule of Law in practical terms means that no person highly placed is beyond the Law and it also implies due consideration for others and a true fear of God. The Courts are the watchdogs of these rights and the sanctuary of the oppressed and will spare no pains in tracking down the arbitrary use of power where such cases are brought before the court. The fruit reaped by respect for the Rule of Law is stability, efficient administration, and economic progress and satisfaction amongst the citizens. Persons in authority and government functionaries should by their good example command and not demand respect.

The judge awarded to Minere Amakiri ₦200 for every stroke of the cane he got, ₦2600 for being detained illegally and ₦2600 for the shave and the pain he got from the defendant. This totalled ₦10 000. Costs were assessed at ₦760.

The Amakiri affair will go down in history as a *cause célèbre* which, in the words of Dr Olu Onagoruwa, a distinguished press lawyer, 'showed to what extent those who are opposed to free press could go in order to achieve their unwholesome aims'. It also showed, said Dr Onagoruwa in his book on the Amakiri affair, 'that press freedom could only be won if those defending it are prepared to fight for it by exhausting all the constitutional avenues available'.[4]

We will never know what effect the question 'What Did Amakiri Do?' published for one month by most of the country's newspapers had on the mind of the judge. But that publication was an unprecedented device to embarrass the government by asking every day what appeared to be a simple question which could attract no legal action. It had the desired effect, thus demonstrating the power of publicity.

In a goodwill message to the fifth annual convention of the Nigerian Guild of Editors held in Kaduna on Monday, 24 February 1975, I said, 'The freedom of the press under a military regime rests on three pillars. The first of these pillars is the professional integrity of the editor. The second is the political consciousness of the Society the press serves. The third is the attitude of the Government of the day.'

It should be added that the first two pillars are far more important than the third. For no government can suppress for long a press that is professionally oriented, demonstrably courageous, and morally dependable, particularly if the people are themselves sufficiently politically conscious to want such a press.

My belief is that by and large the people of Nigeria cherish a free press (even if they do not care enough for the personal liberty of the journalist). The Nigerian press, for its part, managed to conserve its freedom of expression through the most difficult period of its life – the period of military rule. It was an achievement of great historic significance not only for Nigeria but also for the world press as a whole.

7 Foreign policy and military rule

Ray Ofoegbu

Nigeria has lived through three military governments, each of which had its distinctive impact on the country's foreign policy. For purposes of clarity and precision in analysis, it is advisable to discuss separately the periods covered by each military government. These were the periods of

(a) the *first military government* (January 1966–July 1966),
(b) the *second military government* (August 1966–July 1975), and
(c) the *third military government* (August 1975–1979).

Period of the first military government

The brief six-month period of the first military government illustrated vividly that no state which is extremely disturbed and is unstable at home can be effective in international relations. The pressing issues before the government were those of restoring communication and command to the armed forces; dispelling fears and mistrust; building some firm basis for its legitimacy; and undertaking desirable reforms in the constitutional structure, the administration and the economy of the country. Since the government came to office by default, it had no political, economic or foreign policies to implement. Hence, it established many working parties to help it articulate policy positions.

All that it did in the area of foreign policy was largely:

(a) to reassure all nations about Nigeria's commitment to all previous international obligations and commitments;

(b) to plead with foreign investors to continue investing in Nigeria;
(c) to close Nigerian regional offices overseas; and
(d) to stop regions from sending economic missions abroad.

It must be mentioned that it succeeded in restoring command communication to the Nigerian armed forces, but failed to realise that in spite of this, confidence and trust were still lacking, and fears and rumours from the civilian population reinforced the lack of confidence and trust within the armed forces. The government was thus unable to undertake a review of foreign policy, and to reassure the other nations that the domestic situation in Nigeria had sufficiently stabilised to enable Nigeria to operate effectively in the international system.

The second military government (August 1966–July 1975)
The first major rethinking of foreign policy occurred during the second military government. It affected the three main circles of Nigeria's foreign policy, namely, the Commonwealth, the world and Africa, in that order. Nigeria's relations with Britain, its experience with non-alignment, its awareness of the problems of Southern Africa, the British entry in to the European Economic Community, and the Nigerian civil war, severally and jointly caused this rethinking on foreign policy.

The Anglo-Nigerian Defence Pact generated the idea's movement as far back as 1962–3 but its momentum was not sustained. It led to an awareness that informed and politically relevant opinion in Nigeria rejected not just the pact with Britain but any type of military alignment with nations involved in the Cold War. This was done regardless of the fact that all known old friends of Nigeria were militarily aligned to the Western powers.[1] The cost of remaining non-aligned increased and hurt. It became a conscience problem, that is, an obligation on Nigeria to be true to itself and to own up to what it was really doing and believing. Nigeria was thus faced with admitting that it was economically aligned to the West, and could have been militarily drawn into power bloc alignments through the defence agreement with Britain if it had executed its defence pact with that country at a time it was proclaiming non-alignment.

The situation inside South Africa and the Unilateral Declaration of Independence by Southern Rhodesia constituted another set of soul-searching tests for Nigeria. Should Nigeria remain in a Commonwealth defended militarily in part by NATO, and in which there were NATO troops and war equipment, in the face of the dehumanising and reactionary events of Southern Africa?

It was the Nigerian civil war which completely removed the Commonwealth from the dominating position it had occupied in Nigeria's foreign policy between 1954 and 1967, and replaced it with a new emphasis on Africa, a more realistic posture towards Europe, and a genuine cultivation of the friendship of Russia and Eastern Europe.

John de St Jorre's book on *The Nigerian Civil War* stressed the most significant facts on policy towards the USSR. It emphasised that Britain maintained neutrality but continued its 'traditional' (small arms, armoured cars, etc.) and 'purely defensive' (anti-aircraft guns) supplies to Nigeria but resisted federal pressure to sell aircraft, bombs, tanks and heavy field guns to the federal military government of Nigeria. The United States government was confident that Britain would hold the 'Western line against Communist infiltration' in Nigeria. Hence, it declared a formal arms embargo against both Nigeria and Biafra.

Because of this sad experience, Nigeria looked for a nation or power ready to do business by selling weapons and receiving cash. Nigerian missions went to Moscow, negotiated arms and cultural agreements, and by August 1968 broke with tradition by importing massive military equipments from the USSR and Eastern Europe. 'Kano airport was abruptly closed to civilian traffic and Soviet Antonov freighters rumbled in with crated MiG-15 fighter-trainers on board. Two hundred Soviet technicians poured into Nigeria to assemble and test the aircraft. By the end of August the jets were in the air, piloted by Egyptians–rocketing and strafing Biafra, and introducing a new military, psychological and political element into the war.'[2]

Nigeria paid cash or bartered cocoa and groundnuts. The

Russians at first were only prepared to sell small obsolescent aircraft but later supplied MIG 17 fighters, Ilyushin bombers, heavy artillery vehicles and small arms. Russian technicians accompanied all deliveries and often stayed on to train Nigerians. The Soviet presence grew in other ways, notably in the technical assistance field when an agreement was signed in Lagos in November 1968 providing for the construction of Nigeria's first iron and steel mill by Russian technicians and with a Russian loan of ₦120 million. 'A military mission set up shop and Soviet-Nigerian friendship societies proliferated. Left wing trade unionists, the former focus of communist activity in Nigeria, felt the tight official rein loosen a little and quickly adopted a more out-spoken attitude in national affairs'.[3]

The refusal of the Americans and British to supply the arms Nigeria requested, and Russia's assessment of the likely outcome of the war at the end of July when the Nigerian mission went to Moscow, tilted Russia fully towards Nigeria.

> Russia saw that its support of Lagos could not be faulted on either ideological or political grounds, particularly as the Russians deduced from the behaviour of the West, America's diplomatic approval and Britain's limited military support of the Federal government. Soviet commitment would therefore not provoke a dangerous 'Cold War' confrontation in Nigeria. In any case, it was Nigeria that requested Russian aid and trade.[4]

John de St Jorre thus concluded that 'Ironically, British support for Nigeria had been at its weakest in the early part of the war when Nigeria needed it most and at its firmest when Lagos needed it least in the latter stages of the conflict.[5]

Britain thus became expendable in Nigeria's foreign policy decision-making. New friends were made although no drastic break with the past was permitted. The peace initiative by the Commonwealth Secretariat in the Nigerian conflict alienated Nigeria because it was based on a new form of union rather than on One Nigeria. From then on, Britain and the Commonwealth became secondary influences in the making of Nigeria's foreign policy. The British entry into the

EEC reduced further all serious considerations of the Commonwealth in the foreign policy decision-making processes of Nigeria.

The range of EEC external tariffs on Nigeria's primary products before British entry showed a low ceiling of 5 per cent and an upper ceiling of 10 per cent. Commonwealth preferences which Nigerian products enjoyed in Britain on a most-favoured-nation basis lay between 10 per cent and 15 per cent. When Britain entered the EEC, Nigeria was expected to lose, over the years, its Commonwealth preferences in the UK market.[6] This loss would not be all that there was to the problem because Britain would be bound to impose EEC common external tariffs on Nigerian goods. The combined effect of the two measures was capable of creating new tariff limits or ranges theoretically likely to be 5 per cent at the bottom and 25 per cent at the top unless effective diplomatic action was taken to alter the limits of the tariff walls.[7] Within this 5 per cent and 25 per cent range affecting eleven primary products of Nigeria, nine products were to face in the UK market alone external tariffs above 10 per cent. The Nigerian exports involved were groundnuts, cocoa, cotton, rubber, palm oil, hardwood and plywood, hides and skins, groundnut oil and benniseed.[8] These are products that determine the level of income and the general standard of living of millions of Nigerian farmers who constitute a majority of the Nigerian population. With Britain joining the EEC, it became inevitable for Nigerian foreign policy decision-makers to perceive the EEC as the new pivot of Nigeria's foreign economic policy. Arising from these conclusions, we find new objectives of Nigerian diplomacy in Europe which were to seek to reduce, if not eliminate, the economic, political and likely military disadvantages associated with the new European reality. Within Africa, the challenge became more complex. Nigeria had ignored Commonwealth Africa in developing its foreign and African policies, and was unwilling to arouse interest in it after the Nigerian civil war. But Nigeria undertook to bring together Commonwealth and other African states in order to co-ordinate and, if possible, harmonise their policies towards a new and more united Europe. This became a new goal of foreign policy. Furthermore, we may observe that Nigeria discovered that, in the 'seventies, the USA emerged as the single major contributor to Nigeria's foreign exchange earnings through its imports of Nigeria's oil. Because oil revenue commanded nearly 90 per cent of Nigeria's public revenue, the critical role of the USA in the economic life of Nigeria became clear.

Other aspects of Nigeria's foreign policy and, more significantly, Nigeria's thinking about Africa, underwent changes. The most eloquent testimony of this was in respect of West Africa; and by far the most articulate formulation of Nigeria's thinking on the issue can be found in Nigeria's Second National Development Plan.[9]

Firstly, Nigeria undertook to use the nine-station Monrovia Protocol of 1968 as a base for a series of actions geared towards the establishment of a West African Economic Community. It was perceived that the immediate preoccupation of the new states of West Africa was with 'protection': protection of their domestic economies, protection of domestic employment opportunities and concentration on import substitution industries. These states therefore safeguarded their balance of payments and discharged obligations arising from their semi-colonial economic and monetary ties. In this economic environment, it was not possible for them to undertake massive trade liberalisation policies among themselves.

Secondly, Nigeria believed that at this initial stage of wooing African states and socialising them into new ideas such as the harmonisation of economic policies, trade liberalisation, and joint or co-ordinated economic development measures, West Africa required non-discriminatory duties rather than the abolition of duties because this approach would retain customs duties as a major source of income to the new states but would, at the same time, eliminate reverse preferences or favours offered to developed countries by some West African states and found discriminatory against other West African states.

Thirdly, Nigeria perceived that West Africa as a region required the expansion of West African trade in manufactured goods, and was willing to promote this aspect of trade development.

Fourthly, Nigeria argued that time was required to bring

many other West African states to understand the needs, problems and future prospects of West Africa in the same light as Nigeria, and to formulate policies and programmes capable of leading West Africa towards economic unity. It advanced five reasons for this argument, and these were that:

(a) the individual markets of African states were very small, hence time was required to convince these states to plan for bigger markets;
(b) the volume of trade among African states was negligible when compared with Africa's trade with the rest of the world, hence these states were tempted to stress more their expanding non-African trade rather than their negligible intra-African trade;
(c) African states had not diversified their agricultural economies, hence they assumed that the similarity of West African products left them no sizeable agricultural products to export to other West African states;
(d) almost all West African states had per capita incomes that fell below the standard permissible for underdeveloped countries; because of this they could ill afford to aid one another or finance costly supranational structures and agencies, or plan massively, at the West African level, without first laying down the basic infrastructures for their social and economic development at home; and
(e) the fundamental directions of Africa's external trade and economic assistance were basically the same in the post-independence era as they were in the pre-independence colonial era. It therefore required time and courage to break these patterns and chart new ways.

Nigeria sought to point out desirable changes in favour of co-operation, and to warn that considerable time was needed to reorientate others to the thinking of Nigeria. What was very encouraging was that the notes of caution, the catalogues of obstacles, and the list of perceived problems such as limited transport networks, the questions of industrial location and language difficulties, were not seen as decisive obstacles to co-operation. There was confidence in official thinking that these problems can be solved and that the goal of economic unity can be realised.

Another major aspect of the new Nigerian policy on Africa related to style. Nigeria planned and executed official state visits by the Nigerian head of state to Dahomey, Niger, Chad, Sudan, Cameroun, Mali, Guinea, Senegal, Mauritania, Equatorial Guinea and Togo. The primary purpose of these visits was to extend Nigeria's gratitude to these states for the understanding and support which they gave the federal government during the Nigerian civil war. The visits were also used to test the correctness of Nigeria's new thoughts on Africa, and assess the readiness of African states to move away from the limitations imposed on them by the nation state system in Africa, by the realities of their colonial past and their economic predicament.

The second military government normalised relations between Nigeria, Tanzania, Ivory Coast, Gabon and Zambia. These were the African states which recognised Biafra during the Nigerian civil war. This foreign policy performance went a long way in reuniting the Organisation of African Unity thereby saving it from another source of internal divisions that would have assumed, perhaps, more permanent divisive dimensions.

Before the fall of the second military government, it worked successfully to establish the Economic Community of West African States (ECOWAS), and brought African, Caribbean and Pacific (ACP) countries together to negotiate as one group with the European Economic Community. The way it went about the ECOWAS was commendable. It worked jointly with Togo to formulate general outlines and guiding principles. Both states proceeded through effective personal diplomacy in the other thirteen states of the proposed community to explain the community idea, stress its promises, outline the obstacles on the way, and seek the involvement and membership of the prospective members. Later, preparatory conferences were held, a draft charter was agreed upon, and at a meeting of ECOWAS heads of state, the decision to establish the community was taken. The draft charter was subsequently approved, the procedures for ratification of the charter and its coming into force were also approved, and authority was given to ECOWAS officials to start work on the protocols of establishment, implementation and action.

The African, Caribbean and Pacific group initiative represented a determined effort to grapple with an old problem. Since the Rome Treaty and its Association Clause for former French and Belgian colonies, it had not been possible for African states to adopt a common or a harmonised policy towards the European Economic Community. When Britian entered the EEC, this act wiped out, for some African, Caribbean and Pacific states, whatever trading preferences they enjoyed in the British market. Within Europe, in fact in the entire industrialised world, and also within decision circles of the United Nations Conference on Trade and Development (UNCTAD), there were pressures to abandon discriminatory preferences and discuss Third World proposals for a new world economic order. Nigeria's initiative and leadership in bringing all African, Caribbean and Pacific states of the Third World together in order to negotiate as a single body with the European Economic Community was, therefore, significant.

We can sum up the essential features of Nigeria's foreign policy during the second military government as follows.

(a) The priorities of Nigerian foreign policy were changed. Before 1967, the Commonwealth, Africa, Europe and the world in that order were the priority concerns of Nigeria's foreign policy. During the Nigerian civil war, Nigeria removed the Commonwealth from the dominating position it occupied in its foreign policy, relegated Britain to a second position which it shared with the Soviet Union (a new phenomenon in the Foreign Office), and moved Africa to the first priority position.

(b) Even before Britain decided to enter Europe, Nigeria had decided to adopt a more realistic attitude towards Europe by recognising it as the new and principal trading partner of Nigeria in the 'sixties.

(c) Nigeria's new friendship with the Soviet Union, its recognition of Europe rather than Britain and the Commonwealth as its new economic and trading partners, and its limited enthusiasm for renewing warm and close relations with the United States of America, altered in some significant ways the earlier pro-West conduct of its non-alignment foreign policy. When one adds also Nigeria's recognition of the People's Republic of China to these changes, one then realises the lengths to which Nigeria went in order to be more balanced in applying the principles of non-alignment contained in its foreign policy.

(d) Nigeria reviewed its African policy. This review culminated in the establishment of the Economic Community of West African States. It also generated new thoughts aimed at counselling patience and understanding if other African states were not ready to move as fast as Nigeria wanted in seeking solutions to African problems.

(e) Nigeria strengthened relations with its neighbours and with other African states; it also normalised relations with those states that took sides against it during the Nigerian war.

(f) Nigeria offered leadership to the African, Caribbean and Pacific countries in their struggle to negotiate as one body with the European Economic Community and in their efforts, through the Third World countries, to bring about a just, better and more satisfying new world economic order.

What destroyed this government was the bankruptcy and corruption of its domestic policy rather than the foreign policy which it pursued. In fact, in the field of foreign affairs, it would be wrong not to credit the second military government with identifiable achievements and reforms.

Nigeria's foreign policy during the third military government, August 1975–August 1978

The third military government came to power in 1975 and is expected to continue in office until 1979 when it hands over power to a civilian government. In its first year in office the radicalism with which it tackled foreign policy matters shook Nigeria's relations with the major powers. It was forced by the knowledge of what it came up against to undertake what was described as a comprehensive review of Nigeria's foreign policy. Leadership was given by General Murtala Mohammed. In the second and third years of the third military government, these relations were normalised, and new as well as close ties especially with the USA and Eastern Europe were established. These extraordinary changes, if not transformations, took place rather quietly under Lieutenant-General Olusegun Obasanjo as the new leader of Nigeria. Let us review these developments.

FOREIGN POLICY UNDER GENERAL MOHAMMED

Angola and Nigeria–USA relations Severe strains in Nigeria's relations with the USA occurred during the first year of the third military government. The central issue was Angola. Nigeria's perception of the Angola tragedy was fundamentally opposed to the US perception of the same problem. Hence the action which Nigeria took to help effect a settlement ran counter to actions taken by the USA. Initially, Nigeria's initial position was to encourage the three leading groups–MPLA, FLNA and UNITA–to seek to accommodate one another; to agree to receive jointly the independence of their country and to work together for the benefit of their peoples. Nigeria was even prepared to support some delay in the transfer of power in order to achieve the policy goals of securing independence through a government of national unity in Angola. Foreign intervention in Angola completely altered the setting and necessitated an immediate review of policy. A truly independent Angola could neutralise the Caprivi Strip and deprive South Africa and Rhodesia of this military base which they have used to frustrate the independence and Pan-African aspirations of Zambia, Botswana and Zimbabwe. South African and Western economic interests in Angola wanted a 'puppet' government in Angola (a government which would neither threaten their economic interests in this country nor allow Black Africa to utilise the strategic advantages of Angola in the struggle to restore human rights and establish popular governments in Rhodesia, South Africa and Namibia). Because of the strategic and economic interests of the USA in South Africa, the USA perceived Angola more or less from the standpoint of South Africa.

That is, the USA wanted in Angola a government which would neither threaten Western interests in Southern Africa nor seek to force radical political changes on Southern Africa. The USA decided to support the FLNA–UNITA alliance which was being supported by South Africa; overlooked South Africa's military intervention in the Angola crisis, and concentrated any criticisms on the involvement of Soviet and Cuban forces on the side of the MPLA.

As explained earlier, Nigeria did not initially take sides in the Angola crisis. Nigeria did not approve of Soviet and Cuban military involvements in support of the MPLA because all forms of foreign intervention were seen as obstacles to the formation of a government of national unity. Nigeria understood, however, that Soviet aid to the MPLA pre-dated Angola's independence; and knew that the MPLA's armed struggle against Portuguese colonialism was made possible by continued Soviet assistance in money, equipment and men, and that the interests of the Cubans could not be to colonise Angola, seize its wealth, and frustrate the total liberation of Southern Africa. In any case, none of these considerations changed Nigeria's initial policy on Angola.

The change of policy came about because:

(1) South Africa dispatched an invading force into Angola;
(2) and planned 'to crush the most powerful and nationalistic of the liberation movements–the MPLA' and install 'a puppet reactionary regime' of the FLNA and UNITA[10] and
(3) Western economic interests which exploited Angola during colonial times now sought 'to continue to avail themselves of Angola's wealth to their selfish advantage and to the detriment of Angolan peoples even after their independence'.[11]

Nigeria, therefore, decided to support the independence of Angola, to recognise the MPLA government as the legitimate government of Angola, and to assist it in its struggles to unify Angola and defeat the South African invaders and collaborators. It also decided to approve Soviet and Cuban involvements on the side of the MPLA as involvements legitimately requested by the sovereign people and government of Angola, and as actions unlikely to undermine the independence of Angola.

The contradiction between the policy position of Nigeria and that of the USA became dramatic. Regrettably, Nigeria did not launch any diplomatic offensive in Africa to win other African states to its policy position. It was rather the USA which went all-out to fight what it perceived as the dangers of communism and the export of Castro's revolution into Africa through Angola. President Ford wrote personal letters to African heads of state, and along with his secretary of state he dispatched a high-powered diplomatic mission to African governments to explain US policy in Angola. The overall goal of the United States' efforts was to persuade these governments not to follow Nigeria's example, and urge African states that had recognised the MPLA, such as Nigeria, to change their policy. American leaders also used every available opportunity to warn the world and Africa that America wanted the Soviet Union and Cuba out of Angola, and did not cherish an MPLA government in Angola. Nigeria replied in anger to President Ford's letter and made public its angry reply. It cancelled a scheduled visit to Lagos by the American secretary of state, Dr Kissinger. These tumultuous developments in Nigeria-USA relations climaxed the events which began with the Nigerian government takeover of US Information Service buildings and radio-monitoring centres at Lagos and Kaduna respectively.

Anglo-Nigerian relations Many students of foreign policy were perplexed that Nigeria and Britain still maintained diplomatic relations after the events of 1976 in British-Nigerian relations. In 1976, the issue of returning the former Nigerian head of state, Yakubu Gowon, to Nigeria strained these relations to the limit.

When Gowon, the former head of state of Nigeria was overthrown, he took refuge in Great Britain. The new government in Nigeria took extraordinary steps to attend to most of his personal and family needs and comfort in Britain. The fact, therefore, that he was granted political asylum by Britain was not the main issue.

What rocked the basis of Anglo-Nigerian relations during the third military government was a chain of events that did not assume any conclusive or definitive shape.

(1) Gowon was accused of knowing about and being involved in a plot to overthrow the third military government and assassinate its leaders.
(2) He was asked to return to Nigeria and defend himself before a board of inquiry investigating all who were accused of involvement.
(3) When he refused to return, the British government was requested by Nigeria to hand him over to Nigeria for purposes of the investigations. The British government refused to grant Nigeria's request, and argued that if Gowon was unwilling to return, only a court order on him following legal proceedings in Nigeria and Britain could compel Britain to send him out of Britain.
(4) In a move which showed tactlessness and a lack of sensitivity, the British high commissioner in Nigeria, whose embassy building was damaged by demonstrators following the killing of the beloved head of the third military government, compiled a list of the damages done to his embassy and demanded compensation from Nigeria. Nigeria demanded the recall of the British high commissioner and refused to relent on its demand that Yakubu Gowon be returned to Nigeria.

Whether as a result of the strain, or for some other considerations, but definitely during this difficult period, Nigeria decided to diversify its foreign reserves formerly held in sterling. This measure contributed, to some extent, to a run on sterling which prompted industrialised states to rush to the pound's rescue.

Hence, in the very short period of one year, Anglo-Nigerian, and US-Nigerian relations were considerably strained.

Nigeria-Soviet relations Some who were not sufficiently informed either perceived the Soviet Union as the power behind the crises in the relations between Nigeria and the West, or concluded hastily that the Soviet Union was the principal beneficiary of these breaches in relation. Neither perception is correct. In fact Nigerian-Soviet relations have been in crisis since the end of the Nigerian war.

We have stated earlier that in 1968 the Soviet Union and Nigeria signed an Agreement authorising the USSR to establish Nigeria's iron and steel industry. The agreement also provided for a Soviet loan of ₦120 million for the project. As at August 1976, eight years after the agreement, the daily Nigerian papers announced that,

> Nigerian and Soviet technical experts began meeting on the implementation of the nation's iron and steel complex. The Soviet Deputy Minister For Assembly And Specialized Construction Works said that since the problem facing the construction of the complex was a vast one, it became very important and urgent for the contracting parties to sort out things before plunging into the structural aspects of the project.[12]

Dr Hezy Idowu put it mildly when he said, 'The Soviet Union developed cold feet over the iron and steel project and it was not until the advent of the present military administration that her interest in the project was revived'.[13] The situation was one of real crisis in relations, and both countries knew it. Nigeria was no longer interested in the Soviet loan. It was sufficiently capable, from its own resources, of financing the project and paying for whatever materials and services the Soviet Union would provide. This worsened the position because when the Soviet commitment in 1968 was made, Nigeria was dependent on Soviet heavy guns and military aircraft for the country's successes in war, and the USSR had calculated that the goodwill and friendship resulting from this dependence, from the loan of ₦120 million (which was huge in 1968), and from the Soviet-built iron and steel complex, would establish the USSR as the dominant foreign power in the politics, diplomacy and economy of Nigeria after the civil war. That Nigeria drifted back to Britain and

America after the war was extremely frustrating for the Russians.

Even when the second military government was overthrown and the USSR expected the creation of those conditions which it had long anticipated in Nigeria, it was disappointed by many developments which failed to fulfil its anticipations. There were strenuous efforts made by the leaders of the third military government to explain that they would not impose any ideology on the people of Nigeria and would not adopt socialism as their working philosophy even for the interim period of 1976-9. Economic and fiscal measures taken by this government seemed, as it were, to reassure capitalists of predominating roles in the Nigerian economy. There were also government measures which emasculated the working class as a political, social and economic force and movement in Nigeria, and as a force independent of a government that refused to embrace Marxism. There was open hostility towards Russia in parts of Nigeria which accused it of favouring the 'quick kill' rather than the 'peace talks' policy during the civil war, particularly as there was no ideological explanation for its actions in Nigeria. Russia's role in Angola was ignored by Nigeria because Nigeria concentrated on what the Angolans were doing and what Nigeria did to help Angola. Nigeria made no efforts to explain Russia's role in Angola and to present Russia as a friend of Africa.

There is also the little known fact that the way the USSR handled its civil war supplies to the federal army caused grave concern and much alienation. There were fully documented cases of rifles flown in by air while their magazines came much later by sea, of bombs which came by plane while their fuses came by sea, and of vehicles sent into Nigeria without spare parts. These incidents which could have been due to administrative errors generated much unease within decision-making circles. Furthermore, on Angola, and recently on the issue of Shaba province and the Ethiopia-Somalia war, the USSR avoided contact and collaboration with Nigeria in spite of Nigeria's efforts to effect some link-up and to influence major power roles in these essentially African problems.

As of now, Russia's ambition in Nigeria remains unfulfilled. Neither its help to the federal government during the civil war, nor its agreement to build Nigeria's iron and steel mill, nor its ₦120 million loan, nor its unflagging aid to Angola, secured for it and its beliefs, a special position in the post-war management of Nigerian affairs. Nigeria on its part felt it paid for what it bought during the war and did not commit itself to change from a pro-West to a pro-East conduct of its non-alignment policy. It was irritated by the ten years' delay in building the iron and steel mill, and no longer had any need of the Soviet loan.

The Nigerian economy and Nigeria's foreign policy Economic considerations affected the military's review of Nigeria's foreign policy.[14] Primary among these were considerations of national self-reliance and rapid economic development, the realisation of the Economic Community of West African States (ECOWAS), the global problem of a new world economic order, and the review of the economic and political ties between the Arab world and Africa.[15] The government was aware of the fact that in spite of Nigeria's oil revenue, Nigeria still remained a relatively poor country with one of the lowest per capita incomes in the world. Over 60 per cent of Nigeria's population was illiterate, its economic and social infrastructure was inadequate in most areas and shockingly lacking in others, and its economy was not controlled by the Nigerian government and people. Because of this situation, the third military government decided:

(i) to consolidate the country's economic base through indigenisation and the acceleration of national control of oil production, processing and distribution;
(ii) to make conscious and planned efforts to acquire or purchase technology from any country irrespective of ideology; and
(iii) to mobilise the entire population of the country to participate fully in the economic life of the nation.[16]

On indigenisation, the third military government enacted a new decree which involved either the outright selling of some scheduled foreign businesses to Nigerians or mandatory Nigerian participation in such alien enterprises. This programme, though inherited from the second military government, was discovered to have been undercut because many alien companies scheduled to have been taken over by August 1976 had not been sold to Nigerians by that date. Hence, the government announced measures to ensure full compliance with the law, and to accelerate movement into new schedules of companies and enterprises. Many foreign countries whose interests or those of their citizens were affected, protested againt the government's measures. Some, according to the Nigerian Foreign Office, began spreading rumours of economic and fiscal uncertainties in Nigeria. At a meeting between foreign diplomats resident in Nigeria and the Nigerian commissioner for external affairs, the commissioner reassured the diplomats that the country's economy was healthy, and solicited their co-operation in relying on facts rather than rumours or speculations in reporting to their home governments. Nigerian ambassadors abroad were summoned home and given briefings on the domestic situation in Nigeria.

Nigeria-Africa relations The third military government continued to give Africa and African affairs pride of place in Nigeria's foreign policy. The circumstances of its coming into being, that is, the overthrow of Yakubu Gowon while he was attending an OAU summit, created doubts in many African capitals over the new government. Later on, when the government suspended the World Black and African Festival of Arts and Culture (FESTAC), and undertook a massive process of dismissals and retirements that removed known decision-makers and ambassadors from office, the doubts increased.

It was Angola which restored the government to the mainstream of African affairs through Nigeria's recognition of the MPLA; its struggles within the OAU to secure OAU membership for the MPLA; its readiness to incur the displeasure of the USA over Angola and the MPLA; and its clear perception of the link between the Pan-African goals and aspirations of Black Africa in Angola, and the total liberation of Southern Africa especially Rhodesia, Namibia and South Africa. These put the new military government far ahead of many older OAU members on problems of Africa.

On the FESTAC, the government withstood pressures from within Nigeria that the festival should be cancelled. The costs were enormous and Nigeria was virtually bearing them alone; construction works at the festival villages were far behind schedule; the ports were congested, and enormous quantities of foreign food and drink were being imported for the festival. The government was urged either to cancel the festival or scale down its scope and involve other participants in its financing. Any of these moves would have weakened its position and standing in Africa. It must be admitted that for once, Nigeria cast aside rational cost benefit considerations, relied essentially on prestige factors, and decided to set a new date for the FESTAC. Thereafter, it undertook diplomatic action inside and outside Africa to explain its FESTAC policy, revive world interest in it, reconstitute FESTAC's world committees, and fix firm dates for the festival.

In the course of doing this Nigeria encountered considerable differences and disagreements with Senegal. These centred first around whether non-Black Africa should participate in the intellectual aspects (the colloquium) of the festival. The second was the wisdom of spending on the festival alone an amount which was more than the national budget of some members states of the OAU.[17] The third was Nigeria's national control, through its national ministries and departments, of the festival's international secretariat, funds and activities. These concerns led Senegal to allege that Nigeria intended to use its wealth in order to impose its opinion on Africa.

Writing on these developments, Dr Idowu, who has always been critical of Senegal in his comments on African affairs, said, 'Although Africa is the corner-stone of Nigeria's foreign policy and although the Federal Government is determined to promote good relations between this country and other African states it will not tolerate unprovoked hostility, deliberate sabotage and blackmail from any quarters'.[18]

The controversy of FESTAC strained Nigerian-Senegalese relations exceedingly. The objective of policy should not be to carry these differences to breaking point but to seek how best to restore understanding and normalcy.[19]

The Economic Community of West African States

(ECOWAS) also featured prominently in the foreign policy of the third military government. There were fears that ECOWAS rested essentially on the personal involvements and friendships of Yakubu Gowon and President Eyadema of Togo, and that the fall of Gowon, and Eyadema's initial willingness to offer him political asylum, might end all hopes of Nigeria's continued interest in it. These fears have not been borne out. The third military government has argued successfully against extending membership of ECOWAS beyond what the preparatory ECOWAS summit and the treaty agreed upon. It received instruments of ratification from member states, and proclaimed the legal existence of the community following the receipt of the prescribed number of ratifications. It took steps to get work concluded on the protocols of implementation which will govern the establishment of various organs of the ECOWAS, and provide rules and guides of action for the community's personnel.

One disturbing aspect of Nigeria's relations with Africa was Equatorial Guinea, one of the seven immediate neighbours of Nigeria, and one of the three main groups of neighbours lying off the Atlantic coastline of Nigeria. Ever since colonial times, Nigerian labour had emigrated to the Fernando Po Island wing of Equatorial Guinea to work. This colonial labour policy was pursued by many successive Nigerian governments. The conditions under which these Nigerians lived and worked had, from time to time, led to demands in Nigeria for Nigeria's annexation of Fernando Po.[20] The third military government put an end to these problems of Equatorial Guinea by repatriating all Nigerians in that country and resettling them in agriculture and other paid employments within Nigeria.

Finally, Nigeria's role in Angola reassured African liberation movements. What Nigeria emphasised thereafter is that African states must not allow Angola-type situations to arise because they confuse the people and tend to divide the OAU. This was why Nigeria supported the efforts to ignore the quarrelling political leaders within and outside Rhodesia, assist the military wings fighting inside Zimbabwe, and ensure that OAU and outside assistance was channelled only to the liberation fighting forces.

Nigerian intellectuals and foreign policy

No other Nigerian government relied on the Nigerian Institute of International Affairs (NIIA) as the third military government did; and no management of the NIIA has associated scholars of foreign policy and international relations with the work of the institute in research and policy planning, as did the management of Director-General Bolaji Akinyemi. Dr Akinyemi's management of the institute has included the bringing of Nigerian intellectuals in the various fields of international relations and senior policy decision-makers from the universities, the press, the Foreign Office, Defence, Cabinet Office, the institute, and some research establishments, to discuss extensively such issues as:

(1) Nigeria and the world;
(2) Nigeria–Brazil–Angola and the defence of the South Atlantic;
(3) Federalism and foreign policy; and
(4) The Economic Community of West African States.

The institute also created a forum of contact between young External Affairs officers in training and university scholars in various aspects of international relations. In between these activities, it arranged public lectures on major foreign policy issues. Hence, within a period of three years, it was able to do for the country and its foreign policy more than all the past administrations of the institute had done between 1963 and 1975.

There have therefore been tremendous changes in the content and style of Nigeria's foreign policy since the emergence of the third military government. There is no doubt that the policy has been very well received at home, and commands considerable respect abroad especially in Africa. But not much of the sort of objective analysis we have attempted here has been done except, perhaps, for the government's comprehensive review. Hezy Idowu's 'Nigeria's Foreign Policy: A Re-Assessment' was largely sentimental and intemperate in language.

It is necessary to look at the foreign policy as a whole. The fact that our relations with the USA, Britain, the USSR, Senegal, Fernando Po, were all strained at one time or another during the military era should have been a source of worry to Nigeria.

What exactly is happening in Angola? Is Angola no longer the first serious step in the liberation of Southern Africa? Have we re-examined some of the principal ideas of our foreign policy in the light of new world realities? We have so far no answers to these questions. Perhaps by examining the quiet but significant redirection of foreign policy since the death of General Mohammed, we may find the answers.

FOREIGN POLICY UNDER LIEUTENANT-GENERAL OBASANJO

Before the assassination of General Murtala Mohammed on 13 February 1976, some serious inter-agency differences had arisen or were reasonably suspected to exist, especially in respect of Angola, Southern Africa, and liberation movements. These differences ranged the Ministry of External Affairs against Dodan Barracks or State House/Cabinet Office. General Mohammed assumed what seemed to be direct personal responsibility for these subjects. He used his official residence/offices at Dodan Barracks, State House and Cabinet Office (political division) as a mini-Foreign Office. He was thus able to receive unorthodox and non-bureaucratic advice and policy analysis on Angola, the liberation movements and Southern Africa. He also resisted well articulated opinion from the Ministry of External Affairs and outside it suggesting that he should pursue the goals of national unity in Angola rather than take sides with the MPLA.

With his assassination, Lieutenant-General Obasanjo assumed responsibility as the head of state. He retained Brigadier Joe Garba as the commissioner for external affairs, and did not show any very strong inclination towards the continued use of his State House as the nerve centre of foreign policy decision-making on Africa, especially on Southern Africa. Gradually, the Ministry of External Affairs recovered its erstwhile position in the realms of foreign policy, and either working along or in conjunction with, or guided and directed by the ruling military triumvirate of Lieutenant-General Obasanjo, Brigadier Yar' Adua (chief of staff, Supreme Headquarters) and Lieutenant-General Danjuma (chief of staff, army), took rapid, firm but quiet and undramatic steps to change the direction of foreign policy initiated by Murtala Mohammed.

Firstly, Nigeria's relations with Britian and the USA were normalised, and the strains in these relations which were caused by Angola and the Gowon episode were either removed or ignored. Nigeria went beyond the re-establishment of normal relations in many other respects.

Nigeria participated fully in the Commonwealth Heads of State and Government Conference held in London in 1977; arranged state visits of the USA by Lieutenant-General Obasanjo, and of Nigeria by President Carter; and endorsed, with some minor but negotiable reservations, the Anglo-American peace plan for Rhodesia.

Secondly, Nigeria welcomed the far-reaching efforts of the USA to strengthen the United States' economic ties with Nigeria. As at 1978, the USA was buying 60 per cent of Nigeria's oil, and the price it paid was slightly higher than that at which Nigeria's competitors in the field of sulphur-free oil (Libya and Venezuela) were willing to sell their own oil. Because oil contributed about 95 per cent of Nigeria's export earnings, and between 90 and 92 per cent of all non-oil revenue, Nigeria was, therefore, theoretically, dependent on the USA for approximately 54 per cent of 1978 financial resources. The USA further agreed to train young Nigerian technologists, and only recently it established with Nigeria a joint commission to identify other areas of trade, aid and economic co-operation and expansion. This situation is a far cry from the estranged relations of 1975-6 under Mohammed.

Thirdly, while nothing very visible has happened to improve Nigeria–USSR relations, Nigeria's relations with communist Eastern Europe were dramatically improved by Obasanjo. The foci of interest were Romania and Poland. Personal diplomacy at the heads of state level was used; Nigeria sought technology transfer from these countries in the areas of mining, wood/paper industries, and middle level technological education; and jointly Nigeria and Romania made concrete plans for selling Nigeria's oil to Romania. While, therefore, Nigeria's relations with Eastern Europe show remarkable improvements and new directions, its relations with the

USSR seem to persist in a crisis whose existence everyone is eager to deny. We have earlier mentioned that Nigeria's efforts to work out some collaboration with the USSR on Angola failed. On the Shaba Province crisis in Zaire,[21] Nigeria developed peace plans based essentially on African initiatives and African forces, but realised that without Soviet support Angola would reject the plans. Nigeria's plans did not elicit any response whatsoever from the USSR, and this pained Nigeria's decision-makers. When on the issue of the Horn of Africa (the war between Ethiopia and Somalia in 1977-8) Nigeria made contacts and consultations aimed at stopping the war and permitting the OAU to negotiate a settlement, and these came fully before the USSR, what Nigeria received was most embarrassing: there was a cold response, angry restatements of rigid Soviet positions, and expressions of annoyance over Somalia's policy and behaviour towards the USSR. We must also mention that within decision-making circles in Nigeria, there was dissatisfaction that whereas very senior Nigerian officials visited the USSR, senior Soviet leaders and officials were not coming to Nigeria. The general and specific Nigerian–Soviet relationships under Obasanjo could, therefore, be summarised as follows:

(a) Nothing happened in the world or from initiatives taken either by the USSR or Nigeria to alter the strained Nigerian-Soviet relationships which Obasanjo inherited.
(b) The Soviet Union was self-sufficient in crude oil supply and, unlike the USA, had no economic need for Nigerian oil, and could not therefore, like the USA, contribute through oil purchases to the prosperity and development of Nigeria.
(c) The EEC, rather than either Britain alone, the Commonwealth or the Soviet Union, dominated the non-oil export sector of the Nigerian economy.
(d) Jointly, the EEC, Japan and the USA, rather than the USSR, provided the bulk of the imports needed by Nigeria in the consumer goods, non-consumer goods, and capital investment sectors of the Nigerian economy.
(e) Besides the absence of these objective economic bases

for enduring relationships, there was no common ideological understanding predicated, for example, on Marxian socialism between the two states.

(f) Some of the foreign policy actions of the USSR and Cuba in Africa were taken without regard to the positions adopted by Nigeria, and without any serious Soviet thoughts on the likely roles which the OAU could play in them.

Nigeria, under Lieutenant-General Obasanjo, therefore, left its relations with the USSR in crisis. However, it was anxious to demonstrate that it had not gone over completely to the Western powers. Hence, it moved decidedly into Eastern Europe, and began cultivating the friendship of Romania and Poland.

Fourthly, Nigeria's policy on Africa was expected to undergo critical reappraisals in the light of some stark realities which confronted the decision-makers. These realities were many and varied, and included these.

(a) The major world powers and their friends have renewed their diplomatic and military interventions in Africa. France, Britain and the United States of America are prominent in this regard for the West, while for the communists the USSR and Cuba did most to trigger off Western concern and reaction.

(b) Many African states are continually yielding to non-African intervention and manipulation, and are increasingly resisting close integration within the OAU and under OAU auspices.

(c) Because of these outside interventions, the African efforts in Southern Africa are confused and unclear. Angola seems to be adopting anti-Nigeria postures and attitudes and there are incidents in Angola-Nigeria relations of the period which if made public would have led to the termination of Nigeria's aid, assistance and understanding towards Angola. Similarly, both the political and military programmes, activities and achievements of the Patriotic Front do not seem to the Nigerian Foreign Office and press to justify the hopes and aspirations pinned on them, and may not stand close OAU scrutiny if such a scrutiny were to be the basis for continued aid and assistance.

(d) There are no carefully determined OAU policies and attitudes towards the non-African Arab states. The Arabs are not aiding African development and liberation yet they expect to reap political dividends. They pledge assistance but do not release funds, and they reject meaningful co-operation.

In the light of these and other considerations, the government of Lieutenant-General Obasanjo was under constant pressure to review its African policy: to separate emotionalism from reality; pursue realisable goals if these constituted incremental first steps towards the attainment of strategic goals; generally to avoid Angola-type solutions that result in civil war unless these are warranted by outside intervention; to be more outspoken on issues of human rights; and to help organise OAU military efforts in order to make non-OAU foreign military intervention in Africa unnecessary.

It can, therefore, be seen that in these directions Nigeria's foreign policy under Lieutenant-General Obasanjo moved away from what it was in the brief but tumultuous period of General Murtala Mohammed's administration.

8 Mohammed/Obasanjo foreign policy

A. Bolaji Akinyemi

The major focus of this chapter is on those fundamental changes that took place in both the style and content of Nigeria's foreign policy from 1975 onwards under both General Murtala Mohammed and Lieutenant-General Olusegun Obasanjo.

To put these changes in perspective, it is necessary to make reference to what the new regime inherited in July 1975. It is now a well rehearsed history. Under Balewa, while the official line was non-alignment, Douglas Anglin was probably being charitable when he described Nigerian foreign policy as 'Political Non-alignment and Economic Alignment'.[1] The consensus among Nigerian scholars now is that the 1960-66 foreign policy was politically and economically aligned.[2] Evidence has been adduced to show that at independence there was a broad consensus among the political leadership on maintaining close ties with the West.[3] That this consensus was broken by 1962 is also a historical fact. However, whether Chief Obafemi Awolowo and his supporters really underwent a change of mind or whether they simply, as members of the opposition, sought to capitalise on disenchantment with the government is still in dispute. What is not in dispute is the fact that the Balewa regime maintained a consistency between its domestic and foreign policies in the sense that a streak of conservatism ran through both. Even if Balewa had not been a conservative, there is no doubt that the Western-dominated pattern of Nigeria's international economic relations imposed severe limits on possible radical reposturing of Nigeria's political and economic alignment. The capitalist nature of the Nigerian economy which meant that it was individuals and not the government who determined trading partners reinforced the Western alignment. Even the First National Development Plan which was meant to lead to some measure of economic self-reliance initially strengthened the political and economic alignment because the success of the development plan was heavily dependent on the availability of capital from the Western capital markets and consequently upon 'friendly' policies that would not drive the capital away.

Even then, the record of the Balewa regime was not all that bleak. Substantial financial assistance was given to the liberation movements in Southern Africa and in former Portuguese territories. Nigeria voted for the 'right' resolutions in the United Nations that dealt specifically with African issues such as the Resolution on Permanent Sovereignty. Economically, the need to broaden the base of Nigeria's international economic relations was recognised. Various economic agreements were signed with the socialist bloc countries although they did not affect to any appreciable extent the pattern of trade.

The civil war period shattered the foreign policy illusions of the Nigerian élite. More than any of the factors catalogued above, which were not insurmountable, was the perception by the Nigerian élite of the Western bloc as a friend and the Eastern bloc as an enemy. The refusal of Britain to sell aircraft to Nigeria during the war, the refusal of the United States to sell any type of military equipment to Nigeria and the groundswell of public opinion in favour of the Biafran cause came as a rude shock to Nigerians. When the Soviet Union then offered to sell whatever Nigeria needed, the psychological barrier against the Soviet Union was broken.

However, if there were any expectations either on the Soviet side or on the side of the radical elements within the Nigerian élite that the civil war courtship would ripen into marriage, the post-civil war period shattered such expectations. There were several factors why the expectations remained unfulfilled. Firstly, the essentially capitalist nature of the Nigerian economy could not dovetail into the planned nature of the socialist economy. Businessmen could not be forced to change their trading partners and Nigerian consumers could not be forced to change their tastes, selectively. In other words all cars can be banned, or cars over a particular engine capacity can be banned. But the government could not decree that all British or American cars were banned unless it was sure that the Soviet Union would buy all the Nigerian goods which these countries used to buy. Secondly, the personality of Yakubu Gowon was a major factor. To unhinge Nigeria from its Western moorings and transfer it to Eastern moorings needed a major and fundamental overhaul of Nigeria's domestic and foreign systems, and Gowon abhorred taking major decisions, especially those that might lead to fundamental consequences. Thirdly, reconciliation was Gowon's major post-civil war preoccupation in both domestic and foreign policies. Fourthly, while the pyschological barrier against the Soviet Union had been broken, the innate pyschological affinity with the West, especially Britain, was still strong within the Nigerian political, economic and military élite.

On top of all this was Gowon's bewilderment as to what to do about the Nigerian political system in terms of a demilitarisation process which would lead to civilian rule. As long as that issue remained unsettled, the Gowon administration (1) shied away from reaching quick decisions on any issue, foreign or domestic; (2) avoided taking decisions on controversial foreign issues until it was clear which way the African majority on that issue was; and (3) put a premium on cultivating the image of the conciliator rather than an innovator staking out a position and fighting for that position.

This was the environmental background to the foreign policy system which the Mohammed and Obasanjo regime inherited. Even though the Soviet Union had won the contract to build the iron and steel factory which is meant to be the lynchpin of Nigerian industrial revolution, even though the Soviet Union was the main supplier of the striking arm of the Nigerian Air Force and was also responsible for the training of Nigerian Air Force pilots and thousands of Nigerian students, there was an undercurrent of feeling in the country that the Nigerian foreign policy was still too pro-Western.

The July 1975 coup d'état

A military *coup d'état* against a military regime could be a palace revolution – a change of personalities and not of policies. However the July 1975 change which brought Brigadiers Mohammed and Obasanjo to power turned out to be more than a palace coup. That the coup would be a fundamental one was inevitable in the sense that Gowon, as a person, was charming and likeable. It was his policies and in some cases his lack of policies that turned Nigerians against him. Hence it was inevitable that, in order to justify itself, the new regime would have to overhaul Gowon's policies and do it with military despatch since, as has already been pointed out, one of Gowon's weaknesses was tardiness in taking decisions.

Was there any expectation that the overhaul would extend to foreign policy? After all, foreign policy, even in advanced industrialised countries was seldom in the forefront of public opinion. In a developing country, foreign policy would not be expected to be an officers' mess topic of conversation, especially a pro-Western policy among Sandhurst–and Royal College of Defence Studies-trained military officers. But as far back as 1972, both Brigadiers Mohammed and Obasanjo had taken steps to show their interest in international affairs. In 1971, a group of Nigerian scholars had established a Nigerian Society of International Affairs. In 1972, the society sought to increase its membership by throwing open its ranks to those who could be regarded as forming the foreign policy élite in any country – important members of the mass media and officers of the armed forces. Brigadiers Mohammed and Obasanjo were two of the few officers who elected to join the society – an indication of more than just a passing interest in international affairs. This conclusion is further buttressed by the fact that the 1972 annual conference of the society witnessed the presentation of a paper on 'African High Command' by Brigadier Obasanjo as well as a lively exchange of views on the same subject between the two brigadiers. It is quite interesting to note that while Brigadier Obasanjo did not believe in the immediate feasibility of an African High Command, Brigadier Mohammed believed that an African High Command was not only feasible but was of immediate necessity – an administrator confronting a visionary.

Apart from the fact that their involvement was indicative of deep interest in international affairs, that involvement had certain consequences whose importance was to become evident later.

The society was not anti-government *per se*. However, in developing countries ruled by the military, the universities and the press, as two institutions, tend to regard themselves as the loyal opposition. This feeling of being the opposition tends to be reinforced by the alienation of scholars from the decision-making process. It is inconceivable that this feeling of opposition, manifesting itself in views critical of Gowon's foreign policies, would not have rubbed off on both Brigadiers Obasanjo and Mohammed.

On assuming the reins of power, their initial moves on foreign policy confirmed the conclusions drawn above. Firstly, the importance attached to foreign policy was shown by the appointment of Joe Garba, who announced the overthrow of Gowon, as the commissioner for external affairs. Indicative of this spirit was the fact also that it was at the same meeting of the Supreme Military Council that the appointments of a new director-general for the Nigerian Institute of International Affairs and a chief justice of the Supreme Court of Nigeria were made. Secondly, that the new regime was going to tap the intellectual resources of the country outside the civil service for foreign policy ideas was shown by the fact that the director-generalship of the institute which had been vacant for over a year was filled within three weeks of the new regime's tenure in office.

The speed with which the new regime intended to tackle foreign policy issues was shown by the fact that one of the first assignments of the new director-general was to formulate new guidelines for Nigerian foreign policy, with the directive that it should be submitted within a week. The new guidelines were submitted and approved by the new head of state, Brigadier Murtala Mohammed.

A committee was later set up headed by Dr Adebayo Adedeji, the executive secretary of the United Nations Economic Commission for Africa, with the membership drawn from the universities, the mass media and the military to provide an in-depth overhaul of the foreign policy system, substance and apparatus.

If the new regime was hoping for a methodical and gracious transition from a leisurely and somewhat conservative foreign policy to a dynamic one as evidenced by the setting up of the Adedeji Committee, the Angolan crisis came as a rude reminder that foreign crisis is no respecter of domestic political pace.

The Angolan crisis was inherited by the new regime, and for four and a half months, it continued the policy of the old regime of trying to reconcile the three nationalist groups – the MPLA – (Popular Movement for the Liberation of Angola), FNLA – (National Front for the Liberation of Angola) and UNITA – (National Union for the Total Independence of Angola) – and trying to get them to form a national government. In fact, this policy was carried one step further than even the Gowon government might have contemplated. In the course of a trip to East Africa to explore what the Nigerian contribution could be to the efforts at reconciling the three warring nationalist groups, Colonel J. N. Garba, the new commissioner for external affairs, suggested, publicly, that Portugal should postpone Angolan independence to avoid the impending civil war and chaos. This was heresy and many hearts sank in horror and despair. This episode, more than anything else, probably convinced the new head of state, Brigadier Mohammed, and his deputy, Brigadier Obasanjo, that they needed to become more actively involved in the day-to-day management of the foreign policy system.

Pressure from two different sides mounted on the government: from the United States government that wanted Nigeria to maintain its neutrality and from Nigerians, both within and outside government, that wanted Nigeria to throw its weight behind the MPLA. The latter group won. Nigeria not only recognised the MPLA, it gave ₦13.5 million and military supplies to the MPLA government and launched a diplomatic blitzkrieg among African states on behalf of the MPLA for recognition.

This new policy brought the new regime into a confrontational position with the Ford administration of the United

States. Insults were publicly exchanged between the two governments and their relationship plunged to the zero mark.[4] Henry Kissinger, the United States secretary of state, was twice refused permission to visit Nigeria. The diplomatic blitzkrieg by Nigeria resulted in victory for the Nigerian position at the 1976 Extra-ordinary Summit of the Organisation of African Unity held in Addis Ababa to discuss the Angolan crisis.

The word 'victory' is used in the context of OAU politics. Factually, there were two motions before the OAU summit. The first one sponsored by twenty states called for the recognition of the MPLA, while the other also sponsored by twenty states called for a national government. Ethiopia as the host country abstained. Hence, technically, it was a hung jury. But this was the first time in OAU history that the organisation had refused the leadership of the United States in spite of intense lobbying both before and during the conference. To that extent, it was a victory for Nigeria. The situation is akin to guerrilla warfare. The army opposed to the guerrilla needs a kill ratio of 50:1 to maintain credibility. Guerrillas do not have to win a war, all it takes is for the government army to lose.

In another sense, it was a victory for the OAU. At issue were two conflicting approaches to African politics. The United States-sponsored approach saw African politics as an extension of competition between the United States and the Soviet Union, while the Nigeria-sponsored approach regarded the US/USSR competition as being marginal to African politics. Within the context of the Angolan crisis, the two approaches manifested themselves in the United States regarding the MPLA as communist, and UNITA/FNLA as friends of the West; while Nigeria regarded the MPLA as the truly nationalist organisation and the UNITA/FNLA as ethnically based movements. The rejection of the United States' approach was therefore a victory for the OAU.

The combination of these two conclusions, victory for Nigeria and victory for the OAU, has been recognised by the British Africanist, Basil Davidson:[5]

If we are honest among ourselves (and why not be?) we shall

> easily agree that the influence of independent Africa has so far counted for rather little in Great Power decision. . . . Now it may be, though, that something interesting, something new, begins to happen and unfold. Outside pressures and interferences continue, of course, to accumulate in this region or in that. For different individual ends, each and all have the same familiar object of reducing Africa's power to unite for Africa's purposes; and again there is nothing new in that. Yet a counter-pressure, lacking in the past, now starts to shape itself and work within the continent itself. Not for the first time? Perhaps not: and yet for the first time, or so it seems to me, with that degree of force and capability which may be likely to be really meaningful; which may be likely, in other words, to impose their will upon the continent's future.
>
> If I had to pinpoint the onset of this new development of African independence in any general way, I would put my finger on a November day of 1975. That day was when the Nigerian government rejected President Ford's 'advice' to follow America and her allies obediently as before; opted for a foreign policy of independence; and therefore recognised the infant Republic of Angola. The men who took that decision had courage on their side; but they also had vision.

The way and manner the Angolan crisis was handled contained indications of changes in both the style and content of Nigerian foreign policy. Firstly, a bad policy was rapidly changed to a better one. Secondly, there was no attempt to wait for an OAU consensus to emerge before changing the policy. Nigeria was prepared to stake out a position and lobby to create an African consensus around that position. Thirdly, Nigeria was prepared to confront the United States over an African issue, an unprecedented act for Nigeria. Fourthly, the open grant of financial and military aid to the MPLA marked a radical departure from past practice where such aid was small and secretly given. It marked the escalation of the confrontational involvement of Nigeria in Southern Africa.

Nigerian recognition of the MPLA has been defended on, amongst other grounds, the need to react to the South African military invasion of the southern part of Angola. This justification has at times been stressed out of context. Mindful of the dangers of 'if-y' propositions, I still believe that the decision to support the MPLA would have been made even if the South Africans had not invaded Angola, that the decision would still have been made on the basis that, of all the three groups, the credentials of the MPLA as a militant anti-colonial and Pan-Africanist movement, tested on the battleground and committed to the total liberation of Southern Africa, were the best.

From the Angolan decision flowed other decisions. Active involvement in the Zimbabwe crisis crystallised into recognition of the Patriotic Front which was allowed to open an office in Lagos. South-West African Peoples Organisation (SWAPO) was also allowed to open an office in Lagos. Both the African Nationalist Congress and the Pan-African Congress, two liberation movements of South Africa, were also allowed to open offices although only the Pan-African Congress has availed itself of that option. The leader of the Soweto Students Representative Council, Tsesi Mashinini, came to take up permanent residence in Lagos.

The net effect of all this was that Nigeria became the Mecca for liberation fighters in Africa and Nigeria became a front-line state – not physically – for the liberation struggle in Africa.

By and large the policies of the government have commanded acceptance from the generality of Nigerian public opinion. However, the consensus worked out on foreign policy during the Angolan crisis soon broke up over (1) the role of the United States in Southern Africa and (2) Nigerian relations with the United States.

There was always a danger that the wrong lessons would be learnt from the Angolan crisis. On 30 January 1976, I had cause to sound a note of caution in an address to Nigerian scholars.[6]

> There are lessons to be learnt from our policy on Angola and I want, in my own little way, to ensure that the

lessons which we learn are the right ones.

Firstly, we must get one fact clear: there is no intrinsic relationship between success and the justness of one's cause in politics – definitely not in international politics. Therefore, that in recognising the MPLA government in Angola, we backed the winning horse does not mean that we will always be successful in our policies – success being measured in terms of achievement of our objectives. A lot of us would have been bitterly disappointed if the MPLA had been defeated by Western imperialists in Angola. But we would still, however, have been convinced that Nigeria was right in recognising the MPLA. I am also sure, however, that there are some people in this country, who while cheering the government now because nothing succeeds like success, would have been quick to see the failure of the MPLA in Angola as a failure in the conception of Nigerian policy on Angola.

Secondly, while on the Angolan issue we have been quite rightly radical, it is not every issue that lends itself to radicalism. Each issue would have to be judged on its own merits. Where an issue merits radicalism, then definitely, radicalism should characterise the policy. However, where an issue merits moderation, surely it will be an act of folly to disregard moderation and pursue radicalism just for its own sake. To distinguish between a matter that merits radicalism and one that merits moderation is going to task the maturity and judgement of all those who want to see this government pursue the right path in foreign policy.

The net effect was to call for a flexibility that would enable Nigeria to react to changes in the environment surrounding foreign policy issues. The test came over what should be the Nigerian attitude towards the United States. As long as Ford was in the White House and Henry Kissinger was in the State Department, improvement in US/Nigerian relations and co-operation with the United States in solving any African problem was out of the question. However, in November 1976 a new factor came into the situation. Jimmy Carter was elected the president of the United States. He promised a new African policy that would be responsive to African aspirations. He appointed Andrew Young as ambassador to the United Nations and as his unofficial ambassador-at-large to Africa. He sent his vice president, Walter Mondale, to have a showdown with the prime minister of South Africa, John Vorster, at Vienna. At that meeting, Mondale publicly and for the first time committed the United States to a policy of one man, one vote, in South Africa, a pledge which was later repeated at the meeting of the Trilateral Commission by Zbigniew Brzezinski, the national security adviser to President Carter. The Carter administration also stated publicly for the first time that the United States will not fight on the side of the racists in Southern Africa. The new administration dropped its opposition to the admission of Angola to the United Nations.

In addition to these concrete steps, the highest sources within the administration promised to get South Africa to agree to United Nations-sanctioned elections and a United Nations presence in Namibia. The same sources promised to get rid of Ian Smith. In exchange, the new administration wanted SWAPO to agree to the United Nations Namibian plan. It also wanted the Patriotic Front to agree to what has come to be called the Anglo-American plan which basically sought to replace Smith with a British-appointed high commissioner and get United Nations troops into Zimbabwe.

A combination of the actions and the promises of the new administration proved sufficiently convincing for the Nigerian government to agree to a relaxation of tensions between the United States and Nigeria.

Now comes one of those coincidences which often give a mistaken view of cause and effect. General (promoted from Brigadier in January 1976) Murtala Mohammed was assassinated on 13 February 1976. The rapprochement with the United States started in 1977 culminating in the state visit by Lieutenant-General (promoted also in January 1976) Olusegun Obasanjo, the new head of state, to the United States in October 1977 and the return visit by President Jimmy Carter in April 1978.

Critics of the new rapprochement with the United States maintained that General Mohammed would not have permitted it. Another 'if-y' proposition. Maybe yes and maybe not. The confrontation between Obasanjo and Mohammed in 1972 already referred to has shown that while Mohammed was a visionary who believed in taking risks, calculated or otherwise, Obasanjo was the administrator *par excellence*, cautious and calculating. While Mohammed was open, Obasanjo was secretive. The fact remained that while Brigadier Garba, the commissioner for external affairs, recognised the need for open diplomacy, within limits, in recognition of the fact that public support often depended on how much the public understood what the government was attempting to do, Obasanjo gave a low consideration to the role of public opinion in the foreign policy process. There was thus a gap between the rationale for government policy and what the public believed that rationale was. The attempt by the Institute of International Affairs to bridge the gap was often not successful since the same constraint about releasing information operated on it. While the role of the institute was understood by the public, it was a different matter within the establishment itself, a point subtly put by the *New Nigerian*:

> The main weakness of the ministry of External Affairs and to a large extent the government itself today is that it is too secretive and that it takes the Nigerian public for granted. . . . Very little effort is made to enlighten the public on what things are being done and why they are being done. For example, many Nigerians were taken by surprise on the recent rapprochement with Iran. Government functionaries began only to speak up on the matter when critics became vociferous in the denunciations. . . . Perhaps we may have been told much less than we were told last week had the Director-General of the Institute of International Affairs not provoked the critics. In this we owe him some gratitude.

The gap between the government and the critics was influenced by the difference between government perception of the United Nations and that of the critics. The government knew and publicly acknowledged the fact that Nigerian troops had been invited to serve under United Nations command in both Namibia and Zambia. The government also knew that under no circumstances would it permit Nigerian troops to be used in a way detrimental to the cause of African liberation – a point acknowledged by the South African regime which withdrew its support for the United Nations plan in Namibia, citing as one of the reasons the invitation to Nigeria to contribute to the United Nations forces. The critics, on the other hand, remembered only too well the role of the United Nations in the Congo in the early 1960s, especially its dubious role in the overthrow and eventual assassination of Patrice Lumumba, the first prime minister of the Congo (now Zaire). As it was, both the United Nations plan for Namibia and the Anglo-American plan for Zimbabwe were not implemented so that we will never know whether the government was being over-optimistic or the critics over-pessimistic.

There was also another difference in assumption between the government and the critics. The government knew that neither the military operations of SWAPO could force the South African government out of Namibia in 1977/8 nor the military operations of the Patriotic Front force the Ian Smith regime out in 1977/8. The government also knew that its co-operation with the United States was not at the expense of military and financial assistance to the liberation movements. The critics on the other hand believed that both SWAPO and the Patriotic Front were on the verge of military victories and that the various plans were meant to snatch these victories from them. Secondly, the critics also believed that Nigerian co-operation with the United States was a substitute for Nigerian financial and military assistance to the liberation movements. Nothing could be further from the truth, but how were they to know that when everything was under security wraps – the government believing that foreign policy was too important for the public to know the hows, and whys and wheres.

That a discussion of Mohammed/Obasanjo's foreign policy has turned out to deal largely with the issues of Southern African liberation is not surprising. That Africa is the cornerstone of Nigeria's foreign policy has been an article of faith since 1960. Seventy-five per cent of the time and energy of the Foreign Office staff is consumed by African affairs.

Ninety-five per cent of the technical and financial assistance during this period was directed at the continent. Over 75 per cent of the policy differences between Nigeria and other industrialised countries revolve around African issues, especially Southern African issues. For example, the first public rebuke handed down by the new regime to an industrialised country was the criticism of West Germany on 10 September 1975 over an alleged agreement to send a nuclear reactor to South Africa. The warning to multinational companies to choose between Nigeria and South Africa was most certainly an economic sacrifice on the part of Nigeria.

Continuity

On two fronts, the Mohammed/Obasanjo regime continued the policies of previous regimes. These were policies related to the ECOWAS region, and technical and financial assistance to the member states of the Organisation of African Unity.

ECOWAS The area covered by the Economic Community of West African States is not exactly coterminous with the area covered by Nigeria's immediate neighbours. In one sense it is smaller, since it does not include the Federal Republic of Cameroun. In another sense it is larger, since it includes Gambia, Mauritania, Senegal and Guinea-Bissau which are not normally included in the immediate neighbourhood concept.

From 1960 successive Nigerian governments have realised that the size of the country has been perceived as a threat by Nigeria's neighbours. The strategy adopted by Nigeria to neutralise this threat has been to give no cause for offence, to seek peaceful resolution of conflicts between her and her neighbours and to extend generous financial grants to them. This strategy paid off handsomely during the Nigerian civil war when all of Nigeria's immediate neighbours except Benin (formerly Dahomey) refused to give any assistance to the rebel cause. The fact that in the moment of need Nigeria's neighbours supported her cause reinforced Nigeria's belief in her strategy of low-profile neighbourliness.

As the petroleum oil boom widened the relative prosperity – or the appearance of such prosperity – between her and her neighbours, the more thought was turned as to how best to neutralise the consequences of the envy which the seeming prosperity was bound to arouse. A consensus was built around the saying 'Nigeria cannot exist as an oasis of prosperity in the midst of poverty'. The strategy adopted was to extend the neighbourhood concept to cover the West African region within an economic grouping. This decision, taken under the Gowon regime, was pursued with vigour by the new regime. Together with Togo, Nigeria canvassed other West African countries and eventually succeeded in getting a treaty establishing ECOWAS signed. The new regime took off from there and joined in the efforts to reconcile the conflicts blocking the signing of the protocols.

Nigerian membership of ECOWAS is not without its domestic critics. The argument of the critics is that the Nigerian domestic market is sufficiently large to cope with the pace of industrialisation and that Nigeria does not need an export market – at least not in West Africa. The fact that Nigeria pays 33.33 per cent of both the budget and the compensation fund without any corresponding influence in the running of the organisation, in spite of the fact that Nigeria is the seat of the organisation, has fuelled the argument of the critics. The reply of the government is that the institutionalisation of increasing intra-African economic relations, with full Nigerian participation, is a *sine qua non* of lessening non-African influence in that region. As of now, criticism is limited to university scholars. The business community is in full support of ECOWAS. In fact, the Nigerian business community was ahead of the Nigerian government in pushing for institutionalisation of intra-West African economic relations when the Nigerian Chamber of Commerce became one of the leading lights in the formation of a West African Chamber of Commerce before ECOWAS was formed. Against this background, it is difficult to imagine a Nigerian government pulling out of ECOWAS.

Aid programme The new regime was faced with a situation that started under the Gowon regime – a situation which the government handling of the Angolan crisis intensified. Under the Gowon regime, the oil boom was already evident. Nigeria came to be regarded, by other African countries, as a source of aid. This attitude was strengthened by the propaganda war which was being waged against OPEC by the Western industrialised countries, who claimed that since the pricing strategy of OPEC had impoverished the industrialised countries to the extent that they could not afford to meet their aid commitments, OPEC should carry the aid burden. Under the Gowon regime, Nigeria gave out ₦6 743 235 distributed as follows.

Table 8.1

Aid extended to some countries on independence

Guinea-Bissau	₦500 000
Cape Verde	₦ 60 775
Mozambique	₦675 890
Sao Tome and Principe	₦ 60 775

Table 8.2

Aid offered in respect of drought and other natural disasters

Mali	₦ 431 579
Senegal	₦ 333 333
Upper Volta	₦ 407 895
Chad	₦ 320 176
Mauritania	₦ 214 912
Niger	₦ 342 105
Ethiopia	₦ 200 000
Sierra Leone	₦ 20 000
Somalia	₦1107 895

Table 8.3

Aid for various purposes

Niger	₦644 000
Zambia	₦500 000
Sudan	₦400 000
Sao Tome and Principe	₦124 000

Up to that stage, one could say that the African states had only a moral leverage on Nigeria. Nigeria wanted nothing from Africa. Nigeria was not seeking to exercise any influence. This changed when the new regime lobbied other African states for support for its Angolan policies. As Nigeria became more actively involved in African affairs, and sought to influence events and courses of action on the continent, so it looked as if other states expected Nigeria to pay the economic price for the involvement. The requests were varied: to build hospitals, roads and factories; to participate in mining projects; to participate in industrial projects; to sell petroleum at concessionary rates. The requests stunned the Nigerian government, and the response was way below what the other states expected. There were participations in the cement and sugar factories in Benin Republic, in the bauxite and iron ore projects in the Republic of Guinea; roads were wholly financed linking Nigeria and the Republic of Benin, and between Nigeria and Niger; and the two-lane Birni Nkonni bridge in the Republic of Niger was built by the Nigerian government for ₦668 000. Oil was sold at deferred payment schedules to Ivory Coast and Ghana among other states.

The ideological content

I have already pointed out that the basic difference between the Nigerian and the United States approaches to the Angolan crisis was the refusal of Nigeria to see the crisis in ideological terms. This does not mean that Nigeria did not know that the MPLA had a self-proclaimed socialist ideology or that the MPLA was dependent on the Soviet Union for arms and on Cuba for men. All these were regarded as historical accidents. From Nigerian historical experience during the civil war, it was easy to take the approach that a group that is involved in armed conflict is not likely to be too choosy about where the arms come from.

However, those who saw the Nigerian position on Angola as a foretaste of greater things to come in terms of Russo-Nigerian relationship because Nigeria and the Soviet Union were on the same side soon became disillusioned when Nigeria showed no desire for membership of the socialist bloc.

Critics expected that the same intensive consultation that

characterised the Nigeria-United States relationship in the post-Ford/Kissinger period would also extend to Nigeria-USSR relations. To some extent there was justification for this in the sense that hardly a month went by without Brigadier Garba going to Washington or an American functionary coming to Lagos. The fact, however, is that the government was convinced that the United States held the key to the resolution of the conflicts in Southern Africa since it had more leverage over the white minority regimes than the Soviet Union had. It was the United States and the Western alliance that needed to be talked into withdrawing their economic support for these regimes. The Soviet Union had no such economic relations with Rhodesia, Namibia or South Africa. The Soviet Union involvement in the liberation of Southern Africa is an indirect one through supply of military materials to the liberation movements, and this is handled by the liberation movements directly. Having intensive discussions with the Soviet Union would have been like preaching to the converted. 'I come not to call on the righteous but on the sinners to repentance,' was how Jesus put it.

But there was more to the situation than this. In dealing with the Soviet Union, one gets the impression of being asked to find one's place in a set design. In dealing with the United States, one gets the impression of dealing with a state that is prepared to consider several options and of a state that is cognisant of the status of Nigeria as an influential African state.

On a strictly bilateral basis, Nigeria has continued economic relations with the socialist bloc. The Nigerian head of state has paid state visits to Poland and Romania. Nigerian students are studying on government scholarships in the Soviet Union and in all other member states of the socialist bloc. Trade agreements covering extensive commodities exist between Nigeria and the Soviet Union, Romania, Poland, Bulgaria, Hungary and Czechoslovakia. There are companies from the socialist bloc operating in several states in Nigeria.

Conclusion

Under the Mohammed/Obasanjo regime, Nigeria seems to have finally arrived at the role and status which Nigerians have been clamouring for since 1960: influencing events in Africa South of the Sahara, and being widely consulted by world leaders. In 1978 alone ten important dignitaries visited Nigeria, among whom were Jimmy Carter, Helmut Schmidt, Mengistu of Ethiopia, Sekou Toure of Guinea, Manley of Jamaica, the United States chief of army staff, the commander-in-chief of the Soviet Air Force and one of the vice premiers of the People's Republic of China. Nigeria becoming the Mecca of liberation fighters, Nigeria becoming a front-line state in the liberation struggle and Nigeria becoming a respected member of the Organisation of African Unity as witnessed by its involvement as a mediator – on invitation – in practically all disputes between African States.

This effervescent involvement in African affairs backed up by the enormous resources generated by the oil boom, resources which are now being ploughed into the industrial and infrastructural base, has led observers to believe that a continental power has finally emerged in Africa. Not only has this assertion been made by scholars like Basil Davidson, it also received practical demonstration at the United Nations in the famous 1977 Security Council election when a combination of Latin American, Asian, European (both East and West) and North American states voted down the OAU candidate and elected Nigeria to occupy the Security Council seat.

9 Local government and administration

Oyeleye Oyediran and E. Alex Gboyega

When the military seized political power in 1966 one of the most daunting political problems which confronted the new administration was how to reorganise the institution of local government so as to provide a clearly defined scope of authority, responsibility and functions while at the same time maintaining an effective central presence in the localities in order to be able to determine and control the pace and quality of development largely initiated or generated at the local level. At that time there was no local government worthy of the name anywhere in southern Nigeria. In the Northern Region on the other hand, local government (the system of native authorities) was very strong indeed and the emirs and traditional rulers who wielded its instruments were in name and deed the 'government' in their localities.

In practical terms, in southern Nigeria the need was to revitalise and consolidate the local government system; for a variety of reasons which will be discussed later local government had become the object of contempt, perhaps pity as well, but never support. In the Northern Region the need was to modernise the system by emphasising popular participation and control and thereby diffusing the power of the emirs and traditional rulers (potentates, some will say) who tightly controlled the native authorities.

Thus in the south, apart from the early days of military administration when local councils had to be dissolved because the erstwhile civilian governments had packed them with their political minions, attempts at reform of the local government system had positive consequences for the institution and its practitioners. In contrast, in the north, the picture presented was one of a subtle yet decisive and, undoubtedly, imperative struggle to alter power relations at the local level as far as it affected local government. Reviewing the first efforts at reforms here Panter-Brick and Dawson have observed that, 'It would appear, . . . that the balance of forces is by no means on the side of the State Governments. The more powerful Emirates may still prove administratively indispensable and politically influential.'[1]

The local government systems in the north and the south arrived at these disparate conditions largely because their separate developments from the earliest times, but most especially in the period after 1950, were infused with and constrained by different philosophical conceptions of local government.[2] Perhaps it is more correct to say that the differences in conception are rather more of degree or emphasis than of kind. Stated quite briefly, it amounted to this: in the south the governments of the East and the West conceived of local government in extremely liberal terms which led to a rapid and unrestrained adoption of what they considered to be the essence of the British model of local government with its emphasis on popular participation, whilst in the north a more conservative approach led to the adoption of a reform which emphasised functional effectiveness rather than popular participation.

The liberal plunge in the south was led by the Eastern Region which in 1950 replaced the Native Authority Ordinance by a Local Government Ordinance. Under the former ordinance, 'a number of Chiefs and elders were appointed by the Government to form the native authority council of the area'.[3] The Local Government Ordinance of 1950 enabled the majority (80 per cent) of the councillors to be directly elected. But the more important change related to political control. As Holland has observed, 'The keynote of that Ordinance was a change of management – the elimination of control by the administration which had been a feature of the former native authority system and the vesting of power in virtually autonomous councils.'[4] The district officer was kept at a distance from council proceedings and administration; on giving notice in writing, he might visit a council to examine records, and his advice might be sought but none was obliged to accept it.

The structure of the local government system was three-tier, comprising county, district and local councils. The county councils corresponded, in most cases, almost exactly in size to the erstwhile divisional native authorities, and performed major services and functions. The district and local councils covered smaller areas, the former covering a larger area than the latter, but both had powers and functions relative to their size. This brief survey of the main features of the local government reforms of 1950 had to be changed in 1955 along lines and for reasons similar to that which compelled almost exactly the same changes in the Western Region in 1957 of its local government reforms of 1953. Therefore we shall examine the reasons and the changes together later.

In the Western Region the local government reform took place in 1953 with the coming into effect of the Local Government Law 1952 in February 1953. As in the Eastern Region, political control of the local government councils shifted decisively to elected representatives who comprised three-quarters of all council memberships. Here too the district officer might inspect local government records but his advice was in the discretion of the council to accept or reject, even when the council asked for it. Again, as in the Eastern Region, the British-type three-tier structure was adopted and divisional, district and local councils were set up. The divisional councils were coterminous with administrative divisions and performed major functions. The district council came next in status and performed middle range functions while the local council was for a small town or group of villages too small to have a district council. The local council performed only minor functions.

As can be seen from the brief sketch above, the local government systems in the Eastern and Western Regions were very similar in essential features. Underlying the two systems was a philosophical conception of local government which ascribed to local government higher, ulitmate political purposes than the mere delivery of social services and implementation of development projects. The ultimate political purposes served by local government as conceived in the two regions might be said to include political education for local and national leaders, diffusion of political power on an area basis, local self-determination and inculcation of the noble ideals of impartiality, protection of minority rights and integrity, all of which were considered essential to the evolution of a liberal democratic society.[5]

The shortcomings that manifested themselves consequent upon the local government reforms described above were not unexpectedly similar and arose because of the conception of local government the regional governments had and the structural arrangements which that conception entailed. Firstly, there were far too many small-sized local councils which could hardly pay staff salaries and wages let alone provide any services. The desire for local self-determination by various small communities led to fragmentation of many previously compact and large administrative units and this affected overhead costs and dissipated local resources and energies. Secondly, the divisional and county councils were very unpopular as district councils competed with them not only for the same local resources but for prestige as well. The resultant conflict over authority had not been envisaged, as the governments thought they had provided for tiers of functions rather than of authorities, and it was ruinous to harmonious relationships between the divisional and county councils on the one hand and district councils on the other. Thirdly, the absence of close supervision by the regional government gave room for corruption and other abuses of the system which could have been avoided had too much premium not been put on local autonomy.

In 1955 in the Eastern Region the minister for local government was empowered by the provisions of a new local government law to ensure closer scrutiny and supervision of local government activities. In 1958 the county councils were abolished and the district councils became all-purpose local authorities. Thus in the urban and municipal areas local government had only a single tier while rural areas had two tiers of authority – district and local authorities. In 1960 the Eastern Nigeria Local Government Law 1960 further altered the structure of local government as the urban and rural district councils were redesignated urban county and county councils respectively. There now were 107 county councils, two municipal councils and 870 local councils. Thus even with the structural changes there were still too many authorities. It is noteworthy though that in this period local government reforms were undertaken within the same framework of the British liberal model. The course of development in the Western Region was somewhat different.

The Local Government Law 1957 increased the autonomy of local authorities as the local government advisers (formerly district officers) were withdrawn and three provincial local government inspectors were appointed for the entire region thereby making regional government supervision even more remote. (In 1955 the Eastern Region was imposing tighter control.) But in terms of structural changes, the unpopularity of divisional councils and the ineffectiveness of the local councils tended the system towards the evolution of a single tier of authority.[6] One year after the Local Government Law 1957 came into effect it became obvious that there was need for another close look at the local government system and the government commissioned two studies – by the Biobaku Committee and Mr I. D. Cameron. The reports' recommendations did not result in any substantial reforms of the local government system because political crisis within the ruling Action Group party focussed energies elsewhere. But the trend towards a single tier continued; by 1967 eight divisional councils out of fourteen in 1955 had been dissolved and the local councils had been reduced in number from fifty-one to seventeen.

In the Northern Region, on the other hand, the government was cautious, indeed tardy, in democratising the local government system to enable it to embody the political purposes embraced by the southern governments in the 1950s.[7] The native authority law of 1954 not only changed little of substance, merely consolidating existing arrangements, but it even retained the term 'native authority' which elsewhere had been discarded because it was regarded as pejorative.[8] All the seventy native authorities which existed had traditional rulers as their heads.

The law made provisions for five different types of native

authorities, namely:

(a) a chief or other person in council;
(b) a chief or other person and council;
(c) any council;
(d) any group or persons; and
(e) any chief or other person.

The law empowered the premier to appoint to any office of native authority any chief or other person associated with a council as 'a chief or other person in council' or 'as a chief or other person and council', or any chief or other person as the sole native authority – usually as a temporary measure. The composition of any native authority under the designation 'any council' and 'any group of persons' (types (c) and (d) above) was determined by the minister. Thus the government prescribed the composition of native authorities subject only to the expedience of conformity with the native law or custom of the affected area.

The native authority, however composed, might create a subordinate native authority or the government might prescribe it. The relationship between the subordinate native authority and the native authority proper was hierarchical but the superior-inferior relationship which in the Eastern and Western Regions caused so much friction between local authorities only ensured the permeation of rural communities by the authority of the emir or traditional ruler in the Northern Region; as a matter of fact the strength of the native authority system rested upon this chain of hierarchic relationship which reflected closely the traditional power structure.

The very close identity between traditional rulers and élites, and the native authorities, has been elaborately described by others elsewhere.[9] What is deserving of repetition here is that even when popular representation was slowly and grudgingly but increasingly permitted, it did not entail democratisation in the sense of decision-making by majority vote.[10] By far the most important single consideration was not, as was popularly believed, that the government wanted to preserve the institution of traditional rulers but that peace and order were essential to socio-economic development and the traditional rulers were the key, then as before, to achieving that. The liberal democratic consideration of popular representation and participation in the decision-making processes at the local level, which primarily was responsible for the majoritarian local government systems of the Eastern and Western Regions, was of secondary importance in the Northern Region. Consequently when the local government systems in the Eastern and Western Regions confronted the traditional liberal problem of determining the proper scale or, better still, the relationship between size and function, which led to a great deal of disillusionment with the structure of local government in these areas, the local government system of the Northern Region was seen in ambivalent terms.

On the one hand its admirers vaunted its stability and strength while on the other hand its critics pointed to its corruption and undemocratic features. That the entire local government system of the Northern Region rested upon a philosophical belief that the major and perhaps sole purpose of a local government system was the promotion of socio-economic development, in addition to the mandatory maintenance of law and order, was and is not widely appreciated. To be sure this belief had the important consequence of fostering the survival of the institution of traditional rulership and, given the fusion between traditional rulers and élites on the one hand and regional political leaders on the other, might tend to lend credence to the theory of enlightened self-interest. But the unavoidable conclusion is that the direction of causation is more likely to be the other way round; the central political leaders believed more in the validity of native authorities as agents of socio-economic development, and thus fostered them, than in their role as institutions for popular participation and expression of popular will.

The onset of military rule in 1966 marked the beginning of important changes in the system of local governance. It is perhaps here that change has been most profound, as will be elaborated below.

New directions

It was not until the end of the civil war in 1970 that any serious effort was made by state governments to draw up plans for local government. In general, even though each state went its own way, there appears to be three major directions of development. In the Rivers, South Eastern, East Central and Mid-Western States, local administration replaced local government in different shades and colours.[11] The Western State opted for a North American model of council managers. In the northern states the emphasis was on increasing popular representation and the weakening of the traditional hold on the functioning of local political institutions. The rest of this section is devoted to an analysis of the varied approaches within each of these three broad categories.[12]

From local government to local administration As in the South Eastern State, the government of the Mid-Western State replaced the local government system it inherited with a new system called development administration. In the former development was defined as 'comprehensive changes or transformations in cultural, educational, economic, social and political fields'; and 'administration' was seen as 'the harnessing and management of . . . resources in men and materials to meet or bring about these comprehensive changes and transformations thereby administering to the needs and aspirations of communities in the context of the overall development of the state.'[13] The term development administration was chosen as a result of the recommendation of an expert ad hoc committee which examined and advised government on the suitability or otherwise of the system of local government inherited before the war. In the Mid-Western State also the government set up a committee in December 1972 under the chairmanship of Dr G. A. Odenigwe of the University of Nigeria, Nsukka, to examine local government finances, including financial relationships between the state government and the local government councils. In its report submitted in August 1973, the committee found that nearly all the local government councils in the state had failed for lack of funds, effective leadership and dedication to service by their staffs. It therefore recommended the establishment of what it called a development-oriented two-tier system of local administration with emphasis on self-help efforts.

The East Central State government adopted a different

nomenclature for its system of local administration. This was divisional administration which the edict establishing it called,

> a system of local administration intended primarily to coordinate the activities of the State Government functionaries in the Divisions and the local government in such a way as to ensure proper decentralization of functions and actual participation of the local people in the general development and management of their own affairs under the supervision and guidance of the Local Authority.[14]

In each of these states (in particular the South Eastern and East Central States) the philosophy behind development or divisional administration can be summarised as follows. Since the village is the traditional seat of government it is at this level that initiative for development projects lies. Such projects as school buildings, village roads, wells, and so on are things which people need and are prepared to provide for themselves. If, therefore, government wants to carry the masses with it, it is imperative that government gets down to the grassroots, where the traditional seat of government is based. In the words of the Mid-Western State Development Administration Edict, the main objectives of this system of local administration are:

> (a) to provide a framework for effective co-ordination and execution of Government programmes and services in each division and
> (b) to facilitate and encourage the participation of the people of each division in the control and management of their local affairs with the assistance and under the supervision of the government by enabling the people to utilise local community efforts and organizations to raise funds and mobilise resources for the general development of their local areas.[15]

In the East Central State, 'Olu Obodo' was the philosophy designed to stimulate the institutional structure of divisional administration. As the administrator of the state enjoined the citizens in his budget speech in April 1972:

> We must now reject for all time the conception of government as a foreign institution standing outside the community and whose money, property and goals are not the direct responsibility and concern of the community. The community is the government; the government is the community. It is no longer correct to describe the business of government as 'Olu Oyibo'. Government business is truly and properly 'Olu Obodo'.[16]

Structural designs

Even though the structures varied they were designed to achieve the same purpose, that is, state government control of the administration and development of local communities. In the East Central State, a two-tier system of local administration was established. The upper tier was called divisional council of which there were thirty-eight (seven urban and thirty-one ordinary administrative divisional councils). The lower tier which was the primary basis of the new system was called community council. They were constituted at the village group level very much in line with the traditional social and political units. The population of community councils varied between 298 in Ogbaru to 54 891 in Afikpo. Unlike community councils, divisional councils were suspended until, it was claimed, the resumption of political activities. The resident or the divisional officer, who was the state representative in each division, was given the authority to exercise all the powers of such councils.

For the South Eastern State two levels of development administration were established – area development committee and urban or county development council.[17] Each area development committee was made up of a number of villages and dealt with projects requiring the co-operation of more than one village. The county or urban development council covered a number of area committees and served as the centre for development administration. In the Mid-Western State, fourteen development councils and 218 development committees were established, each development council having between eight and thirty-seven development committees as its second tier of administration. As in all the other states, all members of development committees and councils were appointed by the military governor in the Mid-Western State. Each development committee had a ceremonial president (a traditional ruler) and a chairman and between ten and twenty members. A chairman, chairmen of all development committees in the division, and between thirty and forty members constituted each development council. All staff and employees of development councils and committees were designated civil servants. The same was true of the South Eastern and East Central States.

Role of the state representative

What really makes a system local administration rather than local government is the degree of independent and autonomous powers that functional bodies operating it enjoy. It is when we examine the role of the chief representative of the state government in the local communities that this distinction comes out clearly. In the East Central State he was either the resident or divisional officer; in the South Eastern State, he was the development officer, and in the mid-Western State, the resident. Even though there were some differences depending on environmental factors, in general the role of this officer was essentially identical in all the states. He was, as Ronald Wraith has observed, the colonial D. O. with the difference that a Nigerian had replaced the expatriate.

An analysis of the resident in the Mid-Western system gives a good picture of this officer and his functioning within the system of local administration. We can divide the role of the resident into three analytical parts. He was:

(a) the representative of the military governor;
(b) the representative of the Ministry of Development Administration;
(c) co-ordinator of all state activities in his division.

The resident was a senior civil servant whose grade was not lower than that of a deputy permanent secretary or administrative officer grade II. In other words he was of a much higher status than the D. O. under the colonial system of local administration. The post was open to both administrative and professional classes.

As representative of the military governor the resident took precedence over all public officers in the division. He was expected to make time for close and easy relations with people directly responsible to him. He was the living symbol of the presence and authority of the state government in the division. He presided over all official ceremonies. In effect he was a local governor.

He was expected to keep the Ministry of Development Administration fully informed of all the problems affecting the development administration system in the division. In this, his role as representative of the Ministry of Development Administration, the resident served as the chief executive and secretary to development councils. He had power to give to the councils and related development committees such general and specific instructions as appropriate authority might direct. He supervised and inspected council and committee projects and had the power to transfer, appoint, promote and discipline junior officers within the division.

As co-ordinator of all the state activities in his division, the edict establishing the system specified that,

> [The resident] shall be responsible for the co-ordination of all activities of Ministries, departments and agencies (by whatever name called) of government in the division and for ensuring the efficient functioning of such agencies and accordingly all ministries, departments, and agencies of government and all public officers within the division shall be responsible to him in respect of all official matters.[18]

He rendered intelligence reports about all of the various departments in the division and also confidential reports on all senior departmental officers and personnel of corporations and other agencies in his division, except the judiciary. He controlled the vote in his division. In effect he was the head of service in his division.

The replacement of local government with local administration did not last long before a new regime that had more confidence and faith in local government took over control of political power. One of the few serious studies of this era of local government development in these states reported the following findings on the divisional administration system of the East Central State:

(a) that the new system failed to facilitate the establishment of government effectiveness in the communities. Institutions of local governance were viewed by citizens as oriented primarily to revenue collection;

(b) that community councils as the primary participatory channel was not effective mainly because the membership pattern of the councils did not ensure that most of the influential members of a community participated in community decisions;

(c) that the system was afflicted by the problems of co-ordination between the different agencies and bodies involved in local developmental activities. In particular there was a lack of co-operation between the Divisional Officer and the Community Development Officer – a reflection of the traditional antagonism between the generalist and the specialist;

(d) that co-ordination between the activities of improvement or town unions and community councils was lacking. There was also an absence of proper linkage between local development plans and state development plans due to the nature of the state community development programme and the ill-equipped linkage mechanisms.[19]

The replacement of local government with local administration was in essence not to stimulate local development but to strengthen military dictatorship. As Emonfonmwan has pointed out in respect of the Mid-Western State, the development administration system formed part of the institutional structure of military dictatorship designed primarily to ensure political stability in the state. Through the resident who was the instrument of centralised control and stability, the policy of government was monitored in all local communities.[20]

From British to American model

In the Western State, by the time the military took over the control of government, divisional councils – the first tier of local government – had become most unpopular for a variety of reasons.[21] Many local councils were too small to be viable politically and economically. Furthermore local government institutions became the primary institutions for coercing local support for the ruling political party. Finally, committees proliferated and unnecessary meetings were frequently held in order to gain sitting allowances and to get more involved in day-to-day administration of councils. In a sense the British model of local government proved unsuccessful in the state.

By 1967 when the state was created all local government management committees were dissolved and their powers and functions transferred to divisional administrators designated sole administrators. Due to the various problems associated with the system of sole administrator, affairs of councils were neglected except the heavy taxation burden on the citizens. With no visible returns, and frustration due to the absence of effective channels of participation, civil disorder broke out late in 1968 and early 1969 in several parts of the state. One of the major recommendations of the commission that investigated the causes of the civil disorder was that 'Government should undertake as a matter of urgency a review of the existing local government council structure with a view to finding out which councils are viable and which are not, and therefore . . . decide on measures for ensuring that only councils viable and capable of fulfilling their statutory obligations remain.'[22]

The search for a new system of local government was started in 1971. After a series of discussions both private and public, the government decided on an American model of 'council manager' system. In April 1973 the new system was introduced.

Structure of the new system

> 'It is very vital that a council must be financially viable and law and order must be easy to maintain in its area of authority.'

> In the countries where the system operates, there is very little talking in the local government councils. The Councillors do the planning and scheming, and take decisions on matters of general policy. The Chief Executive Officer and his staff execute. . . . The Council Manager is like the General Manager of a limited liability company and the Chairman and Managment Committee are the Chairman and Director of the Company. . . . The Council Manager as the Chief Executive and Administration Officer of the Council shall direct, co-ordinate and supervise the administration of all departments of the council.[23]

These statements and others have led us to conclude elsewhere that the Western State government, like the early twentieth-century American municipal reform movement, was particularly interested in a local government system in which the principal virtues are viability and efficiency. Democracy was on the lowest priority. 'Furthermore government thought that local government could be run like private business and that within the system policy and administration could be neatly separated.'[24]

The existing 114 local government councils of various sizes and stature were merged and consolidated into thirty-nine single-tier local government councils. Each council was made up of a management committee of between twenty and fifty members out of which a standing committee of between seven and fifteen was chosen. Even though the former was in theory the policy-making body it met only four times in a year, whereas the latter met at least once a month. Another important aspect of the structure of the new system was the creation of area committees in each council area with varying populations of between 10 000 and 25 000 and with membership of between ten and thirty. The 320 created were designed to bridge the psychological remoteness of the periphery from council headquarters. It was stipulated that at least 40 per cent of the revenue derived from an area committee was to be spent within that area.

As in the other states discussed above, the colonial D. O. was resurrected not only in name but also in his full glory and power. He was supposed to revert to his pre-1966 position of adviser to local government councils, but the advice of the new D. O. took a different coloration. He served as the government watchdog not only at council meetings but also on council decisions. He was empowered to delay for up to one month the implementation of any council decision which in his view required further clarification. Council meetings were illegal if held in his absence.

Functioning of the system

Unlike the pre-1966 councillors, the members chosen by the military governor to serve on the new councils were of very high calibre. For example, in a study conducted in 1974, it was found that 52.3 per cent of the members of the standing committee of these councils had at least a first university degree, and of the other members of the management committee, one in three was equally qualified educationally. Ten per cent of the standing committee had a postgraduate education. Furthermore 53 per cent of the members of the new councils were teachers or lecturers, 17 per cent were either lawyers or businessmen, and 7 per cent were administrators. This meant that more than three-quarters of the members had a professional background adequate for an understanding of the working of the council manager system.[25]

The high calibre of this new group of councillors was not a strong enough factor for the state government to loosen its hold on the functioning of local government institutions. Budgets of councils had to be approved by the Minstry of Local Government. Even after approval, councils were unable to allocate funds to implement programmes without further approval of the ministry. Councils were forbidden to award contracts to the value of ₦4000 and above without the approval of the ministry.

The great emphasis on control to the detriment of initiative accounted in large measure for the failure of the system. Another important factor was the financial poverty of the councils. These and other related factors were grinding the new system to a halt less than twenty-four months after it was launched. As we have observed elsewhere, it would appear that the adoption of the council manager system was used by the government merely as a 'tactic of negotiation' between the citizens who were demanding a change from the sole administrator system to a system of representative local government.[26]

The move from native administration The process of popular representation in the native administration system in the Northern Region was strongly resisted in the 1950s in the name of efficiency and stability. But by 1963 government decided that all native authority councils should have at least some elected members, and by the time the military took over in January 1966, all native authority councils had some elected members. In some, particularly in the lower north – now Kwara, Benue and Plateau States – elected members formed the majority of members.

Certain policies of the new military regime quickened this gradual reduction in the power and influence of traditional rulers even before states were created in 1967. In February 1966, government announced that all native authority police, prisons and native courts would be taken over by the regional government. The chief justice of Northern Nigeria was asked to prepare plans for a phased takeover of these functions. In the words of the *New Nigerian* this was designed to 'enable the native authorities to concentrate their energies and resources on the provision of social services'.[27]

By April 1968 all these functions were effectively taken over. The importance of this measure can be recognised when it is realised that native authority courts and police in particular provided the traditional rulers with tremendous powers capable of silencing political opponents. As Edward Baun has observed, in effect, 'in the name of justice and efficiency, the political power of the ruling elite could be, and was, drastically reduced'.[28]

Opportunity for the different parts of the Northern Region to go their own ways arose when the region was split into six states in July 1967. In Kwara and Benue-Plateau States, quick action was taken to further ensure popular participation in the government of local communities. Three of the measures designed to achieve this require some elaboration. These are (1) the weakening of the larger native authorities either by outright division or by creating important sub-divisions; (2) the establishment of the principle of election for a majority of local government council members; (3) the reduction of the power of chiefs.

Weakening the larger native authorities

This measure was undertaken by most of the six states. In Benue-Plateau State, the existing thirteen local authorities and three federated ones were reorganised into fifteen local authorities. Eight administrative areas replaced Kano State's four emirate councils. Kano emirate was split into five. The North Central State government created six local authorities out of the existing two emirate councils – Zaria and Katsina. In the North Eastern State, thirty-one development areas were established to complement the existing twenty native authorities; Kwara State replaced the nine former native authorities with eleven divisional or local authorities.

It would be seen that in all these states the term native authority was dropped. Audu Bako, military governor for Kano State, called the term 'derogatory and old fashioned'. Benue State government said the retention of the terminology after independence was an anachronism.

Establishing the principle of representation by election

In general four groups of members featured the new system of administering local communities. These were (a) the chief or emir who served as chairman; (b) a small number of traditional members; (c) a small number of ex-officio or nominated members; and (d) two-thirds elected by popular votes. The implementation of this elective aspect was, however, delayed by the state of emergency in the country.

In Benue-Plateau State, the post of senior councillor was abolished and supervision of a group of departments spread among a number of councillors. Kwara State on the other hand set up council committees which became the principal organs through which business of council was run.

Reduction of chiefs' power

Apart from the earlier measures taken in 1966 other policies were adopted in many of the states to further weaken the power and influence of traditional rulers. One of these was the abolition of the system of chief-in-council and its replacement with chief and council system. The chief-in-council system was introduced in 1952 after the abolition of sole native authorities. The chief-in-council system, as Whitaker has pointed out, means that legally a traditional ruler was obligated to consult his council when taking any decision. Furthermore, the signatures of certain designated councillors were required to supplement that of the emir in all official acts promulgated by a native authority. However, an emir could overrule his councillors even if the majority opposed his position. All he needed to do was to secure the support of the governor. The introduction of the chief and council system meant that the chief or emir had no legal power of veto over decisions made by the majority of his councillors.[29]

Understandably there was resistance to this change. In Benue-Plateau State in particular, this change of status was not favourably taken by the affected emirs and chiefs. They showed great hostility but the popular support for the reform and the determination of government not to yield to pressure were adequate to see the reform through. Furthermore, a serious attempt was made to democratise the methods of selection and appointment of emirs, chiefs and district heads. The Benue-Plateau State government asked communities to submit for its consideration and approval the existing practices in their respective areas. This generated a lot of interest and conflict in some areas. On the selection of district head, government stipulated that, unlike before, these should be indigenous to the district over which they were appointed. Procedures for the selection of such traditional office holders were also harmonised in the state. Not all government measures were to the disadvantage of the traditional rulers. For example, both in Kwara and Benue-Plateau States, salaries of chiefs were revised upwards, and many upgraded chiefs were given enhanced positions within the state traditional chieftaincy structure. In both states, a council of chiefs was inaugurated to the advantage of both the chiefs and government. The council became a forum where chiefs were briefed first hand on government policies and actions.

Without an understanding of the pre-1966 power of the emir in native administration, it may be difficult to realise how profound these changes, which began in the late 'sixties, are within the northern emirates in particular. In its front page comment in 1971, *West Africa* observed:

> In fact one of the most remarkable and least noticed developments in Nigeria in the past five years has been the quiet revolution which has transformed the political system of the former northern region to an extent which in 1966 almost nobody would have thought possible . . .
>
> It is now entirely clear, as it never was to the mass of people in the days of the former northern region, that the state Government rather than the Emir's administration is 'the government' . . .
>
> The Sultan of Sokoto relies for his status not on control of the Sokoto NA but on being recognised as Commander of the Faithful far beyond his emirate. . . . Other rulers, great or small have come to terms with the silent revolution. By their wisdom the rulers may have ensured long life for the institution of chieftaincy in the Northern Emirate.[30]

The Public Service Review Commission on local government

In September 1973 the Public Service Review Commission was set up under the chairmanship of Chief Jerome Udoji. The commission was among other things asked to examine the organisation, structure and management of the public service including local government services and recommend reforms where desirable. In December 1974, the commission's report and government views on it were made public.

The commission was clearly ambivalent in respect of its recommendations on the local government service. The clearest evidence for this can be found in the recommendation on size of local government area or whether or not what is desirable is local government or local administration. As a result each state government was left to go on as before.

The commission recommended, however, that the whole structure of the local government system be re-examined with a view to adopting a single-tier system. This recommendation was turned down by the government. It was the view of the commission that in order to be able to recruit and retain competent staff, the salaries and conditions of service of local government staff should not be less favourable than those of the civil servants. In accepting this recommendation, government added that the qualifications for appointment to local government posts should also be at par with those laid down for appointment to posts graded similarly in the civil service. However, the enhanced salary structure could not, as it was soon found out, give local government the quality of staff necessary. The status of local government itself required considerable enhancement within the total political system.[31] The commission realised this when it stated that functionaries of the state government have tended to apply a colonial style of control at the local level which tended to keep local authorities in a position of inferiority and suspense. This realisation led to the recommendation that a Research and Development Planning Unit should be established in Ministries of Local Government to assist local government in improving the effectiveness of their administration.

In general the commission's recommendations on local government were less far reaching than those on the civil service. As has been observed elsewhere, what makes the situation worse is that on the few issues where the commission's recommendations would have made some significant changes, government in the name of tradition or local differences preferred the status quo.[32]

The 1976 reform

But just as the assumption to office of the military government in 1966 marked the beginning of profound changes in the system of local governance as have been described above, so did the emergence of a new military administration in July 1975. The new military administration included 'a systematic and deliberate reorganisation of the Local Government set up' in its five-stage programme of political action which was announced on 1 October 1975. The reorganisation became effective in September 1976 with the promulgation of the various States Local Government Edicts.[33]

We can only summarise the broad features of the nationwide reforms here, because with nineteen states in the federation to consider, details of differences between states will take up too much space. The reforms provide that local government councils be elected either directly or indirectly. In the event only nine states adopted direct elections to fill their councils in December 1976. In addition the councils have elected majorities, elect their own chairmen subject to government approval and take decisions by majority vote.[34] The local government councils are single-tier authorities with primary and sole responsibility for exercising the statutory powers of the local governments. Thus formal authority at the local level is now unambiguously located in a secular, elected body, though in most parts of the country, but especially in the powerful emirates, it will be some time yet before the local authorities exercise solely and fully all their statutory powers, in particular with respect to control over land. The difficulty here is that the Local Government Edicts of the states provide in identical form on the one hand that the traditional councils (which exist side by side with the local governments) shall have power 'notwithstanding any other provision of this edict to determine the customary law and practice on all matters governed by customary law including land tenure under customary law' and on the other hand vests in the local government 'control of land held under customary tenure'.[35] The confusion is compounded by the constitutionally guaranteed Land Use Decree 1978 (Decree No. 6 of 1978) which vests all lands in the various states and empowers local governments to control non-urban land (designated urban areas being under the direct control of the military governor of each state).

The Constitution of the Federal Republic of Nigeria (Enactment) Decree 1978 which will usher in the Second Republic under civilian administration not only endorses the functions the various States Edicts have assigned to local government in its Fourth Schedule but also guarantees democratically elected local government councils. In the words of the constitution:

> The system of local government by democratically elected local government councils is under this constitution guaranteed; and accordingly the Government of every State shall

> ensure their existence under Law which provides for the establishment, structure, composition, finance, and functions of such councils.[36]

Quite clearly then, the next administration has to preserve the quintessence of the reforms undertaken by the military administration.

The doctrinal ancestry of the 1976 reforms can, of course, be traced to the same wellspring which underlay the local government reforms of the Eastern and Western Regions in the early 1950s. The reforms of 1976, as Brigadier Shehu Musa Yar Adua pointed out, were 'intended to stimulate democratic self-government and to encourage initiative and leadership potential'.[37] Even though pains have been taken to avoid the mistakes inherent in the philosophical conception adopted, namely, fragmentation of units to ensure the maximum possible expression of local democracy, by prescribing the size of the smallest authority to be at least 150 000 in population, the political significance remains paramount for, as Brigadier Yar Adua has observed two years after the reforms, 'Local Government Councils should be viewed as the training ground for democracy'.[38]

The management structure of the local government councils and the state local government relationship instituted by the 1976 reforms are consequential in their broad outline to the basic decision to restore (at least in some parts of the country) and introduce (mainly in the north) the emphasis on the higher ultimate political values of local government and it is against this background that the significance of the achievement of the military in local government reorganisation can be appreciated.

10 The military and the politics of revenue allocation

Oyeleye Oyediran and Olatunji Olagunju

Two fundamental questions have always arisen with respect to revenue-sharing (allocation, adjustment) in all federations. The first question is how do inequalities in size and wealth between units affect fiscal relations between governments? In all federations there are relatively rich and relatively poor units of government. While the poor often favour and struggle for what has been called 'a redistributive system of federal finance', the rich on the other hand are often more interested in autonomy and revenue allocation which is based on the relative contributions of each unit to the federal purse. The second question is to what extent can transfer of revenue between governments be used to promote political stability and even development? From case studies of some federations, it has been found that three basic types of situation may arise in respect of this question: (a) it has not been difficult for fiscal adjustment to be made in federations where a large rich unit is faced with demands from a small poor unit, mainly because the cost to the large unit is relatively small; (b) revenue-sharing is more difficult where a rich small unit is faced with demands from a large poor unit; and (c) fiscal adjustment may be financially feasible but politically difficult where rich and poor units are of roughly the same size.[1]

The object of this chapter is to analyse the extent to which political factors have affected Nigeria's attempt to find solutions to these two seemingly economic questions during the period 1966 to 1979.

Before the military took control of political power in

January 1966, almost every constitutional review was accompanied by a fiscal allocation commission. There were five such commissions between 1947 and 1965. The first which arose as a result of the Richards constitution of 1946 was headed by Sir Sydney Phillipson. In 1951 another, the Hicks-Phillipson Commission was appointed. The need for a second fiscal review commission within five years arose primarily because of the constitutional decision to move towards a quasi-federal system of government under John Macpherson who became governor immediately after Arthur Richards. 1953 was a year dominated by constitutional and political crises in Nigeria. It is not far fetched to suggest that the dissatisfaction by the regions with the revenue allocation system in use at that time played a significant role in these crises. As a result of these crises, the Lyttleton constitution of 1954 increased regional autonomy on the one hand and weakened central power on the other. Following the adoption of this constitution, the Sir Louis Chick Commission was appointed to enquire into and report on the fiscal effect of the new constitution. By 1957 disenchantment with Chick's derivation principle (that is, redistribution based on the contribution of each unit) led to the appointment of a fourth commission, the Raisman Commission. As the Dina Report rightly points out, 'The greatest achievement of the Raisman Commission was its enunciation of the kind of allocation principles which are more conducive to economic and national integration'.[2] The achievement of the Raisman Commission accounts in part for the relatively long interval it took Nigerian political leaders to appoint another commission, which was in 1964 with K. J. Binns as sole commissioner. The Binns Commission was the fifth and last fiscal review exercise before the military came to power.

In this aspect of intergovernmental relations, the strong political content is emphasised by the fact that at every constitutional conference at which a major review of the power relations between units of government was undertaken, there was need to review the fiscal and financial relations as well. Furthermore, almost every commission's report sowed seeds of future political wranglings over revenue allocation. For example, even though Phillipson's report considered two principles, derivation and even development, as the best criteria for revenue allocation, derivation was the only criterion applied. What is more, there were discrepancies between the recommended and actual percentage allocations. The Northern, Western, and Eastern Regions were to receive 46, 30 and 24 per cent respectively by Phillipson's accepted recommendations, but in actual fact the Northern Region's share varied between 40.7 and 34.8 per cent, the Western share between 29.0 and 24.7 and the Eastern between 36.8 and 30.9 in the financial years 1948/9 to 1951/3.[3] This gap between expectation and reality led to bitter complaints from the North and West that their funds were being diverted to develop the East. Apart from derivation, other criteria such as fiscal autonomy, need and national interest were recommended and accepted. Nevertheless complaints of different kinds did not stop. The West, after the Hicks-Phillipson Report, complained against the lowering of the weighting given to derivation; the North was unhappy because inadequate emphasis was given to the principle of need, and the East insisted on the principle of national interest against all others. In other words, there was hardly any principle that enjoyed the support of all units of government at any one point over time. Each government changed its advocacy of particular principles according to the prevailing circumstances. As the Aboyade Report put it, it was more common for different governments to support different principles overtime and for different reasons.[4]

Derivation carried the greatest weight throughout the period 1948-65. However, in the words of Aluko,

> The effect of the derivative arrangements was to intensify interregional controversy about the real volume of interregional trade. It led to the demand, which was fortunately rejected, that the free movement of trade and commerce between one region and the other be controlled so as to prevent customs duties on goods consumed in one region being attributed to the revenue of the other where the original importers or producers were located.[5]

There is no need to point out that the recommendations of

the various commissions before 1966 were in general accepted with only minor modifications. But as Teriba has observed, this was due 'not so much to an undercurrent of unanimity as to a spirit of compromise very greatly helped by the non Nigerian element in the membership composition of the commissions themselves and hence the belief in them as impartial and disinterested arbitrators.'[6] The importance of this point raised by Teriba becomes clearer when we examine the commissions or committees set up during the military era.

Finally, as we shall see below, the rejection of the recommendations of the two commissions set up during the period 1966-79 was based partly on the political implications of the commissions' recommendations. To put it differently, the rejections of the reports were based not on the economic or financial merit of the recommendations, but mainly on the political implications for a federation such as Nigeria. This is more true of the Dina Commission Report which was rejected by the government. The Aboyade Report on the other hand was accepted by government, but rejected by the Constituent Assembly during its deliberation on the draft constitution for Nigeria in 1978.

Basic issues in revenue allocation

Three basic issues which dominated financial and fiscal relations during the period under review are the following. How should federally derived revenue be shared between the centre and the states? What should be the criteria or principles for sharing statutory and non-statutory revenue among the states? Who should have the power to change the taxation system including income tax? The politics of these issues were affected by three major factors. First is the structure of the Nigerian military. The second factor is the increase in the number of governmental units in the federation from four regions to twelve states in 1967 and to nineteen in 1976 and in addition the acceptance of the 299 units of local government as the third tier of government important enough to be taken into consideration in any revenue allocation exercise. Third, the tremendous increase in the importance of oil as the major source of revenue made revenue sharing difficult partly because the rich small units of government were faced with demands from the large poor units.

How these factors affected the basic issues will become clearer below. It is necessary at this stage, however, to examine how the organisational structure of the military affected the politics of revenue allocation during this period. The effects were in three directions: (a) the power relations between the centre and the states; (b) the nature of the reaction of military governors who felt aggrieved by the prevailing revenue allocation principles; and (c) the frequency of changes in allocation formulae.

Based on the Binns Report, the distributable pools account was shared at the beginning of military rule in the ratio of 42 per cent for the North, 30 per cent for the East, 20 per cent for the West and 8 per cent for the Mid-West. The first constitutional amendments made in 1966 vested the federal military government with power to make laws for Nigeria with respect to any matter. This meant that by Decree No. 1 of 1966 the federal arrangement ceased. State governors derived their authority from the head of the military government and were appointed by the Supreme Military Council. This affected what in the Aboyade Report is referred to as 'the free play of intergovernmental relations'. Between 1967 and 1979 revenue allocation in Nigeria was based not only on ad hoc arrangements but also influenced by the subordinate-superordinate relationship between the federal government and other units of government. In a sense, therefore, the Binns Commission could be said to be the end of an era of revenue allocation based on the accepted findings of fiscal commissions appointed unanimously by all the units of government.

The subordinate-superordinate relationship accounted for the low-key statements of military governors who felt dissatisfied with the prevailing fiscal arrangements. For example, when in 1975 the new allocation principles reduced the share of both the Rivers and Mid-Western States from federal source, and politicians in these states formed study groups and other pressure groups to show their displeasure, the military governor of the Mid-Western State was quoted as saying, however, that 'the new allocation formula was agreed upon . . . in the overall interest of the country . . . the nation's interest should take precedence over that of the states'.[7]

During military rule, the allocation formula and the composition of the distributable pools account changed several times. The changes were more frequent between the period 1966 and 1975 than during the previous eighteen years. On the one hand this can be said to be advantageous in the sense that dissatisfaction with an existing system was not allowed to deepen to crisis level before changes were made. On the other hand however, it also points to the fact that fiscal centralism was the accepted system during the period. As Phillips put it, 'The ability of the military government to change the system more frequently, and without recourse to fiscal review commissions is derived principally from the nature of military rule, with its greater command structure, and cohesiveness. It may be unrealistic to expect a continuation of this situation beyond the period of military rule.'[8] It was this fiscal centralism that accounted, at least in part, for the application of different criteria for allocation in 1967. The creation of twelve states out of the previous four regions necessitated a new revenue arrangement. Due to the civil war, an interim revenue arrangement was made in that year to enable the states to settle down and carry out essential services. While population was made the basis of the sharing of the distributable pool account in respect of the southern states, the basis of the allocation of 7 per cent to each of the six northern states was not clear. Yet the decision was accepted by all the states.[9]

The Dina Committee

By the provisions of the 1963 constitution, a fiscal review commission may be appointed only every five years. Since the Binns Commission recommendations took effect from 1965, the earliest time for another revenue allocation commission was therefore 1969. But the political developments in the country – military rule, civil war, state creation – called for a readjustment of the revenue allocation system. This led to the decision of the Supreme Military Council in July 1968 to appoint an interim revenue allocation review committee made up of eight Nigerians – four university teachers and four civil servants. Four of these were economists.[10] The terms of reference of the committee were given as:

> In the light of the creation of twelve states, charged at present with the functions formerly exercised by the Regional Governments to:
>
> (a) look into and suggest any change in the existing system of revenue allocation as a whole. This includes all forms of revenue going to each Government besides and including the Distributable Pool;
>
> (b) suggest new revenue resources both for the Federal and the States Governments; and
>
> (c) report findings within four months.[11]

As Mr A. A. Atta, the then permanent secretary, federal Ministry of Finance, pointed out to the committee during its preliminary meeting, the terms of reference were deliberately made restrictive 'because it was the Federal Government's view at the time they were drawn up that the fundamental structure of the present revenue allocation system should not be changed until a Constituent Assembly had met'.[12] Even with the realisation that its task and the application of its recommendations would be interim, and that a fiscal review commission which 'might comprise experts from abroad' would be appointed later, the committee nevertheless interpreted its terms of reference comprehensively. In the words of the committee,

> We have been guided by the principle that revenue allocation must be seen as the essence of an overall financial and economic settlement, in which all the governments are motivated and geared to the development of one strong and fully integrated national economy within the context of a truly united Nigeria. Thus, we have interpreted our terms of reference in a way that we believe will ensure the development of an integrated economy in the country.[13]

Reviewing past revenue allocation reports, the committee observed,

> Fiscal arrangements in Nigeria appear in the past to have been dictated too much by political as well as constitutional developments. It is our view that this is probably the main source of the weaknesses of the past since this prevented the use of fiscal policy as an instrument capable of alleviating some of the basic problems of economic and national integration.[14]

The attempt to solve the problem of national integration through fiscal allocations and outside of politics led the committee to recommend among other things that: (a) the federal government should assume full responsibility for the financing of higher education, which was on the concurrent legislative list; (b) there should be uniform income tax legislation for the whole country; (c) mining rents in respect of inshore operations should be distributed on the basis of 15 per cent federal, 10 per cent state of derivation, 70 per cent joint account (that is, distributable pool account) – this in effect meant that oil producing states should be allocated 40 per cent less than what used to accrue to them; (d) offshore rents and royalties be distributed on the basis of 60 per cent federal, 30 per cent joint account and 10 per cent special account; (e) the pricing and financial policies of the marketing boards be harmonised; (f) a permanent national planning and fiscal commission 'endowed with effective powers which it could exercise throughout the appropriate agencies of government all over the country' should be established.

The committee's report was submitted in January 1969. From 10 to 12 April 1969, the finance commissioners from all the states of the federation under the chairmanship of the federal commissioner for finance met in Lagos and decided to reject the recommendations of the Dina Committee because it 'exceeded its power and in many respects ignored its terms of reference'.

Dina rejected yet implemented

Was there more to the rejection of the Dina Report than the

announced reason? In our view several other factors contributed. We pointed out earlier that the committee members were all Nigerians, three from the northern states and five from the southern states. It is not impossible that the Nigerian nature of its membership raised the suspicion of a partial and interested arbitrator. The element of suspicion is made stronger by the fact that the committee was chosen by the federal government which came out best *vis-à-vis* the states in the recommendations of the committee. The Dina Report advocated a strong central government in that it argued for more resources and power to the centre at the expense of the states.

Probably of more importance is the fact that in 1969 the commissioners for finance in the federation were mostly seasoned politicians led at the federal level by Chief Obafemi Awolowo, who chaired the meeting at which the report was rejected in April 1969. In the early years of Gowon rule, the regime needed the politicians more than the politicians needed the regime. This was more true of the period of civil war when it was most difficult to release army officers to hold political offices. In other words in 1969, unlike in the years after the civil war when civil commissioners were relegated to the corridors of power by super-permanent secretaries, the politicians played a critical role in governmental decision-making. It should be added that some of these civil commissioners expected a return to civil rule soon after the civil war and because of the opportunity of staying in the limelight during the period they expected to be in a stronger position to determine the nature and pattern of revenue allocation through a commission chosen by them.

In 1970 the federal government, by Decree 13 of that year, introduced the following changes in the revenue allocation formula. (a) The 100 per cent export duties that went to the states of origin was reduced to 60 per cent while 40 per cent was retained by the federal government. (b) The 100 per cent duty on fuel paid to the states of consumption was reduced to 50 per cent. The balance of 50 per cent went to the federal government. (c) The 50 per cent mining rents and royalties formerly paid to the states of origin were reduced to 45 per cent while the distributable pool account was credited with 50 per cent and the federal government retained 5 per cent.

(d) Excise duties were to be divided between the federal government and the distributable pool account. (e) The distributable pool account was to be distributed 50 per cent on the basis of equality of all the states and 50 per cent proportionately according to the population of each state.

In 1971 a more critical change was made. By Decree No. 9, rents and royalties of offshore petroleum mines were transferred from the states to the federal government. Added to the changes in the previous year, the basic theme of the Dina recommendation (transferring greater revenue from the states to the centre) was implemented. The two decrees promulgated in 1975, Nos. 6 and 7, fully endorsed not only the ascendancy of the federal government or the weakening position of the states, they showed that the Dina Report was only ahead of its time. The changes introduced in 1975 included the following:

(1) The 45 per cent mining rents and royalties paid to the states of origin were reduced to 20 per cent while the balance was credited to the distributable pool account.

(2) The federal government retained 65 per cent of import duties on all goods except motor spirit, diesel oil, tobacco, wine, portable spirit and beer. The rest of these duties as well as the duties on motor spirit and tobacco were paid in full into the distributable pool account.

(3) Fifty per cent of the excise duties was paid into the distributable pool account while the rest was retained by the federal government.

(4) The distributable pool account was distributed on the basis of 50 per cent population and 50 per cent on equality of states.

(5) Personal income tax was standardised throughout the federation. In effect the state governments' power to vary income tax rates was taken away from them.

In addition to all these measures, the federal government gradually took over many state functions, the most noticeable of which was education. Universal primary education was introduced by the federal government and financed largely by it. All universities were not only taken over, but no state was allowed to open its own university. The driving force behind all these actions by the federal government was the growth in revenue from petroleum profit tax. As Phillips has pointed out, 'Not only have revenues from this source been growing very rapidly [between 1970 and 1975] but the tax has risen from its position of insignificance in the early '60s to one in which it accounted for almost two thirds of federal revenue in 1974/75.'[15] The effect of this was twofold. Since this productive source of federal revenue continued to be excluded from the revenue allocation system, the federal government continued to pile up surpluses whilst the states had deficits. Even though the volume of both statutory and non-statutory allocation to states grew from ₦245.6 million in 1970/71 to ₦1371 million in 1975/6 these represented only 32.5 per cent in 1970/71 and 26.1 per cent in 1975/6 of total recurrent revenue to the federal government. In other words the proportion of federal revenue that went to the states declined by about one-third during this period.[16] Secondly, it accounted in part at least for the indifference of states to internal revenue sources. Between 1970 and 1974 two of the twelve states, Rivers and Benue-Plateau, derived over 80 per cent of recurrent revenue from statutory revenue allocation; eight states derived over 70 per cent or close to it; only Lagos had a low degree of dependence on this source – about 28 per cent.

Why were measures similar to the Dina recommendations adopted soon after the rejection of the report? Part of the answer lies in the factor analysed above – the unprecedented growth in revenue from oil. Another factor can be traced to the gradual ascendancy of the Gowon government particularly after successfully ending the civil war. Furthermore, the calibre of the political and particularly administrative advisers at the federal level was much higher than those at the state level with the probable exception of one or two states. Finally, soon after the civil war, many powerful political leaders gradually withdrew from public office to their private businesses when they realised that civil rule was to be delayed much longer than they had anticipated. All these factors helped to confirm the subordinate-superordinate relationship between the states and the federal government and with the structure of command in the military, made federal decisions binding on other units of government.

The Aboyade Technical Committee

In July 1975 a new military regime came to power in Nigeria. Almost two years after (June 1977) a Technical Committee on Revenue Allocation was appointed with the following terms of reference:

> Taking into consideration the need to ensure that each government of the federation *has adequate revenue to enable it discharge its responsibilities* and having regard to the factors of population, equality of status among the States, derivation, geographical peculiarities, even development, the national interest and any other factors bearing on the problem, the committee should:
>
> (a) examine the present revenue allocation formula with a view to determining its adequacy in the light of the factors mentioned above and representations from the Federal Government and the State Governments and other interested parties
>
> (b) following from the finding in (a) recommend new proposals as necessary for the *allocation of revenue* between the Federal, States as well as *the Local Governments and also amongst the States and Local Government*
>
> (c) make whatever recommendations are considered necessary for effective collection and distribution of Federal and State Revenues.[17] [our italics]

A number of comments may be made about the terms of reference. It was the first time that a panel was being asked to allocate revenue on the basis of constitutional responsibilities. The committee had therefore been urged to see its task as one of correlating functions (and the subsequent responsibilities generated) with resource allocation. Also it was the first time that specific financial autonomy was being asked to be given to local government as a level of government. This fell in line with the regime's policy statement of August 1976 which stated that 'The Federal Government has . . . decided to recognise Local Government as the third tier of governmental activity in the nation'.[18] This recognition was designed not only to enable local government to get the necessary funds for performing its allotted responsibilities but to raise its status *vis-à-vis* state government in particular. The decision to find correlation between levels of responsibility and revenue allocation was significant because it indicated a search for rational non-political indices for revenue-sharing. This accounted for naming the group given this responsibility the Technical Committee.

Like the Dina Committee before it, this Technical Committee was an all Nigerian affair. Of the six-member committee, four were professional economists (three of them full professors, the other a head of department of economics), one head of a political science department and the other a former managing director of one of the leading daily newspapers in the country. There was ample evidence therefore, at least from the composition of the panel, of a wish to depoliticise revenue allocation. Why should the desire to remove politics out of revenue-sharing be so strongly emphasised? Part of the answer probably lay in the simple notion of revenue sharing as an exercise in statistical projection and quantification. The administration's desire to evolve a 'politics free' but rational formula not only for distributing revenue but also for resolving many public issues was strongly emphasised before this period.

In the committee's report submitted on 30 December 1977, it was revealed that: (a) federally collected revenue rose from ₦282 million in 1967/8 to ₦6100 million in 1976/7 (with a rise from ₦2171 million in 1973/4 to ₦5177 million in 1974/5); (b) during the same period revenue from customs and excise rose from ₦186 million to ₦672 million, an increase of over 360 per cent; (c) revenue retained at the federal level was 65 per cent of the federally collected revenue. But with the creation of twelve states, the percentage rose to 72, and with the increase to nineteen states in 1976, this figure stood at 71 per cent. In the view of the committee three factors have contributed to this federal superiority in revenue allocation. The 'acquisition' by the federal government of functions which were the constitutional responsibilities of the states. This centralisation was encouraged by the buoyant revenue position of the former and partly the need to promote national unity. The net effect of the federal presence was, according to the committee, 'either to abolish completely or reduce considerably the State Governments' independent sources of revenue'. Finally, the psychology and the operational philosophy of the military organisation has tended to contribute to the centralisation tendency.

What then should be done? (1) Responsibilities in the field of agriculture, housing, primary and secondary education, basic health, youth and sports should be returned to state and local governments. (2) Greater efforts should be made by state governments in tax management through increased efficiency in assessment and collection. (3) A return to the position nearer to the division of responsibilities between the centre and the states as contained in the 1963 constitution (with the addendum of local government functions) may help to arrest the 'seemingly inexorable march to centralise and provide an appropriate background for a more rational allocation of national revenues'.

The committee rejected the old principles of revenue allocation either because they were politically controversial and arbitrary or because they lacked statistically concise definition. In all cases when they were used in absolute and unweighted terms, they did not encourage the development of a cohesive fiscal system. The Aboyade Committee broke new ground in the system of revenue allocation. Firstly, its concept of federally derived revenue (all revenue collected from functions allotted to the federal government) was relatively new and derived both from the planning approach of the committee and its interest in promoting a redistribution of income and wealth throughout the country. The rationality, according to the report, was to ensure that all levels of government 'benefit from the proceeds of taxes, the conditions for which collection they have helped to create' and to ensure an even spread of benefits (or loss) among tiers of government in the changing fortune of such a revenue.[19] Secondly, the idea of a local governments' fund was itself a new recommendation by a revenue-sharing committee. However, such a fund was suggested by another panel set up to advise on financing local government. A good deal of that panel's report was accepted by the Aboyade Committee. The local government fund was

composed of 10 per cent from federally derived revenue and 10 per cent of the total revenue receipts of each state government. The committee was of the view that 'by this financial magnitude, the States would be committed to not only the survival but the flourishing of the newly-revived Local Government System.'[20] Thirdly, the committee also proposed new arrangements for revenue-sharing.
The new principles were,

(i) equality of access to development opportunities;
(ii) national minimum standards for national integration;
(iii) absorptive capacity;
(iv) independent revenue and minimum tax effort; and
(v) fiscal efficiency.[21]

For an understanding of the new principles, two new concepts were essential: 'national' and 'state' norms. These norms were defined essentially in terms of sectoral allocations in the 1975-80 National Development Plan. The 'national norm' was defined as the ratio of allocations to sector Y (by both federal and states) as a percentage of the total National Plan allocation. The 'state norm' referred to the ratio of allocation to sector Y as a percentage of a state's total plan allocation. For 'equality of access to development', the committee used the economic sector; and used the social sector as an indicator of national integration. Thus, the levels of development (or lack of it) and national integration (or disintegration) were defined as the distance (positive or negative) of the state norm from this national standard. The national norm is in essence a national mean computed from sectoral allocation of a national development plan.

A number of questions may be raised about the methodology used by the committee in arriving at this formula. Firstly, can development of a nation be defined simply in terms of economic sector allocation of a plan and, even if it can be so defined, are the components of this sector the best indices of development? The same question also applies to the definition of national integration in terms of social sector allocation. Secondly, is it meaningful to define 'development' and 'national integration' in terms of hopes and aspirations? It is a well known comment on development plans that they represent wishes and hopes and that actual performance leaves much to be desired. Furthermore, it is well known regarding planning in Nigeria that plans have been drawn up 'without facts' and have been documents of political compromise rather than of national planning. Thus, the use of sectoral allocation may not only produce an exaggerated 'national norm' but the lack of proven statistical data in drawing up such plans also suggests a false guide to national development and integration. As the committee itself has observed, in connection with another principle, it found that data 'were not consistently of comparable degree of quality and reliability'[22] among the states of the federation and, one may add, among federal ministries. Apart from reliability of data, some of the new principles depend on the presence and quality of manpower, in a state, which the indices have neglected. For example, absorptive capacity and fiscal efficiency of a state depends on availability of skilled personnel.

In spite of the absence of reliable data and the lack of consensus about what the indices do measure – both facts are sources of political arguments, the government went ahead to approve the report and even recommended it to the Constituent Assembly. A number of reasons may have accounted for this: in the first place, the regime genuinely believes that the new arrangement has considerably taken the heat of politics out of revenue allocation. This is partly because the committee did not place undue emphasis on derivation and population principles, and partly because the new formula is capable of generating a new search for facts and reliable figures in the planning process. The military administration may therefore be of the view that, despite inadequate statistical data, the new arrangement will lead to a cohesive fiscal system which, in turn, will promote rational national development. In short, because the view of the committee is in consonance with the national aspirations of the regime and in order to show its faith in the new arrangement government decided not only to implement the formula for the 1979/80 financial year without the factoral weights, but also to recommend it to the Constituent Assembly.

The acceptance of the report may also be attributed to the nature of decision-making under the military regime. The mere fact that the governors of the states are military officers on posting meant that their commitment to the political positions of the states is not as strong as that to the nation. The report, at the time it was considered, was regarded as a technical rather than a political document, and with no political mandate from the electorate its ratification should be easier. Thus, the chance of 'politics' filtering into the decision to approve the report was considerably reduced.

Finally, the hierarchical nature of the military and its decision ethos may have contributed to the easy acceptance of the report. It is probably difficult for the Federal Executive Council (and for that matter the National Council of States) to reject a decision already approved by the Supreme Military Council. Even more difficult is a report emanating from it and on which its position is already known. At best, the lower decision-making bodies can only improve upon questions of detail. For example, the Federal Executive Council suggested that consideration should be given to rewarding community effort.

Both the Aboyade Report and the federal military government's view on it were sent to the Constituent Assembly – an assembly of future politicians. Why was this necessary? Perhaps the government wanted to give the report a democratic blessing, for a large proportion of members were elected from their constituencies all over the country. It is quite possible that government believed that if the Assembly certified the document, revenue allocation would have been taken out of the electioneering campaign and hopefully out of politics in the immediate future. It may also be the case that the SMC simply assumed that enough goodwill and 'nation-feeling' existed in the Assembly to ensure the approval of the document. Government seemed to have forgotten the fact that members of the Assembly were there not simply to recommend a constitutional document for Nigeria but to foster their own political ambitions. Furthermore, the kind of compromise which featured during the consideration of the draft constitution already showed the underlying political rather than technical consideration of the Aboyade Report. The personal ambitions of members of the Constituent Assembly apart, the manner in which, in past years of military rule, revenue allocation issues have been resolved through political accommodation seems to indicate that the Aboyade Report would no longer be received as simply a technical report to be digested, approved and rubber-stamped.

A number of reasons may therefore be suggested for the Assembly, after a full debate, merely 'noting' the report. The presentation of the report by Dr Omoruyi was a tactical mistake, for at the time the report was considered Dr Omoruyi, although a member of the Technical Committee, was a politician and a prominent member of a political organisation called Club 19. Again, his presentation was couched in language which questioned the autonomy and competence of the Assembly. For example, he urged it to approve the report because the Assembly was not competent to produce a substitute. Secondly, the timing of the report was inopportune. It came at the end of the consideration of critical issues such as the creation of more states, the Sharia controversy and the formula for election of the president. These issues already divided members of the Assembly along 'party' or 'issue' lines. Furthermore, the resolutions of these issues were based on those emotional aspects of politics which the Technical Committee had rejected: that is, population and equality of states. Dr Omoruyi had already been known to take sides on these issues. At the time the report was considered therefore, the Assembly was in the mood to reject any report or document which attempted to question its competence.

Thirdly, even if the chairman of the committee had presented the report to the Assembly, and the issues of Sharia, creation of more states and election of the president had not so sharply divided the Constituent Assembly, there was a high probability that the report would have been rejected.[23] Dr Pius Okigbo's 'impressive contribution' (*New Nigeria*, Wednesday, 14 June 1978) represented not only the view of an opposing group of brilliant economists but the political stand of most members of the Constituent Assembly from most of the northern and eastern states.[24]

In a most unfair article in the *New Nigerian*, Candido[25] attacked Nigerian economists. He said,

Assuredly, one of the most powerful groups in our decision-making structure today is that constituted by economists. They have a finger in virtually every pie which the nation bakes.

They monopolise the policy-making process through and through. They are famous for guiding and mis-guiding the political leadership with their piles of figures, computer print-outs, pious assumptions about 'relevant parameters' and passionate appeals to us to believe that 'ceteris' is always 'paribus'. . . .

I do not know what they have in their neatly-packaged revenue allocation formula but I already suspect the worst from the quibble in their opening salvo. Having assured us that they have avoided the old and controversial principles of revenue allocation, they proceed to offer five 'completely new ones' in their stead.

Candido then proceeded to dismiss the five new principles as old wine in new bottles. He went further:

> This brings me to the cause of my grouch with our economists, which is that they are only noticeable when they are appointed to special committees or made heads of specialised centres from where they work themselves half to death misguiding the nation, botching up the economy, travelling to innumerable seminars and basking in the glow of news media reports.[26]

In a follow-up to this piece, five weeks later, Okigbo was praised for his impressive contribution to the debate on the Aboyade Report. In a piece titled 'I doff off my hat to you, Sir' Candido said,

> When on May 3, I took my cudgels against our economists, I did not in any way mean to go in for an out and out condemnation of all our economists. . . .
>
> Having now read Dr Okigbo's impressive contribution to this debate [on the Aboyade Report] I hasten to restate that there are always exceptions to every rule. Dr Okigbo, I doff off my hat to you, Sir.[27]

All this goes to show the extent to which the political atmosphere of the time and the strictly economic nature of the recommendation contributed to the rejection of the report and, indeed, the shelving of the revenue allocation problem for the next civilian regime.

Revenue allocation, like budgeting, though strictly an economic issue, has a high political content. Any attempt to take politics out of revenue allocation is bound to fail. As Wildavsky said to the advocates of budgetary process in the United States, 'If the . . . budgetary process is rightly or wrongly deemed unsatisfactory, then one must alter in some respect the political system of which the budget is but an expression. It makes no sense to speak as if one could make drastic changes in budgeting without also altering the distribution of influence.[28]

The experience of revenue-sharing under the military has also demonstrated the need to take cognisance of political factors. It is true that the nature of military organisation and indeed the growing sense of national awareness have considerably minimised the impact of these factors. The same factors have also made it easier to transfer revenue from one level of government to another. Nonetheless, the conclusion is inescapable that the non-acceptance of a nationally acceptable working formula, even under the military, has been due primarily to political considerations. Thus, the sharing of revenue, like budgeting, is inextricably linked to the political system.

11 Dilemma of military disengagement

J. 'Bayo Adekson

Problem in comparative perspective

The problem of civilian succession to leadership under the military centres on the fundamental question of whether a ruling junta accepts demilitarisation as a desirable goal, and how far it is willing to go in carrying this objective to the logical conclusion by disengaging fully from the political arena.[1] From this central problem, it is possible to abstract other lesser though equally intriguing ones. Suppose a military ruler decides to withdraw, and is actually serious about that, how is the withdrawal to be effected? Who succeeds to power? And how is he to be selected? By 'nomination' or/and 'election'? If by 'nomination', how does the outgoing military junta ensure that its nominee commands popular support? But if the choice is to be determined by 'elections', to what extent should the present incumbents of power seek to dictate the character of the new civilian government? If it is expedient to do so, is it also sound and safe, from the viewpoint of the stability of the political system in the future, that all members of the ex-political class be 'disqualified' and totally excluded from government?

All along it is being assumed that the military regime is actually serious about withdrawing. Of course, one sometimes observes a military ruler who, rather than go all the way to 'total withdrawal' or 'disengagement', merely limits himself to 'partial withdrawal' or even 'non-withdrawal' to speak in relative terms, while at the same time making gestures of token civilianisation. (In the sense in which the term is used here, 'civilianisation' does not mean the same thing as 'demilitarisation'. While 'demilitarisation' in its full sense aims at complete military withdrawal from government, 'civilianisation' or 'quasi-civilianisation' on the other hand merely seeks to inject important civilian individuals or groups into the various decision-making processes, without altering the basic structure of government which remains military.)[2]

However, it should not be inferred from what has been said thus far that all military rulers actually sit down to analyse the issues of demilitarisation or political disengagement in the manner and sequence in which they have been formulated above. To be sure, some rulers may have planned their withdrawal in response to certain personal and professional motivations or/and to given political situations; others may have simply stumbled on to a particular path inadvertently, or may have been forced to take that course, without desiring it, by a fortuitous combination of circumstances. Still another mode of resolving the demilitarisation problem may have resulted simply from a ruler's non-decision or procrastination about issues that should otherwise have attracted commanding attention. Instances of all these abound in the contemporary political history of West Africa.

Types of military disengagement

For example, the withdrawal from government effected by the National Liberation Council (NLC) regime of Ghana in September 1969 was a clear instance of planned demilitarisation. So also is the Nigerian case since 1975, which we discuss in the bulk of this chapter. On the other hand, in Sierra Leone, another ex-military-administered state where civilian rule was restored, it was indecision on the part of the junta as to when to withdraw and who would succeed them that led to their being forcibly thrown out by a counter-*coup d'état* in April 1968.

Admittedly, whatever the style of succession, both the Ghanaian and Sierra Leonean cases, as indeed the still unfolding one of Nigeria discussed below, are instances of full civilian restoration, although this did not, and will not, mean complete termination of military influence over decision-making. However, preceding the earlier Sierra Leonean and Ghanaian examples, there was immediate post-Olympio's

Togoland where ex-Sergeant Bodjello and his men, confronted with the spectacle of exercising rule for which they were apparently unprepared, relinquished power almost immediately on seizing it in April 1963. There is also the example of Dahomey (now Republic of Benin), which has recorded the highest number of civilian restorations consequent upon military withdrawals, with Colonel Alley's withdrawal in favour of Dr Emile Zinsou as civilian president in July 1968, and return to the presidency of the old Maga-Apithy-Ahomadegbe *troika* in 1970 (after Kouandete's coup toppling Dr Zinsou), being to date the most recent instances of these. Dahomey is again back under military rule under Kerekou.

In the Upper Volta, Central African Republic (now Empire), and post-Grunitzky's Togoland, on the other hand, the answer to the problem of demilitarisation was felt to lie in the replacement of the civilian government by a permanent para-military regime.

A close observation of the West African comparative empirical situation, then, suggests that it is possible to group all the various approaches to military disengagement to date into three major forms:[3] (a) countercoup-inspired approach, (b) military-turned-political pattern, and (c) constitutional-evolutionary model. In grouping these approaches, a number of criteria were used, such as the attitudes of the rulers and extent of their commitment to demilitarisation, mode of the power transformation, type of civil-military relations envisaged and why, and nature of the political conditions confronting the soldier rulers.[4] Let us elaborate, briefly, upon each of the forms of demilitarisation typified.

The countercoup-inspired approach While the military may 'civilianise' to a certain extent, this approach results where a ruling junta has no immediate intention of, or are undecided about, withdrawing from politics. The incumbents would wish to stay in power as long as they could. Soon the tenuousness of these soldiers' rule becomes apparent, which, based as it is on a 'legitimacy' that wanes with time, is fraught with much potential insecurity and instability. Even without an added tendency to bask in ill-gotten luxury like the politicians whom they have ousted, this inherent curse of political illegitimacy alone is sufficient to create a big credibility gap for the military rulers. Under the circumstances, a countercoup is hatched to effect the passage of power to other hands. Actually, this form of power transfer may not necessarily aim at civilian succession as such, but may have been carried out by some dissident military faction intent simply on replacing fellow officers. Whether aimed at civilian succession or an intra-military power change, however, the most noticeable feature of this pattern of succession to leadership under the military is the use of counter-military force conjoined, sometimes, with popular revolt.

The military-turned-political pattern The second approach involves a greater degree of demilitarisation than the first, in so far as leadership here divests itself, at least on paper, of the control of the army and seeks a more permanent basis of rule than that initially derived from the power of the bullet. But essentially the regime is still a military-backed one in which members of the ruling junta seek to transform themselves into a new quasi-civilian political élite to permanently replace the former professional politicians. Sometimes conscious attempt may be made to create a national omnibus organisation, party, or movement to canvass mass support for the erstwhile military ruler now turned (or in the process of turning) president through self-nomination. There is a surface change from men-in-uniform (khaki) to soldiers-in-mufti (agbada). The final metamorphosis may be climaxed formally by national elections. However, this pattern of succession, in so far as it aims at prolonging the tenure of the military incumbents beyond the spirit of the original coup, may be designated, borrowing a descriptive term from the vocabulary of Latin American politics, simply as a system of military *continuismo*.

The constitutional-evolutionary model Under this pattern, the military authorities do not limit themselves to mere civilianisation, but seek to fully disengage from the political arena to the extent compatible with the maintenance of a workable relationship between the military and civilian sectors of the society. The rationale behind this approach seems to be that the concept of 'political neutrality' carries with it its own rights and responsibilities.[5] For example, sometimes an army intervenes in, so as paradoxically to be allowed to stay out of, politics; but the obverse side to this argument is the injunction that an army in government ought to hand over as early as possible to a new constitutionally elected body of civilian executives, and withdraw to the barracks to resume its traditional, non-political profession of tending the country's security. Undoubtedly, there may be other pressures at work forcing the military to disengage, such as the increasing political problems facing it, as well as pressures from within the junta and from the 'active' army organisation. On the whole, the emphasis in this type of approach to demilitarisation is on constitutional and methodical procedure of military disengagement. It involves drawing up an elaborate timetable for a phased return to civilian rule, a procedure which features such other processes as the making of a new constitution, summoning of a constituent assembly to debate and ratify the draft constitution, lifting of the ban on political party activities, and finally the holding of national election to determine the civilian successors to the military.

Of the forms of military disengagement just analysed, the last interests us the most, because it best exemplifies the present Nigerian case, which we shall shortly discuss in detail. An earlier example in contemporary West Africa which followed an approach approximating this was Ghana leading to the late Dr Busia's takeover in 1969, although barely within three years that country was to revert to military rule. Variants of the military-turned-civilian pattern of succession are reproduced in most of Francophone Africa, among them Lamizana's Upper Volta, Eyadema's Togo, Bokassa's Central African Empire, and Mobutu's Congo-Leo (now Zaire). General Acheampong's Ghana (1972-8) had, unsuccessfully, aimed at similar quasi-civilian transformation, as was clear from his 'union government' proposals. Finally, we may cite the rank and file revolt which toppled Brigadier Juxon-Smith, and paved the way for the restoration of civilian rule in Sierra Leone, as an instance of countercoup-inspired succession to the military.

However, it should be emphasised that the grouping done here of military-political systems according to their observable patterns of demilitarisation can only be rough and tentative. Nothing is to be interpreted from the foregoing analysis as implying that the three patterns are each autonomous, in the sense of not containing within it elements of others. The opposite is rather true – namely, that in all of the concrete historical cases that have been studied, one observes elements of all three patterns of disengagement mixed up with one another. For example, the pattern presently unfolding in Nigeria did not begin in earnest until after the 29 July 1975 countercoup terminating the previous General Gowon regime that had been noted for its indecision or procrastination on the 'return to civil rule' issue. Similarly, it was the near-successful countercoup attempt of 17 April 1967 which jolted the NLC regime of Ghana from its lethargy and forced it to begin to think about withdrawing. In the latter case, it is interesting that, even in the midst of a supposedly 'constitutional' process of power transfer, Lieutenant-General Joseph Ankrah as chairman of the NLC was still scheming, although unsuccessfully as it turned out, for a military-turned-political type succession, with himself as the new president of post-military Ghana.[6] Finally, although the Sierra Leonean example has been typified as a case of counter-inspired succession, in fact the legality of Siaka Stevens' succession to Brigadier Juxon-Smith had been previously established by the results of the pre-coup, constitutionally held elections of March 1967.[7] These important qualifications should be borne in mind, as we proceed to discuss in great detail the Nigerian case as an example of a constitutional-evolutionary pattern of military disengagement.

The Nigerian case: a constitutional-evolutionary process

Although it had been in power since 15 January 1966 under a succession of rulers, the Nigerian military did not begin in earnest to disengage from political rule until after the 29 July 1975 coup which brought the reforming governments of

Brigadiers (later Generals) Murtala Mohammed and Olusegun Obasanjo into power. In his maiden address as the new head of state, Murtala promised the country a new political programme for a return to civil rule. That programme, which was indeed to be announced three months later on 1 October 1975, is the basis of our characterisation of the Nigerian case as a 'constitutional-evolutionary' approach to military disengagement.

'One important subject' facing the new regime, that the 1 October 1975 address announced,

> 'is of course the question of a Political Programme. . . . The ultimate aim is to forge a viable political system which will be stable and responsive enough to the needs and realities of this country. This is not an exercise that begins and ends in the mere drafting of a constitution. Viable political institutions only emerge from hard experience and practice and the corporate experience of all is what matters. . . . With this in mind, the Supreme Military Council has approved *a five-stage programme* designed to ensure a smooth transition to civil rule by those elected by the people of this country. During the first, the States issue will be settled and any new states created will be fully established. The Committee on States will submit its report in December 1975 and the preliminary steps for the establishment of new states will be completed by April 1976. Meanwhile, a Drafting Committee on the Constitution will be appointed this month and will have up to September 1976 to complete its work on a first initial Draft Constitution.
>
> In stage II, the newly created states will be given time to settle down before the entire Federation embarks upon a systematic and deliberate reorganisation of the Local Government set-up. The reorganisation will lead to elections at Local Government level on individual merit without party politics. Arising from this there will then be a Constituent Assembly partly elected and partly nominated. The purpose of this Assembly is to consider and accept the Draft Constitution after which it would be dissolved. This second stage will last two years, that is, it will be completed by October 1978.

Stage III will be a preparatory stage for elections. The ban on political activities will be lifted in October 1978. Political parties can then be formed in preparation for the final stages in which elections will be held into the Legislatures at State and Federal levels, as prescribed by the new Constitution. The two elections make up Stages IV and V. These two stages are expected to be completed within one year and we intend to hand over power to a democratically elected Government of the people by 1st October, 1979. The present military leadership does not intend to stay in office a day longer than necessary, and certainly not beyond this date.'[8]

Each of the five stages, which are summarised below, represented a different phase in the process of demilitarisation, and yet they were all related, even if not always logically, both to each other and to the overall goal of civilian restoration. We say 'if not always logically', because it seems that some of the task schedules in Phases I and II, dealing in particular with the creation of new states and local government reforms respectively, were concerned more with the restructuring of the federal political system than with the goal of demilitarisation *per se*; while there were other measures dealing directly with this goal, which did not appear on the timetable, such as appointment of civilians into various decision-making positions, and compilation of the corrupt practices of all past leaders, civilian and military, still going on. Already, one had seen the present military rulers immediately on taking over turn their 'anti-corruption' crusade against all the public services and corporations of the federation, retiring in the process hundreds of public servants and employees whom they considered either corrupt or as 'deadwoods'. Admittedly, part of this particular measure might have been aimed by the military at justifying its initial act of intervention (if this needed any 'justifying') as well as consolidating the new regime.

What was the progress report on the demilitarisation programme? A Constitutional Drafting Committee (CDC) nominated to draw up a new constitution for the country, began its meeting on 18 October 1975; and seven more states were added

Table 11.1

Timetable of military return to civil rule in Nigeria, 1975-9

Phases	*Programmes*
Phase I	Creation and establishment of new states (August 1975-April 1976); constitution drafting (October 1975-September 1976)
Phase II	Local government reorganisation, reforms, and elections; summoning of a Constituent Assembly to deliberate on draft constitution (September 1976-October 1978)
Phase III	Electoral constituency delimitation; lifting of the ban on political party activities (October 1978)
Phase IV	Holding of elections to legislative and executive offices at the state level
Phase V	Holding of elections to legislative and executive offices at the federal level; and handover of power by 1 October 1979.

in April 1976 to the twelve-state federal structure inherited from Gowon. But in February 1976 the head of the federal military government and supreme commander of the Nigerian armed forces, Lieutenant-General Murtala Mohammed, was forcibly removed from office in a dastardly act during an attempted countercoup, and one of the inner members of his government, Lieutenant-General Olusegun Obasanjo, sworn in to take his place (13 February 1976).

In spite of this discordant note, the process of return to civil rule continued unchanged. Reorganisation of local governments in Nigeria was carried out, the units were rationalised and streamlined, and elections held into the newly established local councils (December 1976). The Constitutional Drafting Committee submitted its report in

September 1976. The report was thrown open for general debate. On 1 October 1976 the military government appointed a twenty-four-member Federal Electoral Commission (FEDECO) to delimit the electoral constituencies for the country, draw up a comprehensive voters' register, and organise the federal and state elections. Much of the year 1977 was spent by the country, or rather various segments of responsible opinion within Nigeria, including eminent personalities, traditional rulers, scholars, private citizens, and even some soldiers, debating the merits and demerits of the CDC draft document. The debate continued in the Constituent Assembly which was constituted partly by elections and partly by nomination. The Constituent Assembly submitted a by no means consensual document a little over a month earlier than scheduled (29 August 1978).

On 14 July 1978, the head of the federal military government introduced one of the most momentous measures for restoring civil rule in the country.[9] That was the date the government announced the reposting of state military governors as well as some federal military commissioners to the barracks. This particular measure seemed momentous for a number of reasons. For one thing, it directly touched the military *qua* military, whereas all the earlier measures, such as creation of more states, local government reforms, and the constitution-drafting exercise aimed at the wider society. For another, the measure underlined the sincerity of the present military authorities in their oft-stated determination to return the country to civilian politics by 1979. Also, the measure aimed at depoliticising the military before competition for governmental posts by the politicians would have actually begun. The issue of depoliticisation of the military within the overall context of disengagement will be further developed below.

For the moment, it is important to point out that as long as the senior officers concerned remained in their quasi-political positions, they could not be trusted to be non-partisan between the parties or coalitions of parties expected to emerge to compete for office. For example, it is widely believed that some of the previous state governors under the Gowon regime were involved in inflating the 1973 census figures, and helped to turn that exercise, like the previous ones of the 1960s, into a competitive state game of statistical juggling. The fact is that even military men can easily be affected by political issues and start responding to the latter accordingly, once they take up political appointments. So the reposting to the barracks of the state military governors as well as some federal military commissioners was expected to go a long way towards checking this kind of danger, if and when active political campaigns began.

After the 14 July 1978 order was announced, a new Nigerian constitution, submitted by the Constituent Assembly, was promulgated with some important amendments by the Supreme Military Council, the state of emergency as well as the ban on politics in existence in the country since 15 January 1966 was lifted, and political party activities reactivated (21 September 1978). These, it will be recalled, were tasks falling under Phase III of the original timetable. The last two combined Phases IV and V, dealing with controlling competition among the emergent political parties as well as the conduct of elections into executive and legislative positions at both the federal and state levels, were entrusted to the Federal Electoral Commission. These phases began on time, and are expected to end with the investiture of twenty (one federal plus nineteen state) civil governments in the country either a little before, or exactly on, but certainly not after 1 October 1979. In short, the four-year political programme embarked upon by the present military regime in 1975 would have all been completed according to plan.

To conclude this important section of the chapter: the process of transferring power from the military to a new civilian administration in Nigeria offers a very interesting study in the politics of demilitarisation both on its own account and as an exercise in comparative political analysis. It is an unequalled case of a ruling military faithfully presiding, in accordance with a masterpiece formula of detail and method, over the peaceful self-liquidation of their acquired power. Admittedly, the governing soldiers had not been free of pressures both from within and without the government, and had always been conscious, as remarked before, of the inherent tenuousness and instability of their rule based as it is primarily on force. Even so, it is remarkable that the FMG had kept to its promise, especially when one remembers the tendential phenomena noticeable in most of West Africa of soldier-rulers metamorphosing permanently into a new quasi-civilian political class. Also remarkable is the fact that the present FMG had since 29 July 1975 followed its timetable for a return to civilian rule, phase by phase. Nigeria would have recorded a first in the history of demilitarisation, by far surpassing the earlier Ghanaian one in scope, extent and detail, if the on-going methodical, step-by-step, and yet determined process of military disengagement based on constitutional usages successfully eventuated as planned in the hand-over of power by October 1979.

The Military as an interested political referee[10]

The Nigerian military was beginning to develop a professional tradition of political neutrality, when the 15 January 1966 *putsch* took place, thereby nullifying much of the progress made in this area. But, with the promise of a restoration of civil rule and return of the soldiers to the barracks, there is a general desire to see the military resume its search for a politically neutral role after 1 October 1979.

Normally, even if it did not have a baker's dozen years of military rule to reckon with, a demilitarised Nigeria would still have had to contend with the problem that the concept of 'a politically neutral army' is easier to use than define. The fact of the military having been in government for about thirteen years now only serves to exacerbate – but it does not cause – this problem. For, as the present author has shown elsewhere, it is not always clear what the concept of 'political neutrality' means, since it involves at least four analytically contradictory notions each of which is at the same time internally inconsistent.[11] A politically neutral army is sometimes defined the same as (a) an *apolitical* army: namely, a system of formalistic impersonality, existing in a social quarantine, and unaffected by the structure of and conditions within the society (in which it is supposed to operate). Of all the notions of political neutrality, this is the most unrealisitic, and irrelevant to the Nigerian situation.

As commonly used, the concept of neutrality may also

stress simply (b) the *instrumental* role of the army: namely, that, being the ulitmate organ of state power and the defender of its constitution, the army is not permitted to defy the political leadership, nor is it free to separate itself from the body politically (c) *impartial:* namely, to be non-partisan between groups, or coalitions of groups, competing for civil office, while giving their support to every government that is lawfully constituted. Finally, by the requirement of neutrality, one may mean simply being (d) *non-political*, that is, functionally separated from the practice of politics (in the sense in which other professional groups also are).

Now, all the last three notions of political neutrality are internally inconsistent; and, whether viewed as descriptions or prescriptions, can be counter-productive to the goal of civilian control. For example, in a purely instrumental capacity, the military may find itself overthrowing a given constitution by a *coup d'état* while honestly acting to defend it. The requirement that the military be impartial has its corollary that the organisation not be identified as the organ of partisan groups. In the past, failure of many African political governments, including the Nigerian in 1966, to abide by this latter stipulation tended to produce that paradoxical kind of coup by some military members aimed at making their organisation impartial.

Similarly, basic to the non-political stipulation of military role is the injunction of 'keeping politics out of the army'. By this, soldiers expect to be allowed to regulate their own internal affairs by means of such purely functional criteria as autonomy, hierarchy, cohesion and corporatism, without interference from outside. The obverse of this is 'keeping the army out of politics'. Many armies, among them the Ghanaian in 1966, are known to have intervened 'in politics' motivated partly by the desire to stay 'out of politics.

To make matters even more complicated, one particular notion of political neutrality is contradictory of the other. The 'instrumental' may at any given time contradict the 'impartial', which may in turn run counter to the 'non-political', which may also be inconsistent with the 'instrumental'. What happens, for example, if the military sticks, rather legalistically, to a single-track instrumental definition of its role, and refuses to be bothered by an incident of usurpation of power by one political group? Do moralistic or judgemental definitions of the army's duty not impede its effectiveness as an instrumental force? What of the generalisation that armies which are overly concerned with struggles in the political realm, and led to pre-empt political rule, are inherently incapable of defending their countries against foreign attacks? Does the non-political ideal as defined above not, in fact, conflict with the instrumental, with its assumption of soldiers as merely passive instruments in the hands of the political ruler? And how does a society go about inculcating the set of attitudes compatible with such contradictory ideals?

Most of these points, theoretical though they remain now, are going to be very important again after the return to civil rule. For the moment, and in part because Nigeria is still governed *de facto* by the military, it is meaningless to speak of a politically neutral military in the combined sense of the term used above. Even as the country moves towards the restoration of civil rule, all we can hope for or insist upon as a limited goal is that the military be non-partisan between the parties or coalitions of parties that either have emerged or are fast coalescing to contest the impending elections to various federal and state executive and legislative offices. Nor would it be a small achievement if the military succeeded in achieving this minimal objective.

The chances of the military being impartial in the ensuing competition are increased by the observation that Nigeria had managed to escape being divided by any political 'disqualification' debate. The 'age limitation' issue, which would have had effects similar to the latter, was happily avoided as a result of amendment to the Constituent Assembly-produced constitution introduced by the Supreme Military Council. It is also significant that none of the parties that have emerged, as part of its campaign promises, recklessly talks of undoing certain things that the military has done; or embarking upon policies aimed in effect at disbanding the military, and/or creating in the future new para-military bodies that would rival the regular forces. Even those leading politicians, like

Chief Obafemi Awolowo, known for their long-standing opposition to large defence establishment cum budget,[12] have so far kept remarkably silent on such matters. Although Alhaji Aminu Kano, another notable politician, had during the Constituent Assembly debates called for the publication by the military of the state of the country's finances before handing over power,[13] this has also not been made an electioneering issue, at least so far. For, from comparative experience, such talk tends to provide governing armies with an excuse for openly intervening in the succession process, by either championing the cause of certain rival parties and personalities known for their pro-military views and sympathies, or even creating and fielding their own military parties and candidates.

That a given governing military voluntarily withdraws from office is in itself enough of a self-sacrifice if not self-immolation, considering the nature of power, with its irresistible temptation for men of flesh. That, in handing over power, a governing army is able to maintain any semblance of neutrality between competing parties at all is even more praiseworthy. There is no doubt that the issue of who succeeds to 'Caesar's mantle' is a very crucial one, and most retiring armies from contemporary historical experience, even including some that otherwise opted for a constitutional method of power transfer as defined above, end up in effect appointing their own successors, and proceed to use all available machinery of state power to ensure the latter's election (or enthronement).

A recent example from West Africa was that of immediate post-Nkrumah's Ghana (1966-9). There the military to a large extent predetermined the succession issue, by introducing measures aimed to minimise the possibility of challenge from the 'old politicals', by divesting them of their former power and influence; to maintain complete control over the process of competition, and over which political groups or personalities to allow to compete; and to promote the rise of new élite groups or individuals known to be identified with the aims and purposes of the regime, while providing members with opportunities to advance within the framework of the political institutions and governmental structures that the present regime was seeking to perpetuate. The National Liberation

Council (NLC) of Ghana was no doubt blatantly interested in who would succeed them. Not only did they disqualify practically all ex-members of the deposed Convention People's Party (CPP) government, including cabinet ministers, parliamentarians and party functionaries, but the ruling junta even went further, in proscribing any party that it suspected of pro-Nkrumah sympathies, of planning to reinstate Nkrumah in power, or of neo-Nkrumahist revival. Thus it was that practically all leading members of the former opposition United Party (UP) were brought home as *emigrés* from their political obscurity to a new limelight; and their leader, the late Dr M. A. Busia, was made chairman of the Centre for Civic Education, from which position he subsequently moved into the prime ministership. Thus, the role of the Ghanaian military in regulating the succession process had had one central dilemma about it: that of appearing impartial in a case in which the government was both the trial judge and the prosecutor. In the end, it ended up simply taking sides.[14]

Fortunately, at least so far, there is no evidence that the present Nigerian rulers intend to follow such a blatantly interested method of controlling political competition. And FEDECO (that specialised body of civilians headed by Chief Michael Ani set up to supervise this particular phase of the power transfer process) should thank its stars for this! To say this is not to assert that the role of the Nigerian military has been even thus far completely disinterested. Generally, the military has made it clear on numerous occasions that it is 'interested' in the kind of government to emerge after 1979, and that it would not tolerate a return to the politics of opportunism and *immobilisme* of the past. On specific political issues of considerable significance, the military has also made its stand to be known. It would not brook the use of armed thugs or para-militaries for campaign purposes by politicians. Although rather slow on this issue, the present government also aims to keep out of the political race those aspirants who have had their hands tainted with corruption from the past political practices; and it is understood that FEDECO, assisted by officials of the Corrupt Practices Investigation Bureau as well as the Criminal Investigation Department (of the Nigerian police), is in the process of compiling and making public who these particular individuals are.

The military even thought it fit to delete those clauses of the constitution ratified by the Constituent Assembly, which did not accord with its vision of future Nigeria, while re-entrenching others which the Constituent Assembly had rejected. Of the seventeen or so amendments made to the constitution by the Supreme Military Council, before promulgating it into a decree, two are of particular interest to us here:[15] one rejecting the quota principle as a basis of recruitment into the armed forces;[16] and another re-entrenching four particular decrees, which of all the decrees passed since 1966 are obviously dear to the hearts of the present rulers, namely the National Youth Service Scheme (NYSS) Decree, Public Complaints Decree, National Security Organisation (NSO) Decree, and Land Use Decree.[17] The military governments's own *ration d'être* made complete disinterest in such matters well-nigh impossible.

Besides, military men, like other persons in society, have their own (private) political preferences, views, and attitudes which the electoral system, if it is to be stable in the future, must find a way of processing as an input. That is why, in the opinion of this author, it is a good and salutary idea that soldiers are now given the right to vote. Nor would our soldiers be the first in the world to exercise such a right.[18] Like other groups in society, soldiers have a right to contribute to the decision about the awesome problem of who should rule. But once they have exercised this right, soldiers, perhaps more than others, are by virtue of their profession duty-bound to support any government that emerges as lawfully constituted.

Of course, in conformity with their professional tradition, officers and men generally are *not* allowed to form their own or belong to any political parties, run for elections, make speeches or write articles without approval of the army chief of staff, distribute election manifestos, or invite political aspirants to campaign in their barracks. In perhaps one of the most significant measures aimed at disengaging the military from active politics, namely the 14 July 1978 announcement reposting the then state military governors as well as some federal military commissioners to the barracks, to which we have already referred, the government advised those officers who might have been nursing any political ambitions to first resign their commissions. Among other things, the proclamation appeared aimed to prevent creating the phenomenon of officers-turned-politicians who may move in and out of uniform frequently and often use their rank solely for political ends, as obtains in most of contemporary Latin America.[19] So far no senior officers of the Nigerian armed forces still in service are known to have renounced their profession for political office since that proclamation. The indication is that overwhelming numbers still love their profession. It is to be hoped that those few who may well do so before October 1979, together with some long-retired generals already visible in active politics,[20] will not use their ex-military connections to adversely affect the planned (and so far almost flawlessly executed) return to civil rule.

There remains the role which the military authorities may or may not play during the last three days or so before the elections and on the polling day itself. The business here involves not only guaranteeing a law-and-order atmosphere conducive to 'free and fair' elections, but also such other complex tasks as transporting ballot papers to and from voting centres, keeping political parties at a distance from the polling booths, supervising the electoral officers, counting the ballots, and verifying the results. Compressed though they are within the very last days, such tasks are going to be so critical, judging from Nigeria's own past experience, that, unless resolutely and objectively tackled, they may end up marring the whole planned programme of return to civil rule. In this connection, the FMG is going to require the support of all the newly assigned military administrators based at the state capitals, the continued loyalty and discipline of the 200-plus army battalions quartered in various parts of the country, the co-operation of units of the Nigerian police force stationed in all the local government areas, and above all the goodwill of most politicians and people alike.

Sequel to withdrawal – what next?

'He who rides the tiger dares not dismount' is a common

attitude of many a student towards the so-called phenomenon of 'return to the barracks' after a period of military rule. It is a cynical view based on comparative observation of the behaviour of the military in most of Latin America, South East Asia and the Middle East. There are to be found countless regimes of ex-uniformed soldiers donning civilian mufti, which rarely voluntarily retire from office except forced by (the threat of)counter-*coup d'état*, in part because they tend to see themselves as an alternative system of rule to that of the professional politicans whom they have ousted. Expressing a similar view, Professor Samuel E. Finer writes, 'The military engage in politics with relative haste but disengage, if at all, with the greatest reluctance. . . . In most cases the military that have intervened in politics are in a dilemma: whether their rule be indirect or whether it be direct, they cannot withdraw from rulership nor can they fully legitimise it. They can neither stay nor go.'[21]

But available examples from English-speaking West Africa, the world's latest region to have caught the contagion of soldiers in power, warn us against accepting *in toto* this cynical view. Here, beginning with the recent experiences of Sierra Leone (1968) and Ghana (1967-9) and now the continuing one of Nigeria detailed above, we have seen the issue of civilian restoration come to assume a uniqueness that merits some comment by the student of comparative civil-military relations. In the first place, it seems particularly striking that a number of regimes here should have shrunk away from the temptation of clinging to power, and that they should have accepted full demilitarisation as an important value worth being maximised. Of course, those few regimes that attempted to run against this popular trend, including those of Juxon-Smith of Sierra Leone, Ankrah and Acheampong of Ghana at different times, and Gowon of Nigeria, were invariably to rue the consequences.

The ex-British West African approach to the problem of demilitarisation (assuming there is one such approach) is unique for yet another reason: and this has something to do with the general acceptance of and emphasis on the need for at once a constitutional and methodical withdrawal by the military, which the Nigerian case detailed in this chapter clearly exemplifies. As one informed political analyst observed as far back as 1968, commenting on the then Ghanaian example,

> It is to the basic common sense of West Africans that, although so many countries have succumbed to military coups, the need for an early return to civilian rule should be so readily accepted by the soldiers themselves, while neither they nor the civilians want the return to be hasty and unorganised. It is difficult to imagine a similar situation in a Latin American or a Middle-Eastern country.[22]

Admittedly, as that same Ghanaian example referred to suggests, it is one thing to get soldiers to withdraw to the barracks, from power, and quite a different thing to guarantee against their possible political re-entry. For in that Ghanaian case, less than three years after their withdrawal the military came back to recapture the reins of political power. For Nigeria in particular, which is about to return to civilian and democratic politics,[23] one important logical question, sequel to withdrawal, is 'what next the military?' So vital is this question that there seems no better way of concluding this chapter than by taking it up. Needless to say, since the events they purport to cover are things of the future, these remaining discussions can only be conjectural or at best aprioristic.

Part of the problem causing uncertainty about the future derives from the fact that the 'physical' withdrawal of the military in 1979 may or may not necessarily also be accompanied by 'psychological' withdrawal.[24] In the same sense in which these terms are used here, 'physical' withdrawal relates to the overt act of physically taking the military out of politics and re-establishing the principles of professionalism, neutrality, discipline and civilian control, which are known to have been violated by the initial coup, while 'psychological' withdrawal is concerned with disabusing the minds of the military personnel both individually and collectively of the perquisites and privileges of the political power which they once enjoyed. The question here is whether soldiers who had as much been accustomed to being treated like lords as the politicians before them would be content with the drab and unprestigious life of the barracks. This manner of posing the problem makes 'psychological' disengagement more crucial than mere 'physical' withdrawal. And in fact there are countless numbers of military re-entries, often covered by the 'habit of intervention' thesis, that can be explained simply by the fact of psychological withdrawal lagging behind the physical.[25]

The fact is that psychological disengagement is more difficult to achieve than physical withdrawal. Many Ghanaians had also feared this a decade ago and were led to suggest a number of measures to insure, as one analyst put it in June 1968, 'that there is not a too immediate "re-return" to military rule'.[26] This particular analyst had suggested as a panacea for keeping disengaged Ghanaian military and police forces under political control (a) that steps be taken to improve all the barracks in the country and especially all the residences of soldiers above the rank of second-lieutenant, captains, majors, lieutenant-colonels, brigadiers, and so on, as well as those police officers above the rank of inspector; (b) that all members of the (ex-) NLC and other high-ranking military and police officers, then holding various administrative posts in the regions, return to the barracks and depots either on their present or former salaries, whichever was higher; and (c) that immediately on the return to civilian rule, all officers above the ranks of second-lieutenant and inspector be sent to Sandhurst or some police college abroad or a makeshift institution within Ghana for a reorientation course.[27]

All the three suggestions sought to tackle the psychological problem consequent upon the military's physical withdrawal, although the third aimed specifically at a political rehabilitation and retraining, while the first two saw the problem simply in utilitarian terms, that is as a matter of increased donatives and gratuities. The latter set of suggestions is perhaps understandable, considering the testimony of one of the original planners of the 24 February 1966 Ghana coup[28] that concern for better pay, job security, as well as other self-regarding interests, organisational, sectional and personal, had been a major motivation for their action. While the pay motive had been central to that initial coup, as it was also to be in the subsequent 1972 coup marking the military return to power in Ghana,[29] it does not necessarily follow that if only the pay conditions are made bounteous, soldiers everywhere can be kept in control. For such a conclusion assumes that bounteous money gifts would create military discipline, which is doubtful. In fact, on the contrary, if cases such as Obote's Uganda[30] are anything to go by, it is that bounteous pay weakens discipline and encourages military ambition. Nor is this a new finding. Machiavelli, for one, had long called attention to the antithetical nature of 'monetary pursuit' and 'military life'. Whereas military life requires, and is sustained by, moral asceticism, self-sacrifice, and *esprit de corps*, he had argued, the pursuit of pure monetary motive on the other hand breeds, and is infused with, profit-making, avariciousness, and self-seeking.[31]

Informed Nigerians, perhaps influenced by Ghana's experience as well as the vicious oscillation between military regimes and civilian administrations in neighbouring Benin Republic, have of late been haunted by the spectre of military re-entry, even as the country moved nearer to the goal of civilian restoration. However, the solution to this problem came to be felt to lie *not* in increased pay, privilege and gratuities, which most Nigerians know that their military already enjoy anyway relative to other social sectors.[32] Rather, the solution, some Nigerians came to feel, lay in specific constitutional provisions banning coups. Thus, considerable time was devoted by members of the Constituent Assembly towards the end of their sitting to deliberating this. Their deliberations led to chapter I, section I of the draft constitution being finally amended to read thus: 'The Federal Republic of Nigeria shall not be governed, nor shall any person or group of persons take control of the Government of Nigeria or any part thereof, except in accordance with the provisions of this Constitution.'[33]

However, the suggestion for an entrenched constitutional clause outlawing coups is, perhaps, one of the greatest jokes of the last thirteen years. One would have thought the mere fact of having a written constitution based as it is on a government of law under due process – even if such a document does not contain a specific 'no coup' clause – already presupposes this. It should be categorically stated that a written constitution *per se cannot* guarantee against the possibility of *coup d'état* or the spectre of military re-entry. As this author has concluded elsewhere,[34] political control of the military after 1979, to the extent that this is desirable or/and realisable, would not be because of but in spite of formal constitutional provisions.

12 The making of the Nigerian constitution

E. Alex Gboyega

Nigeria's second attempt at civilian political administration commences in October 1979 within a framework whose major parameters have been defined by both the outgoing military administration on the one hand and a motley group of intellectuals, politicians and businessmen on the other. To a very considerable extent careful efforts were made to consult and involve as large and varied a group as possible in the determination of the new constitution.[1] The events and processes whose culmination saw the promulgation of the constitution of the Second Republic of Nigeria have been very extensively analysed and commented upon, particularly those that relate to the demise of the First Republic, and our efforts here will be mainly to take up the analysis from the beginning of military rule as the title of this volume indicates.

The military takeover of political power in January 1966, as was to be expected, led to profound constitutional changes. By the Constitution Suspension and Modification (No 1) Decree 1966, the head of the federal military goverment and commander of the armed forces became vested with all legislative and executive powers.[2] In the regions, the military governors whom he appointed were vested with legislative powers for their regions which they discharged via edicts while federal laws came in the form of decrees. In addition it was provided that any section of the constitution or any law which was inconsistent with a decree was void.[3] Whilst the legal and constitutional changes may have been necessary as a result of the overthrow of the constitutionally sanctioned government, for quite some time prior to the military takeover of political power there had been talk of revision of the constitution.[4]

The constitutional revision envisioned, it needs be added, was pressed as a political issue because of the possibility it offered to alter the geographical power configuration in the country, as Mackintosh observed, and not because of any serious deficiencies.[5] Nonetheless, the new military administration considered constitutional review, alongside administrative reorganisation, as the most important assignments confronting it. Thus at the press conference given by the then head of state and commander-in-chief of the armed forces, Major-General Aguyi Ironsi, in Lagos on 21 February 1966, he announced that he would appoint study groups which world 'submit working papers on constitutional, administrative and institutional problems in the context of national unit'.[6] These three study groups were announced on 28 February 1966. The Study Group on Constitutional Review which comprised M. Buba Ado, Professor E. U. Essien-Udom, Dr Okoi Arikpo and an administrator from each of the four regions was headed by Chief Williams.[7]

At its inaugural meeting, the head of state outlined the terms of reference of the Constitutional Study Group and enjoined it to work within the context of one Nigeria. The Group was

> To identify those faults in the former constitution of Nigeria which militated against national unity and against the emergence of a strong Central Government; to ascertain how far the powers of the former Regional Governments fostered regionalism and weakened the Central Government; to consider the merits and demerits of (a) a Unitary form of Government, (b) a Federal form of Government best suited to the demands of a developing country like Nigeria in modern times and most likely to satisfy local needs without hampering the emergence of a strong, united democratic Nigeria. The Group [was] to suggest possible territorial divisions of the country; to examine voting system, electoral act and revisions of voters register. It [was] to consider the merits and demerits of (1) One-Party System, (2) Multi-Party System, as a system best

> suited to Nigeria, and the extent to which regionalism and party politics fostered tribal consciousness, nepotism and abuse of office; to determine the extent to which professional politics contributed to the deficiencies of the past regime, and the extent to which regionalism and party politics tended to violate traditional chieftaincies and institutions and to suggest possible safeguards.[8]

From the Study Group's working papers consideration was to be given 'to the formulation, at official level, of constitutional proposals to be submitted to a Constituent Assembly followed by a referendum before the new Constitution comes into being'.[9]

The terms of reference were not only a tall order but were fraught with difficulties. As Dudley wondered, would a finding that party politics fostered tribal consciousness, nepotism and abuse of office have 'entailed that "party politics" was then to be abolished?'[10] With the advantages of hindsight one could well answer that question positively.[11] But the Constitutional Review Study Group hardly got started before its significance was undercut by the promulgation of Decree No. 34 of 1966 which made Nigeria a unitary state.

The sole and major impetus behind the measures which turned Nigeria into a unitary state seemed to have been Mr Francis Nwokedi. Mr Francis Nwokedi was a member of the Study Group on National Unity referred to above, charged with the responsibility for recommending on the public services. Other members of this particular Study Group had their specific responsibilities distributed as follows: Mr Justice Stephen Peter Thomas (judicial services); Mr M. O. Ani (statutory corporations, state-owned companies and related organisations), Chief M. O. Udoji (educational services); Mr A. I. Wilson (information services); Yusufu Gobir (police and prisons); Mr O. Bateye (administrative machinery).[12] Mr Nwokedi worked with unusual speed and diligence considering the tardiness of the other members of his National Unity Study Group and the other two Study Groups—Constitutional Review Study Group and Economic Planning Study Group.

It is noteworthy that after its inaugural meeting the Constitutional Review Study Group had not met again before the decree which turned Nigeria into a unitary state was passed. This questionable step fanned the embers of distrust which had been generated in the north by the genocidal killings which took place during the coup in January and increased also the fears of even some groups in the south that the head of state and his closest aides were seeking to achieve total domination of Nigeria by the Ibo. Anyway, since the decisions of 24 May (Decrees No. 33 and No. 34) cut across subjects that were under consideration by the Constitutional Review Study Group, it is a moot point whether Nwokedi's report was acted upon promptly because of its expedition or because of his strong personal connection with the head of state.[13] But perhaps Nwokedi's job was no more than supplying the fine outlines for a predetermined programme. On 19 February 1966 a correspondent of *West Africa* writing on the topic 'Making Nigeria a Unitary State' had said that, 'Obviously in *a unitary state which Nigeria is now destined to be,* there can be only one civil and one judicial service' (emphasis not in original).[14]

Be that as it may, by the provisions of the Public Order Decree (Decree No. 33) of 24 May 1966 all political parties, tribal unions and cultural orginisations with political leanings were proscribed.[15] In all, eighty-one political parties and organisations as well as twenty-six cultural and tribal associations were banned. The decree further invested the head of the federal military government with the authority to ban any society of three or more persons with objectives similar or identical to any of the banned groups, and also made it an offence to form any new party or association.

The Constitution (Suspension and Modification) (No. 5) Decree 1966 (Decree No. 34) was greatly more significant than Decree No. 33 because of the magnitude of the changes it effected. It stated that Nigeria was to cease to be a federation and was to be known as the Republic of Nigeria.[16] The former regions were to become groups of provinces and for the purposes of administration each group of provinces was, subject to the authority of the head of the National Military Government (hitherto Federal Military Government), to be under the general direction and control of a military governor appointed by the former.[17] The existing separate regional public services were unified and constituted into a National Public Service, and a National Public Service Commission set up. Certain offices – judicial offices, economic adviser to the Republic, director of audit of the Republic, etc. – were however not placed under the control of the National Public Service Commission. The Police Service Commission would thereafter be appointed by the head of the federal military government and not the Federal Executive Council.

In announcing these new measures, the head of state had observed that the ban on political parties and organisations would be effective for three years and the unitary measures were described as 'entirely transitional measure' and without prejudice to the work of the Constitutional Review Study Group. But at the same time he added that the meetings of the Supreme Military Council and the Federal Executive Council preceding the announcement of these new measures had also approved the outline of a twenty-year 'perspective development plan' and a five-year 'medium-term plan'. In addition to this a composite 'national budget' was agreed in Lagos.[18] The effect of all these was that despite the fact that the constitutional changes merely rationalised the structure of government since military command structure and rule had effectively put an end to federalism, those who opposed these new measures, particularly in the north, thought that these were dangerous experiments which had to be protested most strongly. These unacceptable measures and the humiliation northerners suffered as a result of the military coup and the euphoric conduct of Ibos everywhere led to riots in several parts of the north on 29 and 30 May during which Ibos were wantonly attacked and killed. On 29 July 1966, the head of state, Major-General Aguyi Ironsi was abducted together with his host, the military governor of the West, Lieutenant-Colonel Fajuyi, and killed.[19] But even before this time there was widespread belief that the constitutional decisions and the reactions to these decisions were grievous enough as to imperil the life of the head of state.[20]

When Lieutenant-General (then Lieutenant-Colonel) Gowon emerged as the head of state after the events of 29 July

1966 he could hardly resist a reversal of the constitutional changes which were the root cause of the recent disturbances.[21] But it was also obvious that the constitutional crisis could not be settled unilaterally on the terms dictated by one side in the conflict. The military governor of the East, Odumegwu O. Ojukwu, challenged the authority of the new head of state, observing that according to military protocol the office should have gone to the most senior surviving military officer, namely, Brigadier Ogundipe. Thus to the constitutional disagreement was added a personality clash.

On 4 August 1966 Gowon announced that an advisory group of civilians would soon be constituted to advise the government. When the Ad Hoc Conference on Constitutional Proposals for Nigeria met on 12 September 1966 it was a gathering of old hands, adept at political bargaining.[22] The delegates comprised Sir Kashim Ibrahim, Mr Joseph Tarka, the North's solicitor-general, Alhaji Buba Ardo (the Etsu Nupe, the Och'Idoma and Alhaji Aminu Kano were advisers to the delegation) for the North; Chief Obafemi Awolowo led the Western delegation which included Professor H. Oluwasanmi who was then vice chancellor of the University of Ife and Chief Olu Akinfosile with the Odema of Ishara, Oba Samuel Akinsanya, Prince Alade Lamuye and the solicitor-general, Dr Ajayi as advisers; the Mid-West's delegates were Chief J. I. G. Onyia and Dr M. N. Odie advised by Mr S. O. Ighodalo, Dr T. M. Yesufu and Mr R. A. Ogbobine; from the East came Professor Eni Njoku, then vice chancellor of the University of Nigeria, the solicitor-general Mr C. C. Mojekwu and Mr E. A. Edem, with Chief Allagoa, Mr M. T. Mbu and Chief Etim of Ahoada as advisers; and finally Dr T. O. Elias, former federal attorney-general, and Alhaji Lateef Jakande, advised by Chief Ishola Bajulaiye, the Eletu Odibo of Lagos, and Mr Femi Okunnu represented Lagos.

The Ad Hoc Conference was enjoined by the head of state to disregard either the creation of a unitary state or the break-up of the country and consider four alternative forms of government: (a) a federal system with a strong central government; (b) a federal system with a weak central government; (c) confederation; and (d) an entirely new arrangement which would be peculiar to Nigeria. The Eastern and Northern delegates were agreed on their preference for a confederation, the Western being prepared for either a federation or a confederation, and the Mid-Western wanting to preserve Nigeria as a federation.[23] The Mid-Western delegation also strongly favoured the creation of new states or regions as did the Western delegation if federalism was accepted, while the North and the East did not want new states or regions created, at least not in the immediate future. At the resumed conference on 20 September, after an adjournment, the Northern delegation amended its position by advocating a federal system with a strong central government and agreeing to the creation of new states, following which the Lagos delegation that previously endorsed Western views struck out a separate identity for itself and announced support for the federal system and the creation of more states, demanding in particular a Lagos state, whereupon the Western delegation came out unequivocally for federalism. Only the Eastern delegation remained undecided about the creation of more states when the conference adjourned on 3 October 1966. Unfortunately, the Eastern delegation was not to return to the resumed conference on 24 October or at any other time before it was adjourned indefinitely as a result of the renewed spate of riots during which Ibos were killed in large numbers in various parts of the North from 29 September.[24]

The next stage in the attempt to resolve the constitutional impasse was the meeting at Peduase Lodge, Aburi, Ghana, where the Ghanaian government hosted the Supreme Military Council on 4 and 5 January 1967. Already the country had reverted to a federation as from 1 September 1966 when the unitary system decree was repealed and the separate public services of the regions were restored (the reversion was merely a matter of legal significance since institutionally nothing had really changed as a result of the unitary measures).[25] So the Aburi meeting was intended largely to rationalise the structure of decision-making within the Supreme Military Council as well as provide some measure of meaningful regional autonomy (in spite of military rule and command structure which conduces more to a unitary system of government) so as to assure Nigerians that no section of the country wanted to or could dominate the rest. The decisions taken at Aburi have received ample analysis elsewhere.[26] Suffice it to say that the Constitution (Suspension and Modification) Decree No. 8 of 1967 which was supposed to embody the Aburi decisions did not entirely do so, which of course left the military governor of the Eastern Region, Colonel Ojukwu, dissatisfied.

As the constitutional crisis deepened with Colonel Ojukwu's repudiation of Decree No. 8 as not reflecting accurately decisions taken at Aburi, fresh efforts were made by the federal government to lay down a programme of return to constitutional civilian rule by 1969. This was to no avail as the Ad Hoc Conference could not reconvene and the country drifted into civil war. But the creation of new states in May 1967, just before arms were joined between the federal and the Biafran sides of the civil war, drastically altered the domestic geo-political relations. By the provisions of the States (Creation and Transitional Provisions) Decree 1967, Nigeria was carved up into twelve states, and thus ended the structural imbalance which existed in the form of huge regional groupings dominated by the three big ethnic groups which used these as bases for ethnic chauvinism.[27] It also satisfied the long-standing demands of the minorities within the regions for some measure of self-rule and autonomy.

While the civil war lasted, of course, the focus of thought and energies was on how to end hostilities—on the battlefield or round the conference table; in the event the former proved to be the case and changed completely the socio-political context within which a new constitution was to be fashioned. General Gowon announced a 'nine-point' programme of six years' duration after which the military would hand over power to civilians in October 1976. The nine items on the programme were reorganisation of the armed forces, national reconstruction (repair of war damage) and implementation of the National Development Plan, elimination of corruption, deciding on creation of more states, revision of the revenue allocation system, provision of a new constitution, a national census, organisation of national political parties, and popular elections to select civilian rulers in the states and at the federal level.[28]

The announcement of the programme was a signal for the resumption of the debate on new constitutional arrangements for Nigeria. The suggestions for a new system of government varied indeed: from Tayo Akpata's one-party rule,[29] Dr Nnamdi Azikiwe's diarchy[30] to Chief Kola Balogun's insistence on a federal structure.[31] But even as the different proposals for new constitutional arrangements were debated, there was always some doubt that the timetable set for a return to civilian rule could, not to say would, be kept. For example, as it was frequently pointed out, can corruption really be eliminated from national life (and how does one determine when)? Much more importantly some sporadic but widely publicised interviews granted by some high-ranking members of the military establishment tended to suggest that there was some disagreement within the top military echelons as to when to hand over power and whether it was to be a partial or complete hand-over.[32] Anyway, on 1 October 1974 General Gowon announced indefinite postponement of the date for a return to civilian rule. As a result of this, civilian disaffection increased and coupled with problems internal to the army produced the change in government on 29 July 1975.[33]

The new government, headed then by Brigadier (later Lieutenant-General) Murtala Mohammed, on 1 October 1975 presented a four-year five-stage programme of return to civilian rule.[34] The first stage involved the creation of new states in April 1976 when the number of states increased from twelve to nineteen and the setting up of a Constitution Drafting Committee with a one-year deadline to complete its assignment which it did in August 1976. In the second stage local government was reorganised and the new local governments (as they are known officially) acted as electoral colleges for the selection of the Constituent Assembly members. Constitution-making comprised the third stage and ended before the October 1978 target date. The last two stages involved elections to fill federal and states offices and the handing over of power to a civilian government in October 1979.

The Constitution Drafting Committee was appointed in

September 1976 and comprised the following fifty people: Chief F. R. A Williams (chairman), Dr. C. S. Abashiya, Dr K. Abayomi, Alhaji Abdul-Rasaq, Dr I. D. Ahmed, Chief R. O. A. Akinjide, Dr S. C. Aleyideno, Mr A. Al-Hakim, Dr A. Y. Aliyu, Professor S. A. Aluko, Mr M. S. Angulu, Alhaji Ardo Buba, Alhaji Nuhu Bamali, Mr P. R. V. Belabo, Alhaji Mamman Daura, Professor T. S. David-West, Professor V. P. Diejomaoh, Mr D. D. Dimka, Professor B. J. Dudley, Professor E. C. Edozien, Chief I. Ekanem-Ita, Dr U. O. Eleazu, Professor E. U. Emovon, Alhaji S. Gaya, Mr R. Gbadamosi, Dr T. O. Idris, Mr Bola Ige, Professor O. Ikime, Mr S. G. Ikoku, Alhaji I. Imam, Mr K. Isola-Osobu, Alhaji Aminu Kano, Alhaji S. M. Liberty, Mr M. A. Makele, Colonel Pedro Martins, Alhaji Shehu Malami, Dr K. O. Mbadiwe, Chief I. I. Murphy, Professor B. O. Nwabueze, Professor G. A. Odenigwe, Dr P. Okigbo, Alhaji Femi Okunnu, Dr S. Osoba, Dr Oye Oyediran, Dr Tahir Ibrahim, Alhaji Talib Ahmed, Dr M. Tukur, Mr G. P. Unongo, Dr Y. B. Usman and Dr Obi Wali. Alhaji Gidado Idris was secretary to the committee.[35] Distinguished and accomplished in various walks of life as these people are, there was no unanimity as to their entitlement to the honour done them. As two radical commentators observed,

> This all-male caucus whose members were nominated on their personal merit include [*sic*] no representative of women, peasants, workers, students and petty-artisans who constitute the vast majority of Nigeria's population. In a country with an average income of less than ₦300.00, the composition of the CDC is clearly an elite of privileged classes that excludes the masses of working people.[36]

But as it was explained by the head of state, the selection had been done not on the basis of class representation, which was the point of most criticism of the list, but on the basis of two representatives each from the twelve states in existence at the time and selection from 'our learned men in disciplines considered to have direct relevance to Constitution-making, namely – history, law, economics and other social sciences, especially political science [and] eminent Nigerians with some experience in Constitution-making were brought in to complete the spectrum.'[37]

At the inaugural meeting of the committee on 18 October 1975, the head of state stated the views of the Supreme Military Council regarding political processes in the past and the expectations of the future. The Supreme Military Council, he said, was committed to a federal system of government and stability founded upon the bedrock of constitutional law. A new constitution therefore should endeavour to 'eliminate cut-throat political competition based on a system of winner takes-all', 'discourage institutionalised opposition to the Government in power', establish the principle of public accountability, decentralise power, ensure free and fair elections, and devise an effective non-political system of census.[38] In order to achieve these aims, the Supreme Military Council came to the conclusion that Nigeria required:

(i) Genuine and truly national political parties. However, in order to avoid the harmful effects of a proliferation of national parties, it will be desirable for you to work out specific criteria by which their number would be limited. (Indeed if there were means to form government without parties that will satisfy the Supreme Military Council.)

(ii) An executive Presidential system of Government in which:

  (a) the President and Vice-President are elected, with clearly defined powers and are accountable to the people...

  (b) the choice of members of the Cabinet should also be such as would reflect the Federal character of the country.

(iii) An independent Judiciary to be guaranteed by incorporating appropriate provisions in the Constitutions as well as by establishing institutions such as the Judicial Service Commission.

(iv) Provision of such corrective institutions as the Corrupt Practices Tribunal and Public Complaints Bureau; and

(v) Constitutional limitation on the number of states to be further created.

These requirements which were urged on the Constitution Drafting Committee are remarkable for their unequivocation about the essentials of a suitable constitution for a new Nigeria, namely, the presidential system of government, cabinet selected to 'reflect the Federal character of the country', Corrupt Practices Tribunal and Public Complaints Bureau, and so on. The report of the Constitution Drafting Committee which was published in two volumes—*Report of the Constitution Drafting Committee Containing the Draft Constitution Volume I* and *Report of the Constitution Drafting Committee Volume II*—and submitted on 14 September 1976 kept very close to these essentials in most important respects.[39]

The Constituent Assembly which considered the Draft constitution was selected through elections conducted on 31 August 1977 with the newly (1976) reorganised local governments acting as electoral colleges. The distribution of seats to the nineteen states of the federation were as follows: Anambra 11; Bauchi 10; Bendel 10; Benue 10; Borno 11; Cross River 12; Gongola 10; Imo 13; Kaduna 13; Kano 16; Kwara 8; Lagos 8; Niger 7; Ogun 8; Ondo 10; Oyo 15; Plateau 9; Rivers 8; and Sokoto 14.[40] Twenty others were nominated into the Constituent Assembly in addition to the seven sub-committee chairmen of the Constitution Drafting Committee. Mr Justice Udo Udoma was appointed its chairman with Alhaji Justice Buba Ardo as his deputy.[41]

The Constituent Assembly had its inaugural meeting on 6 October 1977 and adjourned at the end of the third reading of the Draft Constitutional Bill on 5 June 1978. The proceedings of the Constituent Assembly were more controversial than those of the Drafting Committee and produced some painful drama, perhaps because the majority of the members were elected, even if indirectly, and therefore were more certain of their mandate and also because everybody was imbued with the apparent finality of the decisions taken then. The most heated debates took place over the issue of creation of more states, Federal Sharia Court of Appeal, and the proscription of corrupt politicians or public officers of the past from public office for a length of time. These, and other heated issues during the proceedings, will be examined more closely in their turn.

By far the most important and fundamental decision was the adoption of the presidential form of government. As pointed out above, the head of state had adverted to the presidential system during his inaugural speech to the Drafting Committee, and the latter had adopted it because 'The separation of the Head of State from Head of Government involves a division between real authority and formal authority [which is] meaningless in the light of African political experience and history', the 'clashes and conflicts inherent in the system producing instability in government and society'. The executive presidency on the other hand, it was thought, may by implication provide 'a clear focal point of loyalty, which is indispensable to national integration'.[42] As Panter-Brick has pointed out elsewhere, it cannot be determined *a priori* which form of government, the presidential or the Westminister type, is more suitable.[43] And this was brought to the attention of the Constituent Assembly by some of its members, but especially by Mr A. S. Guobadia who observed that 'whatever defects we may attribute to the Westminster system could easily emanate from the new system now proposed, unless we are prepared to give what it takes to make a success of the Presidential system.'[44] In addition to the symbolic importance of the presidential system within the Nigerian context, which Panter-Brick referred to, may be added the sheer attraction of a system that seems to have served and continues to serve the United States so well. The Watergate episode may have demonstrated the dangers inherent in the presidential system but so did it demonstrate its resilience.[45]

The president of the federation is the head of state, the chief executive and commander-in-chief of the Nigerian armed forces.[46] In order to qualify for this high office, a person must be a citizen by birth and at least thirty-five years old (the draft constitution prescribed forty years) and shall hold office for a period of four years, renewable for another four years only. He should not suffer any disability which would have disqualified him from being a member of the Senate. Where there are only two contestants for the presidency, a candidate is elected when he wins a majority of the votes cast at the election as well as at least one-quarter of the votes cast at the election in each of at least two-thirds of all states. If there are more than two candidates, the winner should have a majority of the votes cast at the election and not less than one-quarter of the votes cast at the election in at least two-thirds of the states. Should the election not produce a clear winner where there are more than two candidates, then the candidate with the highest number of votes and one among the other candidates with the majority of votes in the highest number of states (or highest total of votes cast in a majority of the states where there is a tally) shall have a run-off election. In this second election which shall be held within seven days of the results of the previous elections being declared, the winner shall be determined by an overall simple majority of the votes cast in each House of the National Assembly and in the House of Assembly of every State of the Federation. Under no circumstances can a candidate for the presidency be returned unopposed without elections; when there is only one contestant he has to have a majority of affirmative votes in addition to the minimum prescribed one-quarter from two-thirds of the states. The qualifications for the office of vice president are the same as that for the president and as a matter of fact both have to be elected on the same ticket.

The office of the president is the locus of all federal executive authority, subject only to such restraints as are deemed necessary to prevent the emergence of a dictator. The president determines the size of federal ministries and appoints the ministers, subject to Senate confirmation, appointing at least one from each state. The ministers to be appointed by the president including the attorney-general, who must have at least ten years of legal practice behind him, should also have qualifications that will entitle them to contest election into the House of Representatives. Ministers are not to belong to any of the Houses of National Assembly but may, upon invitation by the legislature, attend to explain the conduct of the affairs of their ministry; the president on the other hand has a right of attendance to address the legislature on national affairs.[47]

The president too appoints, subject to confirmation by Senate, the members (except ex-officio or where the constitution stipulates otherwise) of the following federal executive bodies – Council of States, Federal Civil Service Commission, Federal Electoral Commission, Federal Judicial Commission, National Defence Council, National Economic Council, National Population Commission, National Security Council and Police Service Commission. The president has substantial discretionary powers in the granting or withdrawal of naturalised citizenship.[48]

He also appoints the secretary to the government of the federation (now separate from the Office of Head of Service), head of the civil service, permanent secretaries or chief executives of federal government ministries and departments, and ambassadors, high commissioners or principal representatatives of Nigeria abroad which latter require Senate approval.[49] He appoints and removes the inspector-general of police after consultation with the Police Service Commission; as commander-in-chief of the armed forces he appoints the chief of defence staff, heads of the army, navy and air force as well as direct operational use of the forces,[50] and appoints in his discretion the chief justice subject to confirmation by the Senate through a simple majority.[51] He personally chairs the very important Council of State, National Security Council and National Defence Council. Finally he exercises the prerogative of mercy.

The authority assigned to the president, some of the most important features of which have been listed above, appears *prima facie* formidable. To justify entrusting such powers to an individual in a system hitherto untried here, the method of election requires a fairly broad spectrum of support as indicated above, in a sense making the whole country a single constituency for the presidency and establishing a direct link of mandate between the president and electorate. But even in spite of this, strenuous efforts have been made to diffuse executive authority lest presidential ambitions overstep the bounds of the demands of constitutional government.

Thus, after the president has appointed the non-ex-officio members of the constitutionally established federal executive bodies they may only be removed by him on the basis of an address supported by a two-thirds majority of the Senate asking for a removal—either for misconduct or inability to perform the functions of the office. For members of the National Population Commission they are deemed removed if the president, on the advice of the Council of State, declares their census report unreliable.[52] In addition, the constitution expressly guarantees freedom of action of certain executive bodies and authorities such as the Federal Civil Service Commission, Federal Electoral Commission, National Population Commission and the auditor-general. Interference with these bodies, especially with the conduct of their functions, had been a major source of political and constitutional crisis in the past. Hence the constitutional guarantees are very welcome, but it is necessary to add that how the incumbents exercise their authority, and not mere constitutional provisions, is the real security against presidential tyranny.

These restraints upon presidential authority are reinforced by certain powers granted to the legislature but these are better examined as part of the general provisions for the latter. The constitution provides for a bicameral National Assembly—the Senate and House of Representatives.[53] Section 4 of the constitution vests legislative power for the Exclusive list in this body which also has concurrent powers for stipulated purposes. (The Legislative lists are appended to this volume.) The Senate consists of five senators from each state of the federation (and one from the Federal Capital Territory). Unlike in the United States of America the president of the Senate shall be elected from amongst the senators. The age qualification is thirty years and the usual requirements of citizenship and freedom from legal disabilities such as bankruptcy and conviction apply. Similar provisions apply for membership of the House of Representatives save that the age qualification is twenty-one years. There are 450 seats in the House of Representatives. Both Houses may conduct their business in English, and in Hausa, Ibo or Yoruba when facilities permit it.[54]

A bill may originate in either House and when passed by both Houses has to be assented to by the president within thirty days. If the president fails to assent and the same bill passes each House by a two-thirds majority, then it automatically becomes law. The procedure for a money bill is slightly different: if it is passed by only one House but not the other within two months after the start of the financial year, then the president of the Senate may refer it to a joint finance committee and should the differences still persist he may then refer it to a joint meeting of both Houses. Should the president withhold assent after this procedure has been followed, then the same bill passed by a two-thirds majority of the joint meeting of the Houses automatically becomes law.

The National Assembly (Senate and House of Representatives) approves the Appropriation Bill which authorises governmental spending. It receives the audit report on public accounts from an independent auditor-general. It has power to investigate into:

> (a) Any matter or thing with respect to which it has power to make laws; and (b) the conduct of affairs of any person, authority, ministry or government department charged, or intended to be charged, with the duty of or responsibility for—(i) executing or administering laws enacted by the National Assembly, and (ii) disbursing or administering moneys appropriated or to be appropriated by the National Assembly.

To do this effectively it is empowered to procure necessary evidence. This power of investigation which may be set into motion by resolution of one of the Houses of Assembly, constitutes a veritable instrument of restraint and deterrence to any public officer (the president inclusive) who may wish to overstep the bounds of propriety. Independence to investigate fully an incumbent public officer, especially a president, is enhanced by the fact that from the day of its first sitting the National Assembly is guaranteed a life span of four years which cannot be altered by the removal from office of the president.

Foremost in the minds of the constitution-makers was to devise conditions inconducive to the emergence and survival of an outrageously partisan or sectional president. Could, as has been popularly feared, this negative approach have created a situation in which presidential paralysis is a more probable outcome rather than popular government? It will be rash to say at the moment; prudence and the vagaries of history will determine this.

On the other hand, if the desired harmony and good as well as effective government do not ensue and instead there is constitutional crisis, the provisions for the judicature are intended to provide impartial adjudication. The highest court of law is the Supreme Court of Nigeria, whose head – the chief justice – shall be appointed by the president in his discretion but subject to the confirmation by simple majority of the Senate. It shall comprise the chief justice and not more than fifteen other justices of the Supreme Court. The Constituent Assembly had recommended 'and not less than fifteen other justices' which the Supreme Military Council considered unsuitable. It is a court of original jurisdiction for any dispute between the federation and a state or between states which relates to the existence or extent of a legal right, and of appellate jurisdiction of the last resort.[55] And there is a Federal Court of Appeal which as an intermediate court of appeal, shall determine appeals from the Federal High Court. High Court of a state, Sharia Court of Appeal of a state and Customary Court of Appeal of a state.

The single most controversial issue which confronted the Constituent Assembly is somewhat related to the Federal Court of Appeal. The draft constitution had provided in section 184 for a Federal Sharia Court of Appeal which 'shall have jurisdiction to the exclusion of any other court of Law in Nigeria, to hear and determine appeals from the Sharia Court of Appeal of a State' and in section 179(c) that 'The Federal Sharia Court of Appeal . . . shall consist of a Grand Mufti, a Deputy Grand Mufti and such number of Muftis not being less than three'. Its appellate jurisdiction on matters of Islamic Personal Law were exactly as provided for in the constitution of Northern Nigeria of 1963 (section 53 (a)–(e)). The difference this time is that whereas the Sharia Court of Appeal in 1963 was a regional (state) court, in the draft it was to become a federal institution, presumably because whereas before there was only one region involved, now there are many states.

The Constituent Assembly rejected these two principal provisions regarding the Federal Sharia Court of Appeal and other consequential provisions. A sixteen-man sub-committee headed by Chief Simeon Adebo recommended a compromise provision, namely, that there should be a single Federal Court of Appeal which shall be duly constituted if, in the case of appeals from the Sharia Court of Appeal of a state, it consists of not less than three justices of the Federal Court of Appeal versed in Islamic Personal Law (in the end the provision agreed sustituted 'learned' for 'versed'). In the case of appeals from the Customary Court of Appeal of a state a similar provision was made, thus giving customary law and courts the same constitutional status as Sharia law.

But the real bone of contention in the Sharia issue which produced a dramatic walk-out and boycott of the Assembly proceedings from 6–24 April 1978, was whether the Federal Sharia Court of Appeal would be constituted by judges manifestly more competent in Islamic Personal Law than the Grand Kadi and Kadis whose decisions would be reviewed, hence the provisions of section 179(c) in the draft constitution. For the pro-Sharia group this was the crux of the matter, all other considerations being extraneous.

The anti-Sharia group on the other hand argued variously that Islamic Personal Law was discriminatory against non-Muslims and should not be elevated to federal status; that only a Muslim could become a judge in the Sharia Court; it discriminated against women and thus ran counter to the political objective of equality and that if a parallel Federal Sharia Court of Appeal were granted now it would amount to sanctioning two separate national systems of law and the 'logical progression' in the future would be the creation of a Federal Supreme Sharia Court.

It was obvious that the controversy was not only over religion, custom or a way of life; it involved that, but was also primarily political. The most vociferous and unyielding of the anti-Sharia group were those from Benue and Plateau States, who were non-Muslim yet chafed in the past under the political abuses of the system, perhaps not as individuals but as members of minorities. The Sharia controversy portended far-reaching consequences if an amicable solution was not found as ninety-two members boycotted the proceedings of the Constituent Assembly.[56] On 19 April 1978 the head of state, accompanied by members of the Supreme Military Council, met the Constituent Assembly in an informal session and cautioned them against any course of action which would threaten the stability of the country.[57] Even though the pro-Sharia group returned to the Constituent Assembly on 24 April 1978, it seems that it had not quite given up hope of achieving a more acceptable solution. When the Draft Constitution Bill passed its third reading, spokesmen of the pro-Sharia group on behalf of the entire group dissociated themselves from chapter VII of the constitution and threatened to reopen discussion of the issue at the appropriate time.[58]

Reference has already been made to the provisions regarding the Customary Court of Appeal of a state. It is, like the Sharia Court of Appeal of a state, left to individual states which desire it to set it up and the likelihood is great that this new court will soon come into existence in some states. Then there is provision for the High Court of a state and a Federal High Court. Following recent practice, the states will have chief judges and there will be, of course, the chief justice of the federation.

The more substantive and important provisions concerning the judicature are those intended to enhance its independence and thus ensure its impartiality. Besides the chief justice whom the president appoints in his sole discretion and presents for Senate approval, all other justices of the Supreme Court, the president and justices of the Federal Court of Appeal, the chief judge and other judges of the Federal High Court are appointed on the advice of the Federal Judicial Service Commission and presented to the Senate for confirmation. After appointment these officers shall not be removable until they reach retiring age except that the chief justice can be removed on an address supported by two-thirds of the Senate and for others on the recommendation of the Federal Judicial Service Commission that he is unable to discharge the functions of his office or had misconducted himself or contravened the code of conduct.

The issue of creation of states was also controversial. Some members of the Constituent Assembly were of the opinion that, not only could they pronounce on the conditions for the creation of new states but could actually write the creation of new states into the constitution. This was of course contrary to the oft-repeated determination of the existing military government not to create any new states after increasing the number to nineteen. As the chairman of the Constituent Assembly insistently maintained, 'The power to create more states is obviously not with the Constituent Assembly', because it lacked executive authority and therefore refused to countenance motions calling for the creation of more states.[59] It is of course arguable whether if the motions had been adopted the Supreme Military Council would have altered the provision relating to that in the constitution as it did some seventeen provisions.[60] So while the number of states stands at ninteen, provisions have been made in section 8 of the constitution for the purpose of creating a new one. The first step in order to create a new state is to make a request supported by two-thirds majority of the members representing the area demanding the new state in the Senate, the House of Representatives, the House of Assembly in respect of the area and the local government councils in the area to the National Assembly. It must then secure two-thirds majority approval from the people of the area in a referendum in the area concerned and approval by simple majority of all the states of the federation supported by a simple majority of their Houses of Assembly. Finally, the proposal should be approved by two-thirds majority of members of each House of the National Assembly. These conditions almost certainly will ensure that in only extremely essential cases will it be possible to create a new state. The Supreme Military Council deleted the provision for the admission and incorporation of another state or part of another state as part of the federation ostensibly to make the constitution conformable to Nigerian foreign policy but more probably in order to assuage the fears of domination by Nigeria of its neighbours.

For at least twelve years now (1978) the military have dominated Nigerian government and politics and this fact cannot but leave indelible marks on the future political processes of this country. The reverse of this statement is similarly axiomatic: the notion of an apolitical army is a thing of the past. The Constituent Assembly had sought to reflect this awareness by providing in section 197 (2) that, 'The composition of the officer corps and other ranks of the armed forces of the Federation shall reflect the federal character of the Federation based on the population of each state'. But the Supreme Military Council amendment has deleted 'based on the population of each state' in order not to adversely affect the effectiveness of the armed forces.

The constitution regulates political parties in such ways as are intended to make them national in sections 202–209. Amongst the conditions are that the headquarters of all political parties be at the federal capital, that they hold periodic democratic elections in order to select their governing body which should reflect the federal character of Nigeria, submit their accounts for inspection to the Federal Electoral Commission, shall not receive or having received retain foreign financial aid, and shall not train and maintain thugs. These conditions are designed to ensure that the parties play fair and according to the rules. By the provisions of the Electoral Decree 1977 persons found guilty of corruption or abuse of office by any tribunal with effect from 15 January 1966 are disqualified from participating in the 1979 elections. This rendered obsolete a similar provision dating from 1 October 1960 passed by the Constituent Assembly and which has thus been omitted from the constitution. The Constituent Assembly measure was controversial because it had shifted the date proposed by the draft constitution (15 January 1966) backwards and it was thought this was directed at some top politicians of the First Republic. The Federal Electoral Commission, it seemed, disagreed with this and may have persuaded the Supreme Military Council to stand by the earlier provisions of the Electoral Decree 1977.[61]

Chapter IV of the constitution provides for fundamental rights; of particular interest is the provision (section 40) which prevents compulsory acquisition of property, save for as legally sanctioned and with prompt payment of compensation. This is noteworthy because of the Land Use Decree 1978 which vested all land in Nigeria in the governments of the federation. The legality of the compulsory acquisition of land through the Land Use Decree seemed to have been entrenched by the Supreme Military Council addition to the constitution which says nothing in the constitution shall invalidate the National Youth Service Corps Decree 1973, the Public Complaints Decree 1975, the Nigerian Security Organisation Decree 1976 and the Land Use Decree 1978. The Supreme Military Council has used its power of ultimate sanction decisively against popular (Constituent Assembly) wishes not only in respect of the Land Use Decree but also in respect of the Nigerian Security Organisation.[62]

Two novel aspects of the constitution which deserve mention are the 'Fundamental Objectives and Directive Principles of State Policy' and the 'Code of Conduct' for stipulated public officers. Chapter II of the constitution is devoted to stating the broad social, political, economic, educational, cultural and foreign policy goals to which government shall direct its energies. These, however, are 'non-justiciable'. being merely guidelines for policy formulation. The Code of Conduct contained in the Fifth Schedule to the constitution is intended to ensure some measure of probity in designated public officers. For example the president, the vice president, governors, deputy governors, ministers of the federation, commissioners of the states and members of the National and State Assemblies may not keep foreign accounts. Designated public officers may also not earn another emolument from public office at the same time as they are paid the emoluments of any other public office, nor can they engage or participate in the management or running of any private business, profession or trade. These and other items on the code are intended to minimise possibilities of conflict of interest, greed and corruption. A Code of Conduct Tribunal has been provided for to ensure compliance with it.

Of interest also is the constitutional guarantee given to the 'system of local government by democratically elected local government councils', and more importantly the specification of a separate list of functions for local government within the constitution and financial guarantees through statutory allocation of public revenue by the National Assembly and the House of Assembly of the states.[63] If there is need to pinpoint any single institution which has gained most by the new constitution it is local government. No more can states prohibit, as it were, local government from governing at the local level by locally elected people, as happened before in the Mid-Western, East Central, Rivers and Cross River States. Nor can the functions of local government be gradually encroached upon by the state governments as happened all over Nigeria from the onset of military rule.

The governments of the states are of a similar pattern to the federal government. The governor and deputy governor correspond to the president and vice president at the federal level while commissioners replace ministers in the executive at the state level.

The Constitution of the Federal Republic of Nigeria (Enactment) Decree 1978 which ushers in a new phase of constitutional rule in October 1979 is a document which reflects more the sad experiences of the past than the hopes of the future. The desire for a strong, effective and unifying chief executive is restrained by the fear of unwittingly creating a constitutional Frankenstein's monster. The need to evolve genuinely national political parties leads to regulatory provisions which very nearly contravene the constitutional guarantee of freedom of association. Can the constitutional order so painstakingly designed secure the stable and effective government which is so essential to national development? It is to the Constituent Assembly that we must turn for an indication. As one of its members observed, 'The real problem in our country is the sheer contempt for democracy and our inability to accept democratic decisions. It is this intolerance that mostly constitutes the bane of our society, and consequently, strains Nigerian unity.'[64] Working the new constitution will tax to the utmost the tolerance and ability to abide by democratic decisions of the leaders of Nigeria. It is upon their ability to rise to the high demands of statesmanship which the new constitution will almost inevitably require that the stability of future governments depends.

13 The struggle for power in Nigeria 1966–79

A. D. Yahaya

Military rule in Africa is regarded as an aberration. A normal political system is often regarded as one that is governed, directed and controlled by a civilian political class which has been recruited by popular choice to the decision-making structures of the state. Attempts to provide explanatory schemes for military intervention have induced scholars to focus on the organisational structure, the professional ethos, and the value orientation of the military as the variables which motivate the military to intervene. Nevertheless, the socio-economic conditions of the environment which induce the military to intervene are not neglected. Indeed, one early study of military rule has posited that countries with low or weak political culture are more susceptible to military intervention.[1]

This approach inevitably limits our understanding of the dynamics of politics in a military government primarily because no systematic study of the distribution of power, the process of decision making, the formulation and the execution of programmes are undertaken.[2] This is a serious gap in our knowledge of military rule. The struggle for power during the military regime in Nigeria is an attempt to narrow this gap. This contribution will consequently focus on the dynamics of the political process in a military government.

The military government in Nigeria is divided into phases and each phase coincides with the regime of three different military political groups who assumed control of the country. This division is necessary because the style of government in each of the three military regimes was different. The first phase was an era of military monopoly of political power. The civilian political leaders were displaced and excluded from political participation. The second phase was the era of partnership. A new political coalition of politicians, the civilians and the military political officers was forged. The third phase is the terminal phase of military rule. It is the era of conscious demilitarisation and the general disengagement of the military political clients.

The first phase of military rule

It will be apparent that the first phase of military rule in Nigeria which coincided with the Ironsi regime was the only attempt by the military to rule the country with the collaboration of a select group of experts and technocrats.[3] The civilian political class was totally excluded and even the top military political group was apparently allowed a marginal role in policy making. Members of the Supreme Military Council and the Federal Executive Councils were however officers of the armed forces and the police.[4] The attorney-general was the only civilian officer in the two councils. The exclusion of civilian political leaders from political participation in the military government was however transient.

The military governors of the regions, on the other hand, appointed some top administrative officials into their executive councils. The military government of the East constituted an executive committee of six members.[5] Three out of these six members were permanent secretaries. Other permanent secretaries were co-opted if they had a business before the council. In the executive council of the Mid-West there were eight members but five of these members were civil servants.[6] As in the East, permanent secretaries who had a business before the council would be co-opted. The Western executive council was composed of eight members, six of whom were permanent secretaries.[7]

When the military assumed power the politicians were renounced and discredited. Yet this national condemnation of the political class was short-lived. The major political problems which military intervention unleased glaringly revealed the inadequate political skill of the top military command. This inadequacy led to the eruption of a serious political crisis in the country which compelled the military regime to collaborate with the discredited politicians in their search for a solution.[8]

The reluctance of the military government to share power with other groups during the first phase of military rule was induced by the official conception of the regime. It was the belief of the Supreme Military Council that the government 'did not come to power by the leave of any political party or any section of the country'.[9] It was essentially a 'corrective government' which should not be treated as an 'elected government'.[10] For this reason it was not officially recognised that every government has a political function to perform. When, however, the inclination to restrict participation in government to bureaucrats and army officers was reversed it was too late to prevent the regime from falling. The point at which this reversal of policy was made coincided with the eruption of serious political violence when the government decided to alter the federal status of the country to a unitary form of government on 24 May 1966.

At the federal level it was claimed that the programme of reform introduced by the regime was strongly influenced by trusted aides outside the government. People like Francis Nwokedi, G. Onyike, Dr P. Okigbo and some university academics were said to have greater influence on Ironsi than official groups within the army and the civil service.[11] The influential role of these personal aides rendered the decision-making process non-formal and limited the contribution of political and administrative officials to the policy-making process.

Despite the dependence on personal aides during the first phase, public officials were given specific assignments on the administrative reform programme of the government. These assignments were undertaken either as commissions of inquiry into the administration of federal institutions like the Electricity Corporation of Nigeria, the Nigerian Railway Corporation, the Lagos City Council and the Nigerian Ports Authority, or as study groups. Three study groups were appointed by the government.[12] Nothing came out of the deliberations of these study groups except the 'Guideposts for the New Development Programme' which was prepared by the National Planning Advisory Group.[13]

Reform programmes which included the removal of the old politicians as chairmen and board members of statutory corporations were set into motion.[14] Their places were taken over by civil servants who consequently took over even as chairmen of these corporations. Overall the reform programme of the regime was aimed at eliminating corruption and dishonesty in public life and so politicians were excluded from participating in government and public institutions were probed. The corruption and maladministration of these institutions were exposed but no conscious attempt to undertake a major structural and operational reorganisation of the service was undertaken.

The second phase of military rule

The second phase was the era of the regime of Yakubu Gowon. Unlike the Ironsi regime, Gowon recognised the value of political skills in government and so the regime undertook to conciliate political groups in the country on his assumption of power. Chief Awolowo and other political detainees like Chief Enahoro, Lateef Jakande, Samuel Onitiri, Dr M. I. Okpara, T. O. S. Benson, Chief Fani Kayode, Richard Akinjide and Dr K. O. Mbadiwe were released from detention.[15] Politicians who had been discredited when the military intervened in January were now offered the opportunity to participate in the search for a viable political structure for the country. The first four months of the regime generated intense political discussion in which the politicians, the civil servants and the army featured prominently.

Not every military and police officer was involved in politics but those who were assigned a political role in the regime as military governors, members of the Supreme Military Council and the Federal Executive Council constituted the military political group. The civil service was represented by top administrative officers like permanent secretaries and other professionals in the service. In Northern Nigeria the intelligentsia in the service was known to have had an organised forum where members met. This forum was the Niima Club with prominent civil servants as members.[16]

In June 1966 civil commissioners were appointed at both the federal and state levels. Most of the newly appointed commissioners were prominent politicians but very few had served as ministers with the displaced civilian government. Among the first set of federal commissioners appointed only Shettima Ali Monguno was a minister in the displaced civilian regime. Chief Awolowo who was appointed the vice-chairman of the Federal Executive Council was the leader of the opposition before his conviction for treasonable felony.

The association of civilian politicians with the second phase of the military regime contributed enormously to the legitimacy of the government. The politicians at both the federal and state level featured prominently in the process of government. During the war years (1967-70) they helped to champion the federal cause at the diplomatic front. Initially Gowon took responsibility for External Affairs, but not all the federal government delegations to peace talks were led by him. Civilian politicians led federal government delegations to international conferences and to the peace conferences which met outside the country.[17] Chief Anthony Enahoro led the Nigerian delegation to the Kampala and Addis Ababa peace talks. Chief Awolowo led the Nigerian delegation to the OAU consultative committee meeting on the Nigerian crisis in Niamey even though Governor Audu Bako of Kano State was a member of the delegation.[18] Chief Awolowo also led the Nigerian delegation to the OAU summit conference in Algiers and the Commonwealth conference in London despite the presence of Colonel Hassan Usman Katsina in the latter delegation.[19] Indeed, their immense contribution to the war effort was concentrated on the diplomatic front and the mobilisation of popular support for the federal cause.

During the early phase of the regime commissioners were influential members of the regime. There was no indication of an open political disagreement between the military political group and the commissioners. Even the civil servants who by now had lost their anonymity were still subordinate to their political officers. Thus the glory which the politicians lost when the civilian government was displaced was now revived. The civil war dominated the political scene during this period. The war was interrupted by some positive policy decisions implemented by the regime. One such policy was the reorganisation of local government in all the states of the federation. It is therefore valid to argue that the military succeeded in effecting a major structural transformation in the country with the collaboration of the politicians. The attempt by the first regime to restructure the country was violently opposed largely because the politicians who were also power-brokers were excluded from the political process. However, the influence of the politicians in the government was soon to diminish especially when the role of the government was reduced to an essentially house-keeping function. When the war ended the government directed its efforts to reconciliation, rehabilitation and reconstruction. Rehabilitation and reconstruction are functions that can be more ably implemented by experts and technocrats. The politician was quietly pushed to the background by the military.[20] Before that happened, however, two well known commissioners, Chief Awolowo and Alhaji Yahaya Gusau who served during the war years resigned their appointments after the war and therefore withdrew from the military political scene. The others remained in office until Gowon decided to reshuffle the executive council in January 1975.

The terminal phase of military rule

When Gowon was removed from office, General Murtala Mohammed took over as head of state. The nation was told that the displaced regime allowed the country to drift with no sense of direction. The regime was also accused of 'lack of consultation, indecision, indiscipline and even neglect'.[21] The political indiscretion of discarding 'responsible opinion, including advice by eminent Nigerians, traditional rulers, intellectuals' was condemned.[22] By implication the new regime was to embark on a national reorientation with emphasis on official probity and respect of popular opinion in the process of government. Accordingly, the purification exercise undertaken by the regime was inevitably directed towards the dismantling of the edifice built by the displaced regime.

Public servants were blamed for contributing to the decadence in the society and a state governor stated that he would spare no official who engaged in abuse of office.[23] At the federal level, the head of state decided that permanent secretaries would no longer participate in the deliberations of the Federal Executive Council. They were permitted to attend the meeting of the council in an advisory capacity at the invitation of their commissioners. The regime therefore undertook to disengage civil servants from an active political role. Their subordinate status in the political system was re-established and a massive purge was undertaken. Officers were retired on account of 'old age, inefficiency, poor health, and malpractices'.[24] When it was all over, about 10 000 civil servants had been removed from office.[25] The regime therefore revised the assertive political role of the civil servants to a submissive one. The civil service lost its eminent status in the political system.

The armed forces, however, retained their dominant status. Participation in government was extended to civilian groups but on the whole those appointed commissioners at the federal and state levels were professional and technical experts and not politicians. At the federal level twenty-five commissioners were appointed but only eleven were civilians. The other fourteen were members of the armed forces and police. The civilians were all employed in either the public or private sectors or were academics serving in the universities. Those appointed commissioners at the state level were also drawn from the same professional and technical cadre.

The philosophy of the regime One persistent theme in the objectives of the regime was the determination to inculcate some values in the public life of the nation. Some of these values were discipline, official responsibility and probity. For this reason the regime prominently undertook to introduce some corrective measures in the public sector. Consequently the creative capability of the government was not fully exploited. Thus creative policies were less of a feature of this regime.

The emphasis on corrective policies inevitably induced the government to establish its credibility in the society. All programmes adopted by the government were implemented within stated deadlines. The prompt execution of programmes is an activity which is not heavily dependent on political skills. It is essentially a management and technical function. Thus the role of the political class in a regime with a bias towards efficient execution of functions will be minimal.

The implementation of the programme of the regime seemed to follow a definite pattern. One can in fact identify three strategies. The first strategy was the 'clean-up' campaign. Public officers who were inefficient and were regarded as incapable of surviving in the new order were retired. Public institutions and specific government programmes like the cement order were probed. The findings of these probes revealed the extent of abuse of office or official negligence which was rampant in high offices. This exercise was intended to expose the ills of the displaced regime and to re-establish probity and official responsibility in high office. The popular condemnation of corruption and official malpractice revealed in these probes was expected to guide officials of this regime in their official functions. Yet this corrective posture of the regime was strongly resented by some military officers. This discontent led to an attempted coup in February 1976. The head of state, Murtala Mohammed, was killed but the coup was aborted. General Olusegun Obasanjo took over as the head of state and decided not to change the orientation of the regime. Consequently the regime is being referred to as the Mohammed/Obasanjo regime.

The second stage of the implementation strategy was the execution of the policy recommendations submitted by the specialised commissions appointed by the government. The policy formulation process of the regime deviated from that of the Gowon regime. Major policy decisions were based on the report and recommendation of commissions or panels appointed by the government. Professional and technical experts or highly reputable public administrators were appointed to these bodies. Government policy decisions with regard to the creation of states, the dissolution of ICSA and ESIALA, the establishment of a new federal capital and so on, were all based on reports submitted by the various commissions appointed. The government therefore has demonstrated the considerable value of expert opinion and contribution to the policy formulation procedure.

The third strategy coincided with the implementation of the political programme. These three strategies overlapped one another as, for instance, the implementation of the political programme which was initiated during the clean-up campaign of the regime. It was, however, the political programme of the regime which generated the greatest interest within the political group in the country. On 1 October 1975 in a statement to the nation, the government set October 1979 as the date of transfer of power to civilians. The government set a timetable which if implemented will make the transfer of power possible.[26] The timetable set April 1976 as the date during which new states were to be formally established. Local government was to be reorganised and a uniform structure has now been established throughout the country. A Constitution Drafting Committee, the Constituent Assembly and ratification of a constitution for the country have all been completed within stipulated deadlines. So far the political programme of the regime has been faithfully implemented and the ban on political activities was lifted in September 1978 after the ratification of the constitution.

The politicians as a group never really emerged as a decisive political force in this government. However, they participated prominently in the Constitution Drafting Committee established by the Government.[27] A regime which gave a high regard to skills and professional competence, regarded politicians as qualified to draft a constitution. Their skills were recruited for this political venture.

The emergence of political parties Before the ban on political activities was lifted the government decided to prepare the minds of the people for this change and to recondition the attitude of public officers for the transfer of power to civilian political groups. The first decisive action taken by the government was the significant withdrawal of military presence in the government. A decision in this direction was the reassignment of military governors and military officers holding political office to purely military duties.[28] The withdrawal of military officers from political duties was made compulsory for all officers who do not intend to retire from service at the end of this military administration. Officers in this category relinquished their political posts on 24 July and returned to the barracks. The military governors were replaced by military administrators who were also commanders of their military units. The administrators in addition to their military duties were to serve as the chairmen of their state executive councils. They were to be assisted by civilian deputy chairmen. These administrators were to be resident in the barracks and not in the official state house.

Civilian commissioners who were interested in partisan political activities were advised to resign.[29] Commissioners at both the federal and state levels resigned their appointments by the end of September 1978. However, the number of resignations was not considerable due largely to the fact that only very few active politicians were appointed commissioners by this regime.

The removal of military political groups from office and their civilian clients interested in active political participation was followed by the decision of the government to prepare the minds of Nigerians for a healthy political contest. General Obasanjo therefore organised a series of meetings with influential opinion leaders in the country to advise and appeal to them for support in order to effect a smooth transfer of power. The first meeting was held with traditional leaders who were advised to 'live above partisan politics and parochial interests'.[30] Thirty-eight rulers drawn from all the nineteen states of the federation attended this meeting.

The second set of meetings was held with religious leaders who were asked to collaborate with the government to 'ensure peaceful and painless transition, and help to maintain thenceforth a united, stable, and peaceful nation'.[31] Civil servants were not ignored in this attempt to prepare the minds of the people for a new political order. The civil servants were advised to develop a new awareness, orientation, attitude and approach in the exercise of their duties.[32] It is expected that the norms and the status of the civil service will be adapted in order to make it relevant to a presidential system of government. The fourth group of people whom General Obasanjo met were senior media executives. He called on them to be guided by the principle of 'publish to build and strengthen the nation, and not to publish to destroy or be damned'.[33] Finally, before the Constituent Assembly was dissolved members as elected representatives of the people were called upon to co-operate with the government so that a peaceful and smooth transfer of power can be effected.

The ban on politics was lifted on 21 September 1978 and the Constituent Assembly was formally dissolved. A week after the ban was lifted the formation of not less than six political associations was announced. Among those announced during the first week were the Unity Party of Nigeria (UPN), the Nigerian Peoples Party (NPP), the National Party of Nigeria (NPN), the Nigerian Advanced Party (NAP), and the Nigerian Welfare Peoples Party (NWPP). The quick announcement of the formation of political associations when the ban on political activities was lifted suggests that aspiring politicians must have organised the formation of these parties even during the ban on political activities. The lifting of the ban was therefore preceded by clandestine political activities and the police had at least warned aspiring politicians that the ban was still in force.

The UPN with Chief Awolowo as the leader was the first political association to be declared, a day after the ban was lifted. It was, however, indicated that the political association had existed even before the ban on political activities was lifted.[34] The formation of the UPN was the outcome of regular meetings by the Committee of Friends ostensibly organised as a preparatory group for a future political party. Such social associations became a visible feature of the Nigerian political scene. Almost all the major parties formed were the product of the activities of these social associations.

The formation of the UPN was also preceded by an attempt by Chief Awolowo to make himself acceptable to the people of Nigeria. He published a twenty-five page reply to those he regarded as his critics. He was criticised for some human weaknesses and tribalism; vindictiveness, rigidity and dictatorship were identified as his main weaknesses.[35] Despite this attempt by Chief Awolowo he did not succeed in attracting all his former political associates into his camp. When the UPN was formed, his close political associates like S. G. Ikoku, Chief Anthony Enahoro and J. S. Tarka did not join the party.

On formation of the UPN the four cardinal principles of

the party were announced. These were free education at all levels, an integrated rural development scheme, free health facilities, and full employment for all Nigerians.[36] The party convention was held on 2 October 1978 and Chief Awolowo was adopted as the party presidential candidate while Philip Umeadi was elected his running mate. Chief Awolowo later revealed that his attempt to recruit political aspirants from the northern sector of the country failed and all the prominent personalities he invited to joint his UPN rejected his invitation.

The formation of the NPP followed. The NPP was formed as a result of the coalition of three social associations. These were the Club 19, the National Council of Understanding and the Lagos Progressives.[37] Club 19 was a coalition of members of the Constituent Assembly who were the opponents of the Sharia, the anti-Awolowo elements and the representatives of 'minorities'.[38] To this extent the Club 19 group was largely a protest group brought together because of their common antipathy to some social trends in the country. The fusion of these three groups was announced in August. The prominent members of the NPP included former politicians like Alhaji Waiziri Ibrahim, Mathew Mbu, Chief Olu Akinfosile and Chief Ogunsanya. The NPP, however, was split barely two months after its formation. The split came to the open at the party's first national convention which took place in Lagos on 17 November 1978. Two factions emerged from the split: Alhaji Waziri Ibrahim's faction and Chief Adeniron Ogunsanya's faction. The Waziri Ibrahim faction comprised members of the National Council of Understanding while the Adeniran Ogunsanya faction was made up of members of Club 19 and the Lagos Progressives. Dr Nnamdi Azikiwe later declared for the Adeniran Ogunsanya faction.[39]

Two parties emerged out of the original. The Waziri Ibrahim faction proceeded with the convention and he was nominated the party leader and the presidential candidate while Dr B. U. Nzeribe was elected his running mate. The Waziri Ibrahim faction adopted the Great Nigeria Peoples Party (GNPP) as its official name when it became obvious that the split could not be resolved. The Adeniran Ogunsanya faction retained the NPP and elected Dr Azikiwe as its presidential candidate at the 9 December 1978 convention in Lagos. Chief Olu Akinfosile was elected chairman of the party.

The third major party to be announced was the National Party of Nigeria (NPN) which was an offshoot of the National Movement, an intra-Constituent Assembly group.[40] The NPN attracted a large number of political notables associated with the dissolved political parties and the displaced Gowon regime. Members included Major-General Adeyinka Adebayo, and Major-General Hassan Usman Katsina who were senior political officers in the regime of Gowon. Civilian commissioners under Gowon like Chief Anthony Enahoro, Alhaji Shehu Shagari, Alhaji Shettima Ali Monguno and Chief A. Y. Eke are among the members of the NPN. State commissioners in Gowon's regime like Alhaji Umaru Dikko, Alhaji H. Dantoro and Alhaji Maitama Sule are members of the party.

The fourth major party that emerged was the Peoples Redemption Party (PRP) as the political vehicle of the ideologically oriented group in the society. The prominent members of the party participated in the activities of the National Movement but they withdrew when it was decided to convert the National Movement into a political party. Those who withdrew from the National Movement at this stage included Alhaji Aminu Kano, S. G. Ikoku and other progressives. The circumstances which led to the withdrawal of Alhaji Aminu Kano and S. G. Ikoku were ideological although NPN members argued that they withdrew because they were not assigned important party positions. The PRP was launched in Kaduna on 21 October 1978.

Several other political associations were also launched and it was recorded that over fifty such associations were formed. Some of the well known ones in this group are the Nigerian Advanced Party led by Tunji Braithwaite, the Movement of the People led by Fela Anikulapo Kuti, the Socialist Party of Workers, Farmers and Youths, Nigerian Welfare Peoples Party and Nigerian National Council. These political associations were formed by new men who were either not prominent or who had not actively participated in politics during the civilian political era. These associations were not, however, registered by the Federal Electoral Commission (FEDECO) as political parties.

The Electoral Decree of 1977 made a distinction between a political party and a political association. Political associations must be registered before they can function as political parties. Only political parties are allowed to engage in political activities like the nomination of candidates for election and to canvass for votes for any candidate. To be registered as a political party all political associations must satisfy the following conditions:[41]

names and addresses of national officers must be registered with FEDECO;
party membership shall be opened to every Nigerian, irrespective of place of origin, religion, ethnic group, or sex;
copy of the constitution must be registered with FEDECO, and amendment to the Constitution must be registered within thirty days;
the name, emblem, or motto of the party is national and not ethnic, religious or parochial;
headquarters of the party to be located in the federal capital.

The decree also stipulates that the constitution of the party shall provide for periodic elections to the executive committee of the party at intervals not exceeding four years. Members of the executive council so elected must reflect the federal character of the country by belonging to not less than two-thirds of all the states comprising the federation. Finally it was required that the association must have an equipped and operating office in the capital of not less than thirteen states.

FEDECO fixed 18 December 1978 as the deadline when all applications for the registration of political parties were to be submitted.[42] The deadline was announced on 13 November 1978 to spur political associations into action. Nineteen political associations submitted their applications for registration but only five were accepted by FEDECO. These five are UPN, NPN, NPP, GNPP and the PRP. Out of nineteen political associations that submitted applications for registration only five fulfilled the conditions of the decree and so were officially recognised as political parties.

Each of the five parties can be identified with a dominant

tendency. The UPN emphasises the provision of social and welfare programmes as the primary responsibility of the state. It tends to attract former politicians who were members of the dissolved Action Group. Chief Awolowo who is the leader of the UPN was also the leader of the Action Group. The dominant group within the UPN are professionals and some academics are also known to be members of the party. At this stage there is no indication that big businessmen are in control of the party machine. In fact, even the gubernatorial candidates of the party are professionals and not men associated with big business.

Of all the five registered parties NPN seems to be the party most committed to the maintenance of the existing social order. As indicated earlier, members of the party have been in government either during the civilian political era or during the military regime. One common feature of the leading members of the NPN is that a considerable number of them have been discredited and are all well known political names in the country. Big businessmen have openly identified themselves with the party to the extent that the chairmen of some state wings of the party are businessmen. The NPN has been referred to as the party of 'heavyweights' because of the 'big' names identified with the party.

Some members of the intelligentsia from the northern sector of the country were attracted into the NPN. These members were initially influential within the party but during the party convention in December 1978, members of the old political class emerged as the dominant group within the party. Alhaji Shehu Shagari was elected the presidential candidate and Chief A. M. A. Akinloye was elected the chairman of the party. Both were members of the dissolved Nigerian National Alliance (NNA) which was in control of the federal government between 1964 and 1966.

Electoral contest within the NPN was not based on individual standing. The party adopted a conscious policy which institutionalised the diversity in the country. Specific party positions were allocated to specific sectors of the country. For instance, the office of the party chairman was allocated to the western sector of the country and so the contest for this office was open only to members from this sector. The presidential candidate was to be selected from the northern sector and no member of the party was entitled to stand for party presidential nomination if he was not from the northern sector. This distribution of party office and nomination has come to be referred to as zoning. Zoning has been strongly criticised even by members of the party. The NPN is apparently confident of electoral victory, so much so that the party has been preoccupied with the sharing of the booty of office even before the election is won.

The withdrawal of Alhaji Waziri Ibrahim from the NPP and the declaration of Dr Azikiwe for the party has converted the party into an instrument for the revival of the past political flamboyance of Zik. Some of the top leaders of the NPP are political admirers of Dr Azikiwe and in the past had consistently supported his political cause. Chief Olu Akinfosile, Mathew Mbu, Chief Adeniran Ogunsanya and Michael Ogon were all loyal supporters to Dr Azikiwe. Loyalty to Dr Azikiwe is perhaps the strongest cohesive force within the NPP. Ideologically there is no fundamental difference between the NPP and the NPN and it will not be out of place if members of the NPP ultimately declare for the NPN especially if the NPP fails to achieve an electoral victory.

The Waziri Ibrahim faction took over most of the former NPP branches in the northern sector of the country. The GNPP attracted a large following among the petty bourgeois group especially in the northern sector. It has been claimed that the party has some appeal even to influential traditional rulers in this part of the country. The party, however, has not attracted a large following from the intellectual and professional group in the country. The GNPP like the NPP is not committed to the fundamental transformation of the society.

The PRP unlike all the other parties is committed to the creation of a new social order. The PRP sounds more ideological in orientation than any of the other four political parties. Of particular significance is the policy of the party to replace the present dependent economy with an independent national economy which will uphold the dignity of labour and ensure that the people enjoy the fruits of economic development. The PRP is identified with political ideologies which have some socialist inclination. Alhaji Aminu Kano has been associated with the emancipation of the common man during his days in the dissolved Northern Elements Progressive Union. S. G. Ikoku was closely connected with the ideological reorientation of the dissolved Action Group. Besides these two leaders, the PRP has attracted a large number of university academics and trade union leaders like Chief Michael Imoudu. The primary target of the electoral appeal of the PRP is the common man. It has developed an image of the party of the common man. The party has so far not selected its presidential candidate.

It is significant to note that all these five parties are essentially led and controlled by politicians who had actively participated in politics before the intervention of the military. The expectation that old politicians will be replaced by a 'new breed' has not materialised and indeed old politicians have displaced aspiring political groups as was the case in the NPN. Thus the political class has over the years developed into essential actors in the process of government in Nigeria. Their participation in either the policy-making structures or in specialised commissions or in consultative committees has been found inevitable even in a military regime.

14 Civilian rule for how long?

Oyeleye Oyediran

In his contribution to J. J. Johnson's *The Role of the Military in Under-Developed Countries*, Lucian Pye raises two questions. He asks, 'Is the encroachment of the military into civilian rule a blow to liberal government and civil liberties?' The second question is, 'Has the military established the necessary basis for the growth of effective representative institutions?'[1] The first question may be interpreted to be related to a call for presenting a balance sheet of thirteen years of military rule, while the second question has to do with the after-effect of military rule. These questions will be the themes of this concluding chapter, which is in two parts, of our attempt in this book to assess the impact of military rule in Nigerian politics.

There is no doubt that the military era has been a blessing to Nigeria in many respects. As the preceding chapters show, in many areas of public policy the military has been not only a source of cure for the ills of society, but also a modernising force. The civil war which would have led to the total disintegration of Nigeria as a political entity was prosecuted in such a way that social and economic reconstruction and, more especially, reconciliation were less difficult and painful than they would have been otherwise. As Muhammadu and Haruna point out, the military government proved wrong all the predictions of the Western press that the end of the war would be marked by genocide and mass trials of war criminals.

Restructuring of the public service took place during the period of military rule. The multiplicity of salary scales was abolished and in its place an integrated salary structure was introduced. The age-long dispute between professionals and administrators in the civil service was tackled, though not completely resolved, by making executive administrative leadership of a ministry open to all with the right talents. Comparatively the press fared better in Nigeria than in any other country under military rule. The Amakiri episode was an aberration, and when the press summoned up courage to seek the protection of the law courts, the law was allowed to take its due course. Even though the attempt to take politics out of revenue allocation failed because it was unrealistic, the military era was an era in which the tendency towards equity in the distribution of the financial resources of the country was seriously faced. In particular, the military should be credited with including local government councils in the sharing of federally collected revenue, thereby providing one of the necessary ingredients for improving the quality of life in communities other than state capitals and divisional headquarters.

Most Nigerians will agree that the greatest credit to the military was in the areas of foreign policy, local government, the economy and return to civil rule. In the closing years of military rule, Nigerian foreign policy was something to be proud of. Akinyemi's observation is in general representative of foreign policy observers that 'Nigeria seems to have finally arrived at the role and status Nigerians have been clamouring for since 1960, influencing events in Africa, South of the Sahara, being consulted on events in the country by low and mighty.' These were not all. Liberation fighters, most especially since 1975 saw Nigeria as one of their strongest supporters, financially, morally and psychologically, in Africa.

The constitutional provision that 'the system of local government by democratically elected local government council is . . . guaranteed, and accordingly the government of every state shall ensure their existence under law which provides for the establishment, structure, composition finance and functions of such Council's arose from the commendable and progressive step taken by the military in 1976. By deciding to make local government a third tier of government and by working strenuously to implement this policy decision which arose from the conviction that 'if stability at the national level is to be guaranteed a firm foundation for a rational government at the local level is imperative', the Mohammed/ Obasanjo regime improved the quality of communication between the local communities, state and central governments.

On the economy, the indigenisation and Land Use Decrees are two revolutionary steps successfully taken by the military against all odds. The first was designed to ensure that the economy of the nation is in the control of Nigerians, while the second compelled the few privileged land capitalists to recognise that land belongs to the state and not to individuals or groups of individuals.

Finally, the decision to transfer power to a civilian government, as Adekson points out, is an unequalled case of a ruling military faithfully presiding in accordance with a masterpiece formula of detail and method, over its own peaceful self-liquidation. Despite inside and outside pressures, the military has kept to its promise and from all appearances it has done so without being partisan in the struggle among competing groups of possible successors.

When we consider the other side of the coin, one sees the period of military rule as an era of administrative incompetence, inaction, of authoritarian if not reactionary values. Only a few of the most critical examples need be given. The restructuring of the public service was accompanied not only by salary increases of up to 130 per cent – worse still, part of the package was the payment of unprecedentedly large arrears which were paid in one fell swoop against all intelligent and patriotic advice. The only reason for pumping millions of naira from the public fund into the pockets of 650 000 public servants within a period of sixty days was to buy public political support for a regime that had become very unpopular due to broken promises and inaction. The inflationary consequences of the measure will definitely be inherited by the next civilian government. Moreover, the private sector successfully manoeuvred its way and restored the gap between its salary structure and that in the public sector, thereby negating the whole essence of the salary increases. Government was either unwilling or unable to control the situation. Finally;

even though there is disagreement between inside and outside observers on the actual role of the higher civil servants during the early years of military rule, there is a general consensus that the closing years witnessed a tremendous drop in the morale of public servants in general.

There was overreaction in many respects. Though the aim of the compulsory retirement of about 11 000 public servants within a period of eight weeks in 1975 was to clear the field for an efficient, responsible and polite public service, the result was the loss of able, innocent, devoted and patriotic public servants. As Asiodu points out, the exercise was counter-productive. Many of the civil servants who were lucky enough to escape the purge became reluctant to take either risks or even decisions that were critically necessary. Voluntary retirement as soon as public servants turned forty-five followed to the extent that more than two years after, some state governors had to plead, though discreetly, with the officers to stay longer in the service.

Fear of politics affected negatively the relationship between university institutions and the military rulers. Many instances of this relationship can be given, but the worst example is the directive issued by the executive secretary of the National Universities Commission on behalf of the federal military government on participation of members of university communities in the 1979 political activities. Not only are overt party political activities banned in the universities, students who are allowed to join political parties not as groups but only as individuals are cautioned not to do so to the detriment of their studies. University authorities are required to 'deal with students who neglect their studies in favour of party politics'. Also university staff of all categories are barred from participating in partisan politics 'collectively or individually, in any manner or form, including belonging to political parties, or taking part in political rallies, or undertaking any form of political activities whatsoever'. This is not only authoritarian, it is also reactionary. What is being denied those who work in these institutions goes beyond partisanship, it touches on all the fundamental issues of political participation. As Professor Awa has observed, the real issue is that a section of the intelligent and articulate elements of Nigerian society has been denied political rights, and 'the political system of Nigeria is going to be the worse for it'.[2]

It is difficult if not inappropriate to try and weigh each of the points raised on both the positive and negative effects of military rule in Nigeria. It would appear, however, that in general, it is only in areas which are related to the normal functioning of the military as an institution that success has been much achieved. On issues or policies which are heavily political and require the involvement of the politicians for formulation and/or the support of the citizens for implementation, success has eluded the Nigerian military, or the military rulers have been the reactionary 'guardian of the existing order'.[3] Since the government of any country cannot be run permanently like a military establishment – it requires the support and encouragement of its citizens, particularly the articulate and intelligent elements, if not the involvement of its politicians – military rule in Nigeria can therefore be said to be a failure.

If one accepts that it is this realisation that accounts in part for the decision to hand over power to popularly elected civilian government, what then are the chances that the military will not return soon? Put differently, for how long will civilian government last?

The fear of and in some quarters the desire for a quick return of the military after October 1979 is real.[4] Probably the most concrete evidence for this came out of the debate at the Constituent Assembly in 1978 on the issue of whether or not to include in the constitution a provision against seizure of political power other than as laid down in the constitution.[5] What were the arguments put for and against this attempt to forestall a possible return of the military? Those who supported the inclusion of a provision to ban military coups argued that:

(a) there is need to make the seizure of power by a person or group outside the provisions of the constitution a condemnable treasonable felony;
(b) the intention to stop military takeover of government through the constitution is more important than the method of doing so in that this may have a great psychological effect on the people;

(c) this is a way to maintain civil supremacy and make it a duty for the citizens to rise against any unconstitutional seizure of power.

Those opposed to such a provision argued as follows:

(a) the only guarantee against military or civil coups is good, responsible and representative government which satisfies the needs and aspirations of the people;
(b) military coups cannot be stopped through constitutional means;
(c) the provisions of the criminal code make a military coup a criminal act, so making a special provision in the constitution, the suspension of which is the first act of a military takeover, unnecessary;
(d) military coups are sometimes a reasonable means of correcting national ills.

The outcome of the debate is the provision that 'The Federal Republic of Nigeria shall not be governed nor shall any person or group of persons take control of the Government of Nigeria or any part thereof, except in accordance with the provisions of this Constitution.'[6] As Adekson pointed out in his contribution, a permanent return of the military to the barracks after October 1979 would be not because but in spite of this constitutional provision.

Though reasons for military takeover of political power vary not only from country to country, but also from time to time in any one country, it would be interesting to see if the past is any indication for the future. In other words, have the constitutional and political environments changed positively from what they were in the years preceding January 1966? If they have, what are the chances that they would remain so for long?

In chapter 1 we listed some basic factors which contributed to the 1966 military takeover. These were constitutional problems, north-south and ethnic conflicts, the issue of state creation and a number of 'signposts' that led to the disaster including the structural dilemma of the army. To what extent have these factors or related factors been resolved? Are the constitutional and political environments such that these or other related factors are unlikely to raise their heads at least to such an extent that they will serve as the 'pull' or 'push' for the military?

Let us examine first the constitutional environment. The new constitution which will guide the political behaviour of leaders is in many ways different from the 1963 constitution. At no time in the political history of Nigeria has the opportunity been given to interested Nigerians to discuss openly, over a period of more than twenty-two months, in the mass media, at various conferences and seminars, at committees made up of representatives of various sections of the country, the constitution under which they would be governed. Though there were some days of crisis during the meetings of the Constituent Assembly, the final product was acceptable to the generality of Nigerians. Elsewhere we have examined the points for and against the accepted presidential system of government.[7] In that analysis we concluded that the basic reasons why most articulate Nigerians opted for a change from the parliamentary system of the Westminster type was essentially because of the manner in which executive power is constituted under the presidential system.

Two or three critical aspects of the differences between the old and the new constitutions will suffice as evidence for the assertion that the constitutional environment is positively different from that before 1966. One of these is the relationship between the military and civilian decision makers. This point was the theme of the speech of the chief of staff, supreme headquarters, Brigadier Shehu Yar' Adua to the students of the Command and Staff College at Jaji, Kaduna, on 20 December 1978.[8] In the old constitution it was not clear which of the two leaders, the president as ceremonial head, or the prime minister as the head of government, had the authority to determine the occasions on which the military should go into action. The president in that constitution was the commander-in-chief of the armed forces, though the military was responsible to the prime minister as head of government. The ambiguous relationship of the military with the two heads was an important issue in the 1964-5 federal election crisis. As Yar' Adua put it, 'A critical factor in the stability of our country is the nature of the civil-military relationship and whether or not that relationship is governed by rules and norms prescribed by the constitution.' He went on, 'A stable institutional relationship presumes a clear definition of roles and an understanding and acceptance of such roles both by the military and civilian government.'[9]

In the new constitution, the ambiguity of the 1963 constitution has been removed. The president as the chief executive and commander-in-chief of the armed forces has the power to determine the operational use of the armed forces Not only that: the president in section 198, subsection 2, of the new constitution also has the power to appoint the chief of defence staff, heads of the army, navy, air force and of such other branches of the armed forces as may be established by an act of the National Assembly. In order to drive the point home to his colleagues, Brigadier Yar' Adua concluded, 'The plain fact of the new constitution is that the military is subordinate to and is under the control of the civilian authority.'

One of the major political issues between 1951 and 1966 was that of creation of more states. The lopsided nature of the federal components affected the resolution of other major issues such as representation in the federal parliament and revenue allocation. With the reorganisation of Nigeria into twelve states in 1967 and nineteen states in 1976, much of the venom has been taken out of the argument of agitators for state creation. This is not to suggest, however, that the issue was thereby finally resolved. Both at the Constitution Drafting Committee and the Constituent Assembly pressures were brought to bear on members to change the conditions laid down for state creation. Although the conditions in the 1979 constitution are as stringent as in the 1963 constitution, the political atmosphere is completely different with regard to this issue.[10] At the 1957 constitutional conference claims for fifteen states were put forward. If granted, this would have made Nigeria a federation of eighteen states. In the new constitution, Nigeria is a federation consisting of nineteen states and a federal capital territory. In short, the issue of creation of states has been considerably weakened.

The third and final evidence of a different constitutional environment is the question of role and election of the president in the new constitution. It has been argued that a plural executive as in the parliamentary system undermines responsibility in two ways. First, through the weakened authority of the prime minister to enforce collective responsibility and second, by making it difficult to determine on whom the blame or punishment for error should fall. Furthermore, the separation of a head of state from a head of government often results in a clash of personalities and of interest.[11] Unlike in the old constitution, where the head of government was determined by the party with the majority in the House of Representatives, in the new constitution the chief executive will be popularly elected by the Nigerian electorate at an election in which as many political parties as are registered by the Federal Electoral Commission can compete. In addition, both majority and minority ethnic groups in the country would have a say in who is finally president. According to sections 124 to 126 of the 1979 constitution, a candidate who is declared elected as president must have a majority of votes cast at a presidential election and those votes must be spread in such a way that he has not less than one-quarter of the votes cast in each of at least two-thirds of all the states in the federation. A chief executive so elected can, unlike in the past, legitimately claim to have the mandate of Nigerians to rule.

When one moves to the political environment the situation is cloudy. There are so many factors that may counteract the positive elements in the constitution. Two of these factors are critical. The first is the basis for political party formation. The second is the calibre and behaviour of political leaders whether or not they hold elective office.

Conditions for the formation and recognition of political parties are prescribed both in the constitution and the electoral decree.[12] Only political parties are allowed to canvass for votes for any candidate at an election. Cultural, social, ethnic, occupational or religious groups are forbidden to contribute to the funds of political parties or the election expenses of any candidate at an election. Apart from these, special restrictions are laid down for formation of political parties. These include non-recognition as a political party of any association

(a) which is not open to every Nigerian;
(b) whose emblem or motto has ethnic or religious

connotation or whose activities are confined to a part of the geographical area of Nigeria.

A political party is considered open to all Nigerians only if the Electoral Commission is satisfied that it has a properly established branch office in each of at least two-thirds of the states in the federation and that officers have been elected or appointed to run the affairs of each such branch office. Although by and large FEDECO has been accepted as a non-partisan umpire, there is no assurance that this relative objectivity will be maintained as the present electoral commissioners are to leave office after the 1979 election for a new team. Even if they are retained political pressure may be brought to bear on them. If a partisan group controls this institution it could be a source of trouble in the future.

Five political parties are recognised by FEDECO for the 1979 elections. These are the Unity Party of Nigeria (UPN), National Party of Nigeria (NPN), Great Nigeria Peoples' Party (GNPP), Nigeria Peoples' Party (NPP), and Peoples' Redemption Party (PRP). These started as three political associations. GNPP and NPP were originally one and PRP arose out of disagreement within the NPN. Since the leadership of these political parties is essentially dominated by the politicians who ruled the country during the First Republic, it is being said by some observers that political parties of the past have been resuscitated. It is correct that some of them were conceived by former comrades but the type of political system to be operated has necessitated going beyond former groups of supporters. In short the ethnic appeal of pre-1966 political parties cannot yield positive electoral results in the new system.[13]

In the First Republic many legislators behaved like political bats, changing party affiliation in accordance with the political fortune of their group. This made a mockery of the rules of the political game. In order to put a stop to this type of behaviour, legislators are not now allowed to change their party affiliation in the legislature. If they do, their seats are declared vacant and a new election is held to fill the vacancy. This is not the only rule to guide future behaviour. It is very difficult to remove an executive head of a government once he is elected into office. During the Action Group crisis of 1962, the party leadership was bent on removing Akintola as premier on a simple motion of no confidence. His very few supporters resorted to violence so as to stop the House of Assembly from meeting peacefully, thereby preventing the passage of the motion. A motion of no confidence passed by a legislature is not enough to remove a government, neither is personality nor ideological conflict within a majority party enough excuse to dissolve a legislative house in the new system of government.

Apart from these two factors there are some important yet potentially crisis-oriented political issues unresolved. These include revenue allocation and population count. As pointed out in the chapter on revenue allocation, the military did not succeed in carrying the politicians along in the attempt to take politics out of that issue. Not only that, one of the strongest presidential candidates for the 1979 election has promised an immediate review of the principles of revenue allocation if he is elected. The only attempt by the military to get involved in population count in 1974 was a terrible failure. Its handling contributed to the unpopularity of Gowon as head of state and his eventual fall in 1975. One of the terms of reference of the subcommittee on the economy, finance and division of power of the Constitution Drafting Committee was 'to examine and make recommendations on the Constitutional arrangements suitable for ensuring accurate and reliable population count as often as may be considered necessary in the national interest and, in particular, to consider in what ways population count can be depoliticised'. As a member of this subcommittee the present writer can reveal that much time was devoted to devising possible ways of handling this issue. All that we succeeded in recommending, and which could not be improved upon by either the Constituent Assembly or the Supreme Military Council, was the setting up of an independent National Population Commission whose chairman and members would be appointed by the president and confirmed by the Senate. This provision in the constitution is no insurance against crisis. In short, unless these and other issues are resolved with political maturity and the interest of the nation as the dominating factor, they could become signals for an early return of the military.

Undoubtedly the most important unpredictable factor is the military. The issues of demobilisation and military expenditure could easily lead to confrontation between the military leadership and a civilian government. Even if it is accepted that these issues have diminished in importance with the revelation of General Obasanjo in a national television interview that the numerical strength of the army had been reduced from 230 000 to 180 000 over a period of three years, because the government realised the burden of maintaining a large army in peace time,[14] two other elements in the military factor remain critical. The military leaders who are now holding political power are retiring before the end of 1979. Are the successors bound by the promise of their predecessors? To what extent will the seizure or continued control of political power by the military in other African countries affect the behaviour of the successors? This re-emphasises the problem of psychological withdrawal raised by Adekson in the chapter on the dilemma of military disengagement. As he puts it, the problems of psychological withdrawal are more crucial than those of physical withdrawal. It is the unpredictability of the military factor that makes a long civilian rule in Nigeria very doubtful.[15]

Notes

Chapter 1

1 Claude E. Welch Jr (ed.), *Soldier and State in Africa* (Evanston: Northwestern University Press, 1970).
2 Morris Janowitz, *The Military in the Political Development of New Nations: A Comparative Analysis* (Chicago: University of Chicago: University of Chicago Press, 1964) pp. 27-9.
3 *Ibid.*, p. 1.
4 Samuel P. Huntington, *Political Order in Changing Societies* (New Haven: Yale University Press, 1968), p. 194.
5 J. 'Bayo Adekson, 'Towards Explaining Civil-Military Instability in Contemporary Sub-Saharan Africa: A Comparative Political Model', mimeographed, Department of Political Science, University of Ibadan, 1978.

Adekson's position is supported by Welch in his list of a number of salient factors that precipitate military takeovers. These factors vary in importance in different circumstances. They include the following: declining prestige of the major political forces; the weakening of the broadly based nationalist movements that had hastened the departure of the former colonial power; lessened likelihood of external intervention in the event of military uprising; domestic social antagonisms; economic malaise leading to austerity policies; corruption and inefficiency of government and political party officials; heightened awareness within the military of its power to influence or displace political leaders, Welch, in *Soldier and State in Africa,* pp. 18-34.

In a recent review of the literature on military coups and military regimes in Africa, Decalo concludes that the personal ambitions of military officers or what he calls 'the personal and idiosyncratic elements in military hierarchies' is probably more important than any other explanations of military interventions in Africa. Samuel Decalo, 'Military Coups and Military Regimes in Africa', *Journal of Modern African Studies*, 11, 1 (1973), pp. 105-27.

6 A. H. M. Kirk-Greene, *Crisis and Conflict in Nigeria: A Documentary Sourcebook 1966-1970* (London: Oxford University Press, 1971), vol. 1, pp. 1-24.
7 For the distinction between traditional and modern nationalism see James S. Coleman, *Nigeria: Background to Nationalism* (Berkeley and Los Angeles: University of California Press, 1958).
8 *Ibid.*, p. 275.
9 Kalu Ezera, *Constitutional Developments in Nigeria* (Cambridge: Cambridge

University Press, 1960), pp. 76-84. Okoi Arikpo emphasises the fact that although the constitution gave forceful constitutional validity to the administrative division of the country with three regions, these divisions existed since 1939. Furthermore the constitution did not divide Nigeria into three immutable autonomous regions. The policy of regionalism was directed more to administrative devolution than to political separation of the various groups. Okoi Arikpo, *The Development of Modern Nigeria* (London: Penguin, 1967), pp. 51-2.

10 Obafemi Awolowo, *Path to Nigeria Freedom* (London: Faber and Faber, 1947), pp. 124-34 in particular.

11 For the protest campaign of the only existing country-wide political party, the NCNC, on the constitution, see Coleman, pp. 218 f.

12 Kalu Ezera provides the best account of the various stages of the process in his *Constitutional Developments in Nigeria.*

13 See Coleman, Eme Awa, *Federalism in Nigeria* (Berkeley and Los Angeles: University of California Press, 1964) and O. Awolowo, *Awo – The Autobiography of Chief Obafemi Awolowo* (Cambridge: Cambridge University Press, 1960).

14 Kirk-Greene, p. 11.

15 P. C. Lloyd, 'The Ethnic Background to the Nigerian Civil War' in S. K. Panter-Brick (ed.), *Nigerian Politics and Military Rule: Prelude to Civil War* (London: Institute of Commonwealth Studies, 1970) pp. 1-13.

16 F. E. O. Schwarz Jr, *Nigeria: The Tribes, the Nations, or the Race,* (Cambridge: Massachusetts Institute of Technology, 1965), p. 51.

17 For ethnic rivalry that extended to football matches, publicity of academic achievement of group members in the newspapers, etc. see O. Awolowo, *Awo*, pp. 138-41.

18 See his speech as president of the Ibo State Union, *West African Pilot*, 6 July 1949.

19 See Government of Nigeria; *Proceedings of the General Conference on the Review of the Constitution* (Lagos: Government Printer, 1950).

20 Kirk-Greene, p. 9.

21 See John O. Mackintosh, *Nigerian Government and Politics* (Evanston: Northwestern University Press, 1966), chapter xii on the ethnic complexion of electoral trends in Nigeria.

22 Ezera, pp. 148-64. Ezera, however, realises that except Zik, all members from Lagos constituency were Yoruba – Adeleke Adedoyin, Ibiyinka Olorunnimbe, T. O. S. Benson and A. Adebola.

23 See in particular, Sir Ahmadu Bello, *My Life: The Autobiography of Alhaji Sir Ahmadu Bello, Sardauna of Sokoto* (Cambridge: Cambridge University Press, 1962) pp. 111 f.

24 The figures given by Sir Ahmadu Bello are slightly lower. See *ibid.*

25 Obafemi Awolowo, *Path to Nigeria Freedom,* p. 54.

26 Schwarz, p. 92.

27 Kirk-Greene, p. 92.

28 Even though attention is focussed on (a) Action Group crisis and the treason trial, (b) the census controversy, (c) the 1964-5 federal election and (d) the 1965 Western Election, it is not being suggested that these were the only 'signposts to disaster'. Others such as the Workers' Strike of 1964 and the Lagos University Crisis of March 1965 had their impact on the Nigerian political system.

29 See K. W. J. Post, *The Nigerian Federal Election of 1959* (London: Oxford University Press, 1963) for full details.

30 For details of the formation of the coalition government, see Mackintosh, pp. 420-27.
31 Kenneth Post and Michael Vickers, *Structure and Conflicts in Nigeria: 1960-65* (London: Heinemann, 1973).
32 See *Report of the Coker Commission of Inquiry into the affairs of certain statutory corporations in Western Nigeria, 1962* (Lagos: Ministry of Information, 1962).
33 NNDP was the name used by Herbert Macaulay's group between 1920 and the early 'forties.
34 There is some justification in the conclusion of Mackintosh that Balewa's full backing of Akintola throughout this crisis can be seen in the former's disappointment in Awolowo's behaviour as leader of opposition in the federal legislature, particularly his role on the defence pact.
35 Kirk-Greene, p. 16.
36 This of course did not result in the dissolution of the NPC/NCNC coalition at the federal level. The NCNC members of the federal cabinet for various tactical reasons remained in their posts.
37 Kirk-Greene, p. 21.
38 See *Daily Times*, 2 April 1964 for the charges against the Railway Corporation and Ikejiani's reply.
39 Soon after the NNA came into being, two members of the NNDP, (Rosiji and Akinloye) in the House of Representatives were appointed federal minister by the prime minister without any consultation with NCNC, the other partner in the federal coalition government.
40 This is not the first time that secession has been used as a political weapon. As pointed out above, Northern political leaders used it in 1950 and again in 1953, the West used it on the issue of separation of Lagos from Western Region in 1957.
41 The distribution of seats was as follows: North 167, East 70, West 57, Mid-West 14 and Lagos 4.
42 Douglas G. Anglin, 'Brinkmanship in Nigeria: The Federal Election of 1964-65' *International Journal*, Spring 1965, p. 173.

Three weeks before election day the president in a 'Dawn Address' to the nation had advised the leaders that 'if they have decided to destroy our national unity, then they should summon a round-table conference to decide how our national assets should be divided before they seal their doom by satisfying their lust for office.' He concluded, 'Should the politicians fail to heed this warning, then I will venture the prediction that the experience of the Democratic Republic of the Congo will be child's play, if it ever comes to our turn to play such a tragic role.' *West African Pilot*, 11 December 1964.

On 28 December 1964, the army paraded round Lagos as a warning to all. The following day the prime minister met with all heads of the armed forces to discuss precautionary measures. The misconception of the president that he had control over the armed forces was corrected by the service chiefs.
43 Anglin, p. 187.
44 Mackintosh, p. 550.
45 B. J. Dudley, 'Western Nigeria and the Nigerian Crisis' in Panter-Brick, pp. 94-5.
46 After the election, the price was reduced to ₦130.00 per ton — ₦50 below selling price.
47 *Nigerian Daily Sketch*, 13 September 1965.
48 William Gutteridge, *Military Institutions and Power in the New States* (London: 1964), p. 105.

49 See J. 'Bayo Adekson, 'Military Organisation in Multi-Ethnically Segmented Societies: A Theoretical Study', Ph.D. dissertation, Brandeis University, Waltham, USA, May 1976, especially pp. 88-130.
50 *Daily Times,* 11 December 1964.
51 A. R. Luckham, 'The Nigerian Military: Disintegration or Integration?' in Panter-Brick, p.63.
52 *Ibid.,* p. 77.

Chapter 2

1 Mahmud-M. Tukur, 'Values and Public Affairs: The Relevance of the Sokoto Caliphate Experience to the Transformation of the Nigerian Polity', Ph.D. thesis, Ahmadu Bello University, Zaria, 1977.
2 See, however, A. H. M. Kirk-Greene, *Crisis and Conflict in Nigeria: A Documentary Sourcebook, 1966-70* vol. I, pp. 115-24.
3 Only one Ibo army officer is known to have been killed in the January coup.
4 It has been observed that even though he was a congenial man, Ironsi was never regarded as very intelligent. His position as General Officer Commanding was earned not because of his ability but his seniority and political considerations. See J. P. Mackintosh, *Nigerian Government and Politics*, pp. 589-96.
5 B. J. Dudley has put it this way: 'Faced with possibly conflicting opinion and advice, and educationally ill-equipped to assess and evaluate them, Ironsi might be expected to turn to some group for advice and suggestion . . . such group . . . was made up of men like Mr. Francis Nwokedi, Mr. Gabriel Onyuike, and Dr. Pius Okigbo.' See B. J. Dudley, *Instability and Political Order: Politics and Crisis in Nigeria* (Ibadan: University of Ibadan Press, 1973) pp. 118-19. For an exhaustive analysis of some of the actions taken by Ironsi, see *Ibid.*, chapter 6.
6 *Ibid.*, p. 132.
7 See *Verbatim Report of the Proceedings of the Supreme Military Council Meeting, Aburi, Ghana, 4-5 January 1967.*
8 See Kirk-Greene for Ojukwu's terms to the National Conciliation Committee.
9 *Ibid.*, pp. 427-44 for Ojukwu's address to the Consultative Assembly.
10 See Oyeleye Oyediran, 'Reorganisation of the Nigerian Federation: Its Background and Administrative Problems', *Philippine Journal of Public Administration*, XVIII, 3, 226-44 and A. A. Ayida, 'The Nigerian Revolution: 1966-1976', presidential address delivered at the 13th Annual Conference of the Nigerian Economic Society, April 1973, for the government strategy in the reorganisation.
11 Dudley has observed that many of the foreigners who reported on the war had a limited knowledge of West Africa and in particular Nigeria. 'Inescapably then', he continues, 'their activities displayed varying degrees of ignorance if not bias.' e.g. Auberon Waugh and Suzanne Cronje, *Biafra: Britain's Shame* (London: Michael Joseph, 1969). Dudley, p. 202.
12 John Stremlau, *The International Politics of the Nigerian Civil War* (Princeton: Princeton University Press, 1977).
13 *Ibid.*, p. 221.
14 Dudley, pp. 205-6.
15 It was believed in federal quarters that £7 million had been paid by a French

oil company to the Eastern Regional government in December 1966.
16 G. Thayer, *The War Business* (London: Palladin, 1970).
17 Dudley, p. 207.
18 See Kirk-Greene, vol. II, pp. 58ff for the various British pressures.
19 *Ibid.*, p. 56.
20 Kennedy Lindsay, 'Political Factors in Biafran Relief', *Venture*, vol. 22, no. 2, February 1970.
21 Kirk-Greene, p. 56.
22 For an exhaustive analysis of the role of British pressure groups on the Nigerian civil war see William A. Ajibola, *Foreign Policy and Public Opinion* (Ibadan: Ibadan University Press, 1978). Other writings by Nigerians on the international involvement include Jide Aluko, 'The Civil War and Nigerian Foreign Policy', *Political Quarterly*, April 1971; Oye Ogunbadejo, 'Civil Strife in International Relations: A Case Study of the Nigerian Civil War, 1967-70', Ph.D. thesis, University of London, 1974.
23 *Observer*, 28 April 1968.
24 De Gaulle said during an interview in Paris in September 1968 that even though France supported Biafra, 'she has not performed the act which to her, would be decisive of recognizing the Biafran Republic, because she regards the gestation of Africa as a matter for the Africans first and foremost'. Kirk-Greene, vol. II, p. 329.
25 J. de St Jorre, *The Nigerian Civil War* (London: Hodder and Stoughton, 1972) p. 347.
26 See de Gaulle's interview referred to in note 24, where he asked 'Why should the Ibos, who are generally Christians, who live in the south in a certain way, who have their own language . . . depend on another ethnic fraction of the Federation?'
27 Stremlau, p. 116.
28 See B. J. Dudley, chapter 8, titled 'The Paradox of Misplaced Agreement' for a full discussion of the Aburi agreement.
29 Stremlau, p. 46.
30 *Ibid.*, p. 92.
31 See full details of the OAU resolution and the communiqué issued at the end of the OAU consultative mission visit in Kirk-Greene, p. 172-4.
32 *Ibid.*, pp. 229-32.
33 *Ibid.*, pp. 221-8.
34 *New Nigerian*, 13 September 1969.
35 Stremlau, p. 294.
36 Quoted in *ibid.*, p. 233.
37 See the proceedings of a Conference on National Reconstruction and Development held at the University of Ibadan, 24-29 March 1969 in A. A. Ayida and H. M. A. Onitiri (eds.) *Reconstruction and Development in Nigeria* (Ibadan: NISER, 1971).

Chapter 3

1 The Nigerian experience between 1966 and 1969 is a vivid example. This is elaborated upon later in this chapter.
2 The only politically uncertain period between 1970 and 1979 was the February 1976 abortive coup in which the then head of state, General

Mohammed, was assassinated. The 1975 coup was essentially a peaceful palace coup.

3 The government now owns 55 per cent of equity in oil-producing companies and, through the Nigerian National Petroleum Corporation, engages in oil prospecting and exploitation.

4 For a critique of the role of the modernising soldier with respect to developing countries, see Adekson (1978).

5 See B. J. Dudley, 'The Military and Development', *Nigerian Journal of Economic and Social Studies*, 13, 2 (1971), and J. 'Bayo Adekson, 'The Nigerian Military and Social Expenditures' in *Democracy in Nigeria: Past, Present and Future* (Proceedings of the 5th Annual Conference of the NPSA at Ife, 1978).

6 See O. Aboyade, 'The Economy of Nigeria' in P. Robson and D. Lury (eds.) *The Economics of Africa* (London: Allen & Unwin, 1969).

7 The population data used is based on the 1963 census.

8 This is a defective index since it covers only urban areas and neglects the rural areas which have a greater share of the population. The implicit GDP deflation is even less reliable in Nigeria.

9 The basic balance concept is used here (current + capital account). This is a more relevant economic concept when dealing with the performance of an economy.

10 The development objectives are stated fully in the First National Development Plan 1962-68.

11 The marketing boards contributed significantly to the exploitation of the peasant farmer. See Helleiner (1966).

12 The National Supply Company was created by the federal government to import food on a massive scale so as to dampen rising food prices. The activities of the company have had little impact on food prices.

13 The liberal food import policy of the government has even stifled local production – for example, of rice.

14 Due to inadequate domestic supply of oils the government banned the export of groundnut oil and palm oil in 1977.

15 The decree allows an individual to own up to 500 hectares of farming land and up to 5000 hectares of grazing land through the acquisition of a Customary Right of Occupancy. Some politicians have expressed their wish to abolish the decree if they come to power in October 1979, for selfish reasons.

16 See Industrial Survey 1970 published by the Federal Office of Statistics.

17 See the proceedings of the symposium organised by the Nigerian Economic Society in 1974 on the indigenisation decree. See also P. Collins, 'The Policy of Indigenisation: An Overall View', *Quarterly Journal of Administration*, ix, 2 (1975).

18 Approximately ₦1 billion each was allocated to the power sector and telecommunications and ₦7 billion for the transport sector. In other words, about one-third of total capital expenditure in the Third Plan period was devoted to infrastructural development.

19 For an in-depth analysis of the power sector, see A. Iwayemi, 'Public Sector Participation in Economic Activity – The Electric Power Supply Industry', presented at the Annual Conference of the Nigerian Economic Society, Lagos (1979).

20 See Adekson for comparison with social expenditure.

21 The data on defence/GNP for Canada in 1971 was 1.8, Brazil 2.5, West Germany 2.9, France 3.1, South Korea 5.1. The source of the information is G. Kennedy (1975).

Chapter 5

1 Quoted in A. A. Ayida, *The Federal Civil Service and Nation Building* (Lagos; Federal Government Press, 1976), p. 6.
2 See H. H. Gerth & C. W. Mills, *From Max Weber: Essays in Sociology* (New York: O. U. P., 1946), p. 43.
3 Fred W. Riggs, 'The Structure of Government and Administrative Reform' in Ralph Braibanti (ed.) *Political and Administrative Development* (Durham, N. C.: Duke University Press, 1969), p. 244.
4 The common note in the varied definition of Development Administration is that it refers both to the 'efforts of a government to carry out programmes designed to reshape its physical, human, and cultural environment, and the struggle to enlarge a government's capacity to engage in such programmes'.
5 Milton J. Esman, 'CAG and the Study of Public Administration' in Fred W. Riggs (ed.), *Frontiers of Development Administration* (Durham, N. C.: Duke University Press, 1971), p. 62.
6 Brian Loveman, 'The Comparative Administration Group, Development Administration and Anti Development', *PAR* no. 6 (Nov./Dec. 1976), p. 619.
7 C. O. Lawson, 'The Role of Civil Servants in a Military Regime' and 'Army, Civil Servants have a stake in Government' in *Daily Times*, 11 and 12 December 1973.
8 See among others, Abdo I. Baaklini, 'The Military-Civilian Bureaucracies, the Middle-Class and Development: An Organisational Perspective', *Occasional Paper Series, CADSC*, SUNNY, Albany 1974; and Ruth First, *Power in Africa* (New York: Pantheon Books, 1970).
9 Esman, p. 71.
10 Quoted in Robin Luckham, *The Nigerian Military, 1960-1967* (Cambridge: Cambridge University Press, 1971), p. 254.
11 Such considerations influenced the Udoji Commission in creating middle and senior management positions in the civil service in harmony with the practice in the private sector.
12 See among others, R. C. Fried, *Comparative Political Institutions* (New York: Macmillan, 1966), pp. 60-67; Ruth First, p. 113; Gerald A. Heeger, *The Politics of Underdevelopment* (New York: St. Martin's Press, 1974), pp. 107-28. The same conclusion is served by the analysis of the organisation and structural characteristics of the Nigerian military attempted by Robin Luckham, pp. 96-8.
13 See Ayida.
14 Top Ibo federal civil servants were alleged to have inspired the programme for sectional hegemonic interests.
15 See S. O. Olugbemi, *Military Leadership and Political Integration in Nigeria, 1966-1976*, unpublished D.P.A. dissertation, State University of New York, Albany, 1978, pp. 106-7 and 137-8; also see *Federal Republic of Nigeria, 1966* (Lagos: Federal Ministry of Information, 1967).
16 Particularly those of them who fled the federal public service from July to October 1966.
17 Some civil servants or public officials at least were alleged to have encouraged the inflation of the returns from some of the Northern states.
18 P. C. Asiodu, *The Future of the Federal and State Civil Services in the Context of the Twelve States Structure* (Benin City: Mid-West Newspapers Corporation, 1971), p. 12.
19 This view of the pre-military political class is widely shared in the civil

service. See for instance, M. A. Tokunboh, 'The Challenge of Public Service' in *Quarterly Journal of Administration*, Vol. 11, No. 2, (Jan. 1968), pp. 71-8.

20 See Esman; and W. F. Ilchman and N. T. Uphoff, *The Political Economy of Change* (Berkeley: University of California Press, 1970), pp. 131-2.

21 Esman.

22 *Ibid.*

23 Federal Republic of Nigeria, *Third National Development Plan, 1975-80* (Lagos: Federal Ministry of Economic Development and Reconstruction, 1975), pp. 11-16.

24 See Olugbemi, p. 304.

25 The failure of the leadership to demonstrate selfless and dedicated leadership to the 'nation' must account for the widespread indiscipline which characterised much of the military interregnum.

26 The questions to be asked are (1) whether these 'facts after the event' were not known to the officials at the planning stage; (2) if they were known, what reasons compelled the officials to stretch their capability to the extent manifest in the plan documents?

27 See these newspaper editorials: *New Nigerian* of 1 August 1974 and the *Daily Times* of 12 August 1974 on misplaced priorities in our national development efforts.

28 See Federal Republic of Nigeria, *Second National Development Plan, 1970-74* (Lagos: Central Planning Office, Federal Ministry of Economic Development and Reconstruction, 1970), p. 145.

29 For a sample of such disappointing performances, see Olugbemi, pp. 250-51.

30 *Ibid*, pp. 215-52.

31 *Ibid*, p. 252.

32 Fred W. Riggs, *Thailand: The Modernisation of a Bureaucratic Policy* (Honolulu: The East-West Centre Press, 1966), p. 131.

33 See Olugbemi, pp. 258-61.

34 *Ibid*, pp. 241-5.

35 O. Aboyade, 'Approaches to Industrialisation; The Cases of Mexico and Nigeria', paper presented to the Dakar Conference on Strategies of Economic Development in Africa Compared with Latin America, 1973.

Chapter 6

1 *Nigerian Tribune*, Wednesday, 19 March 1969.

2 *Sunday Times*, Sunday, 23 March 1969 (emphasis is ours).

3 *Nigerian Tribune*, 28 August 1974.

4 Olu Onagoruwa, *The Amakiri Case* (Lagos: Daily Times Publication, 1977).

Chapter 7

1 Douglas G. Anglin, 'Nigeria: Political Non-Alignment and Economic Alignment', *Journal of Modern African Studies*, 2, 2 (1964), pp. 147-263.

2 John de StJorre, *The Nigerian Civil War*.

3 *Ibid.*

4 *Ibid.*

5 *Ibid.*

6 P. N. Okigbo, *Africa and the Common Market* (Longman, Green and Co. Ltd, 1967), pp. 94-8.

7 Adebisi Ajayi, *Daily Times*, 17 March 1972.

8 Between 1960 and 1968, Nigeria's world exports rose by £42 million. During this same period of growth in total Nigerian world exports, Nigeria's exports to the UK dropped by £18.8 million and this represented a 19.2 per cent drop in the UK's share of total Nigerian exports. But Nigeria's exports to the EEC appreciated by £43.7 million and represented a 14 per cent increase in the EEC's share of total Nigerian exports. If one combines EEC and UK share of Nigeria's exports in 1968, one finds that the expanded or new EEC that included Britain commanded £155.9 million out of the £211 million of Nigeria's world exports. This showed an impressive 73.9 per cent of all Nigeria's world exports. Thus the new EEC emerged as a market which Nigeria could hardly ignore or treat lightly.

9 *The Second National Development Plan, 1970-74*.

10 Speech by the Honourable Commissioner for Industry at the opening of the national conference on 'Nigeria and the World', NIIA, Lagos, 27 January 1976.

11 *Ibid.*

12 *New Nigerian*, 7 August 1976.

13 H. Idowu, *Times International*, 2 August 1976.

14 J. N. Garba, 'Foreign Policy and Problems of Economic Development', an address presented at the University of Ibadan, 19 February 1977, by the federal commissioner for external affairs. See *Daily Times*, 24 February 1977.

15 *Ibid.*

16 *Ibid.*

17 The cost of FESTAC excluding some capital and recurrent costs incurred by the Federal Government Agencies came to ₦141 million.

18 Idowu.

19 Nigeria-Senegal relations improved in September 1976 when Senegal returned to the FESTAC.

20 Some of the main reasons which led to this demand for annexation were that by the early 'sixties Nigerians formed a mjority of the island population of Fernando Po, and the security of Nigeria from the sea was threatened by Fernando Po being in the hands of a hostile power.

21 Opponents of Zaire struggling for Katango (Shaba) independence, trained in Angola, and used Angola as a base to attack Shaba and seek to capture it.

Chapter 8

1 Douglas G. Anglin, 'Nigeria: Political Non-alignment and Economic Alignment'.

2 A. B. Akinyemi, *Foreign Policy and Federalism: The Nigerian Experience*, Ibadan University Press, 1974: Caleb I. Akinyele, 'Angola-American Liberalism as a Dominant Factor in Nigerian Foreign Policy, 1960-1966', Ph.D. thesis, University of Washington, 1969; Ibrahim Gambari, 'The Domestic Politics of Major Foreign Policy Issues in Nigeria', Ph.D. thesis, New York, Columbia University, 1974.

3 Akinyemi.

4 One statement on US–Nigerian relations at this time was officially headed 'Federal Government Condemns Attempt to Insult the Intelligence of African Nations'. The *Daily Times* captioned it 'SHUT UP', 7 January 1976. The *Daily Sketch's* editorial was titled 'Shameless America', 8 January 1976.

5 *West Africa*, 23 October 1978, p. 2077.

6 After-dinner speech delivered to the participants at the Nigerian Institute of International Affairs conference on 'Nigeria and the World'. Text in NIIA library.
7 *New Nigerian*, 14 February 1978, p. 1, 'Brigadier Garba's Annual Report'.

Chapter 9

1 S. K. Panter-Brick & P. F. Dawson, 'The Creation of New States in the North' in S. K. Panter-Brick (ed.), *Nigerian Politics and Military Rule: Prelude to Civil War* (London: University of London for the Institute of Commonwealth Studies, 1970) p. 138.
2 Local government in Nigeria as much as in Great Britain pre-dated central government. But it was only after the famous despatch from the Secretary of State for the Colonies, Rt Hon. A. Creech-Jones, to the Governors of the African Territories on 25 February 1947 that local government began to evolve a modern, representative character. After the adoption of the Macpherson constitution in 1951 the Regional Governments in Enugu, Ibadan and Kaduna in that order reformed their local government system and it is from these reforms that we should date the philosophical conceptions referred to.
3 E. E. Akpan, 'The Development of Local Government in Eastern Nigeria', *Journal of Administration Overseas*, IV, 2 (April 1965), pp. 118-27.
4 S. W. C. Holland, 'Recent Development in Local Government in Eastern Nigeria', *Journal of Administration Overseas*, 11, 1 (January 1963).
5 There has been some controversy over the relationship between local government and democracy. The debate is summarised in (i) L. J. Sharpe, 'Theories of Local Government' in L. D. Feldman & M. D. Goldrick (eds.), *Politics and Government of Urban Canada* (Toronto: Methuen, 1969), pp. 348-58; (ii) Brian C. Smith, 'The Justification of Local Government' in L. D. Feldman & M. D. Goldrick.
6 See E. A. Gboyega, 'Local Government and Political Integration in the Western State 1952-1972', unpublished Ph.D. thesis, University of Ibadan, 1975, pp. 95-9.
7 Brian C. Smith, 'The Evolution of Local Government in Northern Nigeria', *Journal of Administration Overseas,* VI, 1 (January 1967), pp. 28-42. See also Ronald Wraith, *Local Government in West Africa* (London: George Allen and Unwin, 1964), p. 128.
8 L. Gray Cowan, *Local Government in West Africa* (New York: Columbia University Press, 1958), p. 81.
9 See for example: (i) C. S. Whitaker Jr, *The Politics of Tradition: Continuity and Change in Northern Nigeria* (Princeton: Princeton University Press, 1970), pp. 177-309; (ii) B. J. Dudley, *Parties and Politics in Northern Nigeria* (London: Frank Cass, 1968), chapter VII.
10 Dudley, p. 256.
11 By local administration we mean the governing of local communities essentially by means of local agents appointed by and responsible to the state or central government.
12 South Eastern State Official Document, No. 7 of 1973.
13 Divisional Administration Edict No. 18 of 1971, East Central State of Nigeria Official Gazette, no. 33, vol. 2, 9 August 1971.
14 Ibid.

15 Development Administration Edict No. 26 of 1974, Midwestern State of Nigeria Gazette, no. 72, vol. II.
16 1972/73 Budget Speech by the Administrator, East Central State News Official Text No. 28 (Enugu: Ministry of Information, 24 April 1972).
17 The government claimed that the different levels were not tiers of local administration but channels of control, contacts and co-operation with the people. This can only be regarded as a play on words.
18 Section 5 (2) of Development Administration Edict 1974, No. 26, Midwestern State of Nigeria Gazette, no. 74, vol. II.
19 See Emmanuel E. Osuji, 'Community Development and Political Development in the East Central State of Nigeria', unpublished Ph.D. thesis, Department of Political Science, University of Ibadan, September 1975, especially pp. 227-349.
20 Richard Victor Emonfonmwan, 'Aspects of Local Government: The Role of the Resident in Development Administration in Benin East Division Bendel State', unpublished essay, Department of Political Science, University of Ibadan, June 1976.
21 See *An Introduction to the New System of Local Government Council System in the Western State of Nigeria* (Ibadan: Government Printer, 1971).
22 *Report of the Commission of Inquiry into the Disturbances which occured in certain parts of the Western State of Nigeria in the month of December 1968* (Ibadan: Government Printer, 1969), p. 113.
23 *An Introduction to the New Local Government Council System in the Western State of Nigeria* (Ibadan: Government Printer, n.d., pp. 2 and 11.
24 Oyeleye Oyediran, 'Council Manager Plan: The Experience of Western Nigeria', *Philippine Journal of Administration*, XXI (forthcoming).
25 Oyeleye Oyediran, 'The Chosen Few: Policy Makers in the New Local Government System in Western Nigeria', *Quarterly Journal of Administration*, VII, 4, (July 1974).
26 Oyediran, 'Council Manager Plan'.
27 *New Nigerian*, 22 February 1967.
28 Edward Baun, 'Recent Administrative Reform in Local Government in Northern Nigeria', *Journal of Developing Areas*, VII, 1 (October 1972), p.8.
29 C. S. Whitaker Jr, *The Politics of Tradition: Continuity and Change in Northern Nigeria, 1946-1966* (Princeton: Princeton University Press, 1970), p. 271.
30 'The North's Silent Revolution', *West Africa*, no. 2819, 25 June 1971.
31 Ali Yahaya, 'Enhancing Local Government Performance: Udoji Recipe', *Journal of Public Affairs*, vol. V (May/October 1975).
32 Oyeleye Oyediran, 'The Public Service Review Commission on Local Government and Administration' in Ladipo Adamolekun & Alex Gboyega (eds.), *Leading Issues in Nigerian Public Service* (Ile-Ife: Ife University Press, forthcoming).
33 Nearly all the edicts were actually promulgated in December 1976 or soon after, but all of them had retroactive effect from September 1976.
34 The proportion of elected members varies from state to state and ranges from 75 per cent to 90 per cent.
35 This double investiture is extracted from the Borno State's Local Government Edict 1976. But the situation is the same for all states.
36 Constitution of the Federal Republic of Nigeria, 1979, Section 7 (1).
37 *Guidelines for Local Government Reforms* (Kaduna: Government Printer, 1976,) Foreword.
38 Text of address delivered by Brigadier Shehu Musa Yar 'Adua, chief of staff,

Supreme Headquarters, at the meeting of commissioners for local government at Port Harcourt on Tuesday, 21 November 1978. *Daily Times,* 23 November 1978, p. 26.

Chapter 10

1 R. J. May, *Federation and Fiscal Adjustment* (Oxford: Oxford University Press, 1969), p. 161.
2 *Report of the Interim Revenue Allocation Review Commission* (Apapa: Nigerian National Press Limited, 1969), p. 23. Henceforth referred to as Dina Report.
3 *Ibid.*, pp. 6-8.
4 *Report of the Technical Committee on Revenue Allocation*, (Lagos, December 1978), vol. 1, p. 48 (mimeographed).
5 S. A. Aluko, 'Nigeria Federal Finance: A General Review', *Quarterly Journal of Administration*, IV, 2 (January 1970), p. 79.
6 O. Teriba, 'Nigerian Revenue Allocation Experience, 1952-65: A Study in Intergovernmental Fiscal and Financial Relations', *Nigerian Journal of Economic and Social Studies*, 8, 3 November 1966), p. 362.

Professor Samuel Aluko, an economist, has further emphasised the political content of revenue allocation particularly in Nigeria when he said, 'The problem of federalism in Nigeria is not really the problem of the financial weakness of the federal government vis-à-vis that of the states . . . but that of the lack of political will and the administrative incompetence which the federal government has always demonstrated even during this period of military emergency and centralised rule'. He continued, 'In all federations, the structure of the political parties, more than the distribution of fiscal and constitutional powers, has determined the constitutional and fiscal effectiveness of the federal government. This is why the *political imperatives have to be recognised in any serious discussion of the federal-state fiscal relations.'* (Emphasis is ours). Aluko, pp. 81-2.

7 *New Nigerian*, 15 March 1975.
8 Adedotun O. Phillips, 'Revenue Allocation in Nigeria, 1970-80', *Nigerian Journal of Economic and Social Studies*, 17, 2 (July 1975), p. 4.
9 As Oyovbaire has pointed out, the three most populous of the northern states resented this discriminatory treatment. These were Kano, North Eastern and North Western states. This may have been one of the reasons for the Dina Commission the following year. Samuel Egite Oyovbaire, 'The Politics of Revenue Allocation' in S. K. Panter-Brick (ed.), *Soldiers and Oil: The Political Transformation of Nigeria* (London: Frank Cass, 1978), p. 228.
10 It was the committee itself that decided on its chairman, Chief I. O. Dina.
11 The Dina Report, p. 1.
12 *Ibid.*, p. 2.
13 *Ibid.*, p. 3.
14 *Ibid.*, p. 5.
15 Phillips, p. 8.
16 *Ibid.*
17 *Report of the Technical Committee*, pp. 2-3.
18 *Guidelines for Local Government Reform.*
19 *Report of the Technical Committee*, pp. 85-6.
20 *Ibid.*, p. 87.

21 The federal military government accepted the new arrangements but rejected the weighting allotted to each principle on the grounds that 'the relative weighting of the five new criteria is a political decision'. See *Government Views on the Report of the Technical Committee on Revenue Allocation* (Lagos: Federal Ministry of Information, 1978), p. 7.

22 *Report of the Technical Committee*, p. 94.

23 Members of the Technical Committee were asked by government to be available to present their report to the Constituent Assembly. The latter, however, rejected the offer, claiming that enough competent economists are members.

24 See *Proceedings of the Constituent Assembly*, No. 96, Monday, 29 May 1978, for the contributions by Omoruyi and Okibgo.

25 Candido is a pen name used by a top member of the management group in the New Nigerian Newspapers which has its headquarters in Kaduna.

26 *New Nigerian*, Wednesday, 3 May 1978.

27 *New Nigerian*, Wednesday, 14 June 1978.

28 Aaron Wildarsky, 'Political Implications of Budgetary Reform', *Public Administration Review*, vol. 21 (Autumn 1961), pp. 183-90.

Chapter 11

1 A modified form of the general and theoretical base of our discussions here was formulated in J. 'Bayo Adekson, 'Succession to Leadership under Military Regimes in West Africa: A Comparative Analysis', unpublished manuscript, Department of Politics, Brandeis University, Waltham, Mass., 1970.

2 Cf. Samuel E. Finer, *The Man on Horseback: The Role of the Military in Politics* (London: Pall Mall, 1962), *passim*.

3 For a recent typology surprisingly paralleling our own here, see Valerie P. Bennett, 'Patterns of Demilitarisation in Africa', *Quarterly Journal of Administration*, IX, 1 (October 1974), pp. 5-15.

4 Professor Finer has postulated that the drive behind military disengagement is provided by what he describes as 'the culmination of three conditions: the disintegration of the original conspiratorial group, the growing divergence of interests between the junta of rulers and those military who remain as active heads of the fighting services, and the political difficulties of the regime', *The Man on Horseback*, p. 191. Actually, the Finer thesis applies more to soldiers operating under conditions defined by our first and second types of disengagement. For one thing, it rules out those soldiers who, either because they remain genuinely professionally oriented (their initial intervention in politics notwithstanding), or because they belong to that rare category of men who have power without wanting it (i.e. the *cincinnati* of this world), tend to voluntarily withdraw from political rule at the slightest opportunity. Such soldiers are invariably found operating in our third-type conditions of disengagement.

5 See below for a further elaboration on this point.

6 For this, he was removed and replaced by Brigadier A. A. Afrifa as chairman. See *Legon Observer*, 11-24 April 1969.

7 Thomas S. Cox, *Civil-Military Relations in Sierra Leone: A Case Study of African Soldiers in Politics* (Cambridge, Mass.: Harvard University Press, 1976).

8 This programme, setting out the timetable for the military's phased withdrawal from political rule, was the crux of Murtala's 1 October 1975 national address, as reported in *Daily Times*, 1 October 1975.

9 On this, see the front page comment written by this author, entitled 'Towards Disengaging the Military from Politics', in *The New Nationalist*, 5, nos. 3 & 4, (University of Ibadan, June & July 1978), p. 1.

10 This section is expanded from J. 'Bayo Adekson, 'The Role of the Nigerian Armed Forces in the Ensuing Competition between the New Political Parties', *Afriscope* (forthcoming, November 1978).

11 J. 'Bayo Adekson, 'Military Clauses of the New Nigerian Draft Constitution: A Critical Analysis', mimeographed, Institute of Administration, Ahmadu Bello University, Zaria, 1977, pp. 19-21.

12 For proof of this, see, for example, *Awo: The Autobiography of Chief Obafemi Awolowo*, and the address he delivered as the then chancellor of Ife, *Daily Times*, 21 August 1975.

13 And was widely reported at the time by most Nigerian national dailies.

14 Perhaps the very nature of the pre-coup Ghanaian political situation rendered it wellnigh impossible for the succeeding military government to appear impartial if it so wished. In a country once governed by a one-party regime, legislated into being in spite of articulate opposition from other civilian groups, no successive government could appear impartial whose very justification for existence was opposition to the former regime.

15 The said amendments were announced by Lieutenant-General Obasanjo in his 21 September 1978 speech promulgating the new Nigerian constitution, lifting the state of emergency, and reactivating political party activities. Quoted, *New Nigerian*, Friday, 22 September 1978, pp. 1, 3, 13, 15.

16 For an analysis of the old 50-25-21-4 military quota principle under the four-regional federal political system in use before 1966, and the contribution of this to the subsequent inter-ethnic crisis and conflicts in the 1966-70 period, see J. 'Bayo Adekson, 'Military Organisation in Multi-Ethnically Segmented Society: A Theoretical Study, with Particular Reference to Three Sub-Saharan African Cases', Ph.D. dissertation, Brandeis University, Waltham, Mass., (May 1976), ch. IV.

17 The original draft which was submitted by the CDC had similarly called for the entrenchment of some of these provisions. See *Report of the Constitution Drafting Committee Containing the Draft Constitution*, vol. I (Lagos: Federal Ministry of Information, 1976), ch. VI, part II. The entrenchment of the NYSC provision may be said to have been implied in ch. II, par. 9 as well as ch. IV, part VIII, para. 169 (1) and (2). The only new addition, then, is the Land Use Decree which was promulgated after the original draft constitution had been submitted.

18 Soldiers have the right to vote, for example, in India, Britain, USA and France.

19 Edwin Lieuwen, *Generals Vs. Presidents: Neomilitarism in Latin America* (New York: Praeger, 1964).

20 Including Major-Generals Adeyinka Adebayo, Hassan Usman Katsina and Olufemi Olutoye, Brigadiers George Kurubo and Benjamin Adekunle, Colonels Hillary Njoku and Anthony Ochefu, Lieutenant-Colonel T. Oyedele, as well as Inspector-General of Police Sam Kalem and Deputy Inspector-General of Police T. A. Fagbola. These are easily the most visible ones. Besides, there are hundreds of other senior officers either dismissed or retired for their participation in the 'Biafran' war after 1970, for involvement with the former Gowon regime immediately following the 29 July 1975 coup, or as part of the 'general purge' of November 1975. For now, most of these are politically dormant. In addition, one should mention the thousands of NCOs, infantrymen, and temporarily recalled ex-servicemen discharged, though in piecemeal, as part of the post-war demobilisation exercise. The political role

of all these ex-military individuals will make a very interesting study, but can probably not be done thoroughly until more details of their involvement become available.

21 Finer, p. 243.

22 *West Africa*, no. 2647, Saturday, 24 February 1968, p. 209.

23 Although Lieutenant-General Theophilus Danjuma, as the army chief of staff, has argued that strictly speaking, since pre-1966 Nigeria was not a 'democratic policy', one cannot talk of a 'return' to democracy in Nigeria after 1979. See his foreword to Brigadier David Jemibewon, *Combatants in Government* (Ibadan: Heinemann Educational Books, 1978).

24 This distinction was also made by K. A. B. Jones-Quartey in 'An Interview with the Prime Minister of Sierra Leone Siaka Stevens', *Legon Observer*, IV, 10 (9-22 May 1969), p. 11.

25 This, of course, will be in addition to three other major sets of explanatory variables postulated in J. 'Bayo Adekson, 'Toward Explaining Civil-Military Instability in Contemporary Sub-Saharan Africa: A Comparative Political Model', mimeographed, Department of Political Science, University of Ibadan, 1977.

26 *Legon Observer*, III 12 (7-20 June 1978), p. 18.

27 *Ibid.* However, this 'concessions against re-entry' thesis was rejected by the well known Ghanaian historian Professor Adu Boahene among others because, as he put it, 'it is not brigadiers and commanders of army alone who can stage coups – in fact they hardly do'. See his rejoinder in *Legon Observer*, IV, 18 (1-5 September 1969), pp. 6-20.

28 A. K. Ocran, *A Myth is Broken* (London: Longman, 1968).

29 W. F. Gutteridge, *Military Regimes in Africa* (London: Methuen, 1975), pp. 82-3.

30 Michael F. Lofchie, 'The Uganda Coup – Class Action by the Military', *Journal of Modern African Studies*, 10, 1 (1972).

31 For further elaboration of this, see J. 'Bayo Adekson, 'Machiavelli and the Military: The Prince and the Psychology of Empty Power', in *Planning Strategy for Nigeria in the Eighties* (NISER & Federal Ministry of Economic Development, forthcoming).

32 J. 'Bayo Adekson, 'The Nigerian Military and Social Expenditures', in *Democracy in Nigeria: Past, Present and Future* (Proceedings of the 5th Annual Conference of the NPSA, 1978).

33 Federal Republic of Nigeria: *The Constitution of the Federal Republic of Nigeria 1979* (Lagos: Ministry of Information, 1979).

34 Adekson, 'Military Clauses of the New Nigerian Draft Constitution', p. 22.

Chapter 12

1 As will be pointed out later, opinion was not unanimous about the representativeness of the Constitution Draft Committee.

2 The Constitution (Suspension and Modification) Decree 1966 (Decree No. 1, 1966).

3 See E. A. Keay, 'Legal and Constitutional Changes in Nigeria under the Military Government', *Journal of African Law*, 10, 2 (Summer 1966).

4 See for example J. P. Mackintosh, *Nigerian Government and Politics*, 1.

5 *Ibid.*, p. 51.

6 *West Africa,* 5 March 1966, p. 279.
7 The other Study Groups were on (i) National Unity, and (ii) National Planning.
8 *West Africa*, 2 April 1966, p. 391.
9 *Ibid.*
10 B. J. Dudley, *Instability and Political Order: Politics and Crisis in Nigeria* (Ibadan: Ibadan University Press, 1973), p. 121.
11 Acheampong's military government in Ghana attempted to impose on Ghana precisely that through the Union Government concept.
12 *West Africa*, 12 March 1966, p. 303.
13 Dudley, pp. 118-43.
14 *West Africa*, 19 February 1966, p. 205.
15 The Public Order Decree 1966 (Decree No. 33 of 24 May 1966). Supplement to Official Gazette Extraordinary No. 51, 24 May 1966 – Part A.
16 The Constitution (Suspension and Modification) (No. 5) Decree 1966. Supplement to the Official Gazette Extraordinary No. 51, 24 May 1966.
17 The incumbents of the positions continued in their offices.
18 This was altered as it affected the eastern group of provinces by the military governor, Lieutenant-General O. Ojukwu.
19 The rebellion resulted in the death of several other Ibo military officers in other military locations outside the eastern group of provinces.
20 Major-General Ironsi had to issue a statement to dispel rumours that he was dead in June. See *West Africa*, 11 June 1966, p. 9.
21 Dudley, pp. 134-43.
22 Gowon intimated in a 4 August broadcast that in order to involve civilians in the search for a solution to the political and constitutional crisis, 'leaders of thought' had met in the various regions and delegates were selected to represent their regions in the Lagos talks.
23 The Western and Lagos delegates adopted a common stance.
24 The negotiations at the Ad Hoc Conference are well analysed by Dudley, ch. 7.
25 The Constitution (Suspension and Modification) (No. 9) Decree 1966. Supplement to Official Gazette Extraordinary No. 85, Vol. 53, 1 September 1966 – Part A.
26 See for example, S. K. Panter-Brick, 'From Military Coup to Civil War, January 1966 to May 1967' in his *Nigerian Politics and Military Rule: Prelude to Civil War*. Also Dudley, *Instability and Political Order*.
27 States (Creation and Transitional Provisions) Decree 1967. (Decree No. 14, 1967). Supplement to Official Gazette Extraordinary No. 37, Vol. 54, 27 May 1967 – Part A.
28 For a discussion of this programme, see, Valerie P. Bennett & A. H. M. Kirk-Greene, 'Back to the Barracks: A Decade of Marking Time' in S. K. Panter-Brick (ed.), *Soldiers and Oil: The Political Transformation of Nigeria*, pp. 13-26.
29 *The Nigerian Observer*, 23 May 1974, p. 17.
30 Dr Nnamdi Azikiwe delivered the Samuel Jereton Mariere Inaugural Lecture entitled 'Stability in Nigeria after Military Rule: An Analysis of Political Theory' at the University of Lagos on 27 October 1972. For the full text, see *Democracy With Military Vigilance* (Nsukka: African Book Company Ltd, 1974).
31 *The Renaissance* (Enugu) 1 April 1974.
32 See for example the text of the interview granted by Brigadier Ogbemudia published by the *New Nigerian* 22 March 1974.

33 These are discussed in: (i) Ian Campbell, 'Army Reorganisation and Military Withdrawal' in S. K. Panter-Brick (ed.), *Soldiers and Oil*; (ii) Oyeleye Oyediran & Alex Gboyega, 'The Nigerian Political Scene, 1975' in O. Oyediran (ed.), *Annual Survey of Nigerian Affairs* (Oxford University Press, for the Nigerian Institute of International Affairs, forthcoming).

34 See *A Time for Action*, a chronological presentation of General Murtala Mohammed's speeches as head of state (Lagos: Ministry of Information, 1976), pp. 30-32.

35 Chief Awolowo who was also chosen as a member declined to serve.

36 E. Osagie and B. Onimode, 'Economic Interpretation of the Draft Constitution', unpublished seminar paper presented at the Department of Political Science, University of Ibadan, on 8 November 1976.

37 Federal Republic of Nigeria, *Report of the Constitution Drafting Committee Containing the Draft Constitution* Vol. I (Lagos: Federal Ministry of Information, 1976), pp. xli-xliii.

38 *Ibid.*

39 The draft constitution has been carefully analysed by S. K. Panter-Brick in 'The Constitution Drafting Committee' in his *Soldiers and Oil*, pp. 291-350.

40 See *West Africa*, 12 September 1977, pp. 1857 and 1859 for the election results.

41 Only one woman, Mrs Akinrinade, won election (in Oyo State) while four of the nominated members were also women.

42 Draft constitution, para. 7.1-3 and 7.1-4 p. xxix.

43 Panter-Brick, *Soldiers and Oil*, p. 312.

44 The *Nigerian Tribune*, 13 December 1977, p. 9.

45 The attractions of United States institutions began much earlier; at the political level, as far back as 1973 the Western State of Nigeria had opted for the American council manager model in preference to the British model.

46 Constitution of the Federal Republic of Nigeria (Enactment) Decree 1978 (Decree No. 25 1978). Official Gazette Extraordinary Vol. 65, No. 43, 30 September 1978, Chapter VI, Part I. Subsequent references to the constitution will be to relevant sections or chapters of this decree.

47 Section 63.

48 Chapter III.

49 Section 157.

50 Sections 196(2) and 198(1)-(2).

51 Section 211.

52 Section 144.

53 Chapter V and Section 264.

54 The options of Hausa, Ibo and Yoruba when facilities permit is one of the reference alterations to the constitution by the Supreme Military Council. For a full list and reasons for the changes, see the *Daily Times*, 22 September 1978, pp. 11 and 24.

55 Chapter VII.

56 The number quoted varies from eighty-three to ninety-three, ninety-two being preferred because it is often repeated. See the following newspapers for more details of this controversy: *New Nigerian*, 2/12/77, 7/4/78, 11/4/78; *Nigerian Tribune*, 30/12/77; *The Punch*, 5/4/78; 7/4/78; *Daily Times*, 6/4/78, 7/4/78; *Nigerian Herald*, 7/6/78.

57 For the full text of the speech, see the *Daily Star*, 21 April 1978, p. 19.

58 *Nigerian Herald*, 7 June 1978, p. 1.

59 See the *Daily Sketch*, 2 June 1978.

60 *Daily Times*, 22 September 1978.

61 See the *Nigerian Tribune*, 22 June 1978, p. 1.
62 The Government had proposed to the Constituent Assembly to embody the Nigerian Security Organisation in the constitution and had been rebuffed.
63 See section 7, and Fourth Schedule to the constitution.
64 Dr Obi Wali. See the *Nigerian Tide*, 19 December 1977, p. 9.

Chapter 13

1 S. E. Finer, *The Man on Horseback: The Role of the Military in Politics* (London: Pall Mall Press, 1962).
2 Henry Bienen and Martin Fitton, 'Soldiers, Politicians and Civil Servants' in S. K. Panter-Brick (ed.), *Soldiers and Oil: The Political Transformation of Nigeria*, p. 27.
3 B. J. Dudley, *Politics and Crisis in Nigeria* (Ibadan: Ibadan University Press, 1973), pp. 118-19.
4 A. H. M. Kirk-Greene, *Crisis and Conflict in Nigeria: A Documentary Source Book, 1966-1970*, pp. 133-4.
5 *Ibid.*, p. 147.
6 *Ibid.*, p. 149.
7 *New Nigerian*, 18 February 1966.
8 Martin Dent, 'The Military and Politicians' in S. K. Panter-Brick (ed.), *Nigerian Politics and Military Rule: Prelude to Civil War*, p. 78.
9 Kirk-Greene, p. 185.
10 *Ibid.*, p. 185.
11 Dudley, p. 119.
12 *New Nigerian*, 2 March 1966. See chapter 11 for the membership and terms of reference of these study groups (*Editor*).
13 Dudley, p. 122.
14 *New Nigerian*, 19 February 1966.
15 *Daily Times*, 4 August 1966 and 5 August 1966.
16 *New Nigerian*, 29 July 1966.
17 *Daily Times*, 5 July 1967. See chapter 2 for further details on this (*Editor*).
18 *West Africa*, 27 July 1968.
19 *West Africa*, 11 January 1969.
20 See the chapters on the civil service (*Editor*).
21 *Daily Times*, 1 August 1975.
22 *Ibid.*
23 *Daily Times*, 6 August 1975.
24 *New Nigerian*, 25 August 1975.
25 Dent in *Nigerian Politics and Military Rule*, p. 119.
26 *New Nigeria*, 2 October 1975.
27 Out of the forty-nine members, about eleven were well known politicians. *Reports of the Constitution Drafting Committee*, vol. II (Lagos: Federal Ministry of Information, 1976), pp. 5-7.
28 *New Nigerian*, 15 July 1978.
29 *New Nigerian*, 2 August 1978.
30 *New Nigerian*, 12 September 1978.
31 *New Nigerian*, 15 September 1978.
32 *New Nigerian*, 16 September 1978.
33 *New Nigerian*, 18 September 1978.

34 *New Nigerian*, 20 September 1978.
35 *New Nigerian*, 18 August 1978.
36 *New Nigerian*, 25 September 1978.
37 *Daily Times*, 30 November 1978.
38 *New Nigerian*, 23 August 1978.
39 *Daily Times*, 23 November 1978.
40 *New Nigerian*, 26 September 1978.
41 Electoral Decree No. 73 of 1977.
42 *New Nigerian*, 15 November 1978.

Chapter 14

1 Lucian W. Pye, 'Armies in the Process of Political Modernisation' in John J. Johnson (ed.), *The Role of the Military in Under-Developed Countries* (Princeton: Princeton University Press, 1962), pp. 69-89.
2 Professor Eme Awa, 'University Staff: A Special Class in Political System', *Daily Times,* 13 January 1979, p. 7.
3 Samuel P. Huntington, *Political Order in Changing Societies* (New Haven: Yale University Press, 1969), p. 221 (paperback edition). As Huntington puts it: 'In the world of oligarchy, the soldier is a radical; in the middle class world he is a participant and arbiter; as the mass society looms on the horizon he becomes the conservative guardian of the existing order.'
4 In a radio interview on the Broadcasting Corporation of Oyo State on 17 December 1978, Dr Nnamdi Azikiwe said that one of the reasons he returned to partisan politics is to forestall the return of the military after 1979. Professor Chike Obi, in the same medium and on the same day, forecast that the military would return within eighteen months. See also *The Punch*, 26 January 1979, where Godwin Daboh, of the Tarka-Daboh scandal during the last year of the Gowon regime, was alleged to have advised the federal military government to draw up a contingency plan to return to power.
5 See *Proceedings of the Constitutent Assembly*, Official Report vol. II, 9 January-21 March 1978 (Lagos: Federal Ministry of Information, 1978), pp. 1457-73.
6 *The Constitution of the Federal Republic of Nigeria*, 1979, chapter 1, part 1, section 1 (2).
7 Oyeleye Oyediran, 'Executive, Legislative and Judicial Leadership in Nigeria' s Proposed Government', *The Nigerian Accountant*, forthcoming.
8 *New Nigerian*, 10 January 1979, p. 7.
9 *Ibid.*
10 Section 8, subsection 1 of the 1979 constitution.
11 Oyediran.
12 See Electoral Decree 1977 (Decree No. 73 of 1977) as amended by Decree No. 32 of 1978.
13 See chapter 13 for more details on the five political parties.
14 *Daily Times, New Nigerian, The Punch*, 18 January 1979, front page.
15 It is General Obasanjo's view, however, that 'what determines whether the military remains or does not remain in the barracks is not the doing of the military itself. It is the doing of the political leaders and sometimes coupled with the system.' See *Daily Times*, 2 February 1979.

Select Bibliography

Each chapter has a good number of references. This selected bibliography is therefore to be used along with these references. But these two sources do not by any means give a complete listing of all material on each particular subject. For more comprehensive material interested readers should consult *Nigerian Publications, 1950-70* (Ibadan: Ibadan University Press, 1977).

Background to military rule and the civil war

1 Okoi Arikpo, *The Development of Modern Nigeria* (London: Penguin, 1967).

2 James Coleman, *Nigeria: Background to Nationalism* (Berkeley and Los Angeles: University of California Press, 1958).

3 B. J. Dudley, *Parties and Politics in Northern Nigeria* (London: Frank Cass, 1968).

4 B. J. Dudley, *Instability and Political Order* (Ibadan: University of Ibadan Press, 1974).

5 Ruth First, *Power in Africa* (New York: Pantheon Books, 1970).

6 A. H. M. Kirk-Greene, *Crisis and Conflict in Nigeria: A Documentary Sourcebook, 1966-1970* (London: Oxford University Press, 1971), vols. I and II.

7 John P. Mackintosh, *Nigerian Government and Politics* (Evanston: Northwestern University Press, 1966).

8 James O'Connell, 'Inevitability of Instability', *Journal of Modern African Studies*, 5, 2 (September 1967).

9 S. K. Panter-Brick (ed.), *Nigerian Politics and Military Rule: Prelude to Civil War* (London: The Athlone Press, 1970).

10 F. A. O. Schwarz Jr, *Nigeria: The Tribes, the Nation or the Race* (Cambridge: Massachusetts Institute of Technology Press, 1965).

11 A. R. Zolberg, *Creating Political Order: Party States of West Africa* (Chicago: Rand Mcnally, 1966).

The Nigerian military

1 J. 'Bayo Adekson, 'Military Organisation in Multi-Ethnically Segmented Societies: A Theoretical Study with Reference to Three Sub-Saharan African Cases'. Unpublished Ph.D. thesis, Brandeis University, Waltham, USA (1976).

2 J. 'Bayo Adekson, 'The Nigerian Military and Social Expenditures' in *Democracy in Nigeria: Past, Present and Future* (Proceedings of the 5th Annual Conference of the Nigerian Political Science Association, 1978).
3 A. A. Ayida, *The Nigerian Revolution* (Ibadan: Nigerian Economic Society, 1973).
4 Leo Dare, 'Military Leadership and Political Development in the Western State of Nigeria'. Unpublished Ph.D. (thesis, Carleton University (1972).
5 Samuel Decalo, 'Military Coups of Military Regimes in Africa', *Journal of Modern African Studies*, II, 1, (1973).
6 Edward Feit, 'Military Coups and Political Development: Some Lessons from Ghana and Nigeria', *World Politics*, 20, 2 (January 1968).
7 Robin Luckham, *The Nigerian Military 1960-1967* (Cambridge: Cambridge University Press, 1971).
8 N. J. Miners, *The Nigerian Army, 1956-1966* (London: Methuen, 1971).
9 Oyeleye Oyediran (ed.), *Survey of Nigerian Affairs, 1975* (Ibadan: Oxford University Press for the Nigerian Institute of International Affairs, 1979).
10 S. K. Panter-Brick (ed.), *Soldiers and Oil: The Political Transformation of Nigeria* (London: Frank Cass, 1978).
11 Margaret Peil, 'A Civilian Appraisal of Military Rule in Nigeria' *Armed Forces and Society*, 2, I (Fall 1975).

The economy

1 O. Aboyade, 'The Economy of Nigeria' in P. Robson and D. Lury (eds.), *The Economics of Africa* (London: George Allen and Unwin 1969).
2 C. K. Eicher and C. Liedholm, *Growth and Development of the Nigerian Economy* (Michigan State University Press, 1970).
3 A. Ayida and H. Onitiri, *Reconstruction and Development in Nigeria*, NISER (1971).
4 World Bank, *Nigeria: Options for Long-Term Development* (Baltimore: The Johns Hopkins University Press, 1974).
5 World Bank, Nigeria: Economic Memorandum Report No. 1235–UNI (1976).
6 International Monetary Fund, *Surveys of African Economics*, vol. 6 (Washington: 1975).
7 S. B. Falegan, 'Trends in Nigeria's Balance of Payments and Policy Measures for Self-Reliance' presented at the NISER Workshop on Trade towards Self-Sufficiency and Self-Reliance in the Nigerian Economy, Ibadan (1978).
8 Federal Ministry of Finance, 'Declining Government Revenue and Measures for Mobilization of Internal Resources for Economic Development and Self-Reliance' presented at the NISER Workshop on Self-Sufficiency, Ibadan (1978).
9 Federal Government of Nigeria, *First, Second and Third National Development Plans* (Lagos: 1962, 1970 and 1975).
10 Central Bank of Nigeria, *Annual Report and Statement of Accounts* 1960 to 1976.
11 Central Bank of Nigeria, *Economic and Financial Review*.
12 Federal Office of Statistics, *National Accounts of Nigeria 1960/61-1975/76* (1978).
13 Federal Office of Statistics, *Economic Indicators*.
14 O. Aboyade and A. Ayida, 'The War Economy in Perspective', *Nigerian Journal of Economic and Social Studies*, 13, 1 (1971).

15 Nigerian Economic Society, 'Nigeria's Indigenisation Policy', proceedings of 1974 Symposium organised by the NES on the subject – Indigenisation: What have we achieved? (1974).
16 M. Kaldor, 'The Military in Development', *World Development*, 4, 6 (1976).
17 B. J. Dudley, 'The Military and Development', *Nigerian Journal of Economic and Social Studies*, 13, 2 (1971).
18 J. 'Bayo Adekson, 'On the Theory of the Modernising Soldier' in *Current Research on Peace and Violence*, 1, 1 (1978).
19 J. 'Bayo Adekson, 'The Nigerian Military and Social Expenditures' in *Democracy in Nigeria: Past, Present and Future* (Proceedings of the 5th Annual Conference of the Nigerian Political Science Association, 1978).
20 G. Kennedy, *The Economics of Defence* (London: Faber and Faber, 1975).
21 A. Iwayemi, 'Public Sector Participation in Economic Activity – The Electric
22 P. Collins, 'The Policy of Indigenisation: An Overall View', *Quarterly Journal of Administration,* IX, 2 (1975).
23 M. O. Ojo, 'Food Supply in Nigeria 1960-1975', Central Bank of Nigeria: *Economic and Financial Review*, 15, 2 (1977).
24 G. K. Helleiner, *Peasant Agriculture Government and Economic Growth in Nigeria* (Illinois: Richard Irwin Inc., 1966).
25 A. Morgan *et al., Report of the Commission on Review of Wages, Salary and Conditions of Service of Junior Employees of the Governments of the Federation and in the Private Establishments 1963-64*. (Lagos: Federal Ministry of Information, 1964).
26 F. I. Adesanoye, 'Nigerian Defence Policy', Lecture to the Second Senior Officers Course, Army Command and Staff College, Jaji (1977).
27 G. Kennedy, *The Economics of Defence* (London: Faber and Faber, 1975).

The civil service and local government

1 Ladipo Adamolekun, and E. A. Gboyega (eds.), *Leading Issues in Nigerian Public Service* (Ile-Ife: Ife University Press, forthcoming).
2 E. A. Gboyega, 'Local Government and Political Integration in the Western State 1952-1972'. Unpublished Ph.D. thesis, Department of Political Science, University of Ibadan (1975).
3 Samuel Humes, 'Local Government', *Quarterly Journal of Administration*, V, 1 (October 1970).
4 Emmanuel Osuji, 'Community Development and Political Development in the East Central State of Nigeria'. Unpublished Ph.D. thesis, Department of Political Science, University of Ibadan (1975).
5 Oyeleye Oyediran, 'In Search of Power Structure in a Nigerian Community', *The Nigerian Journal of Economic and Social Studies*, 14, 2, (1972).
6 Oyeleye Oyediran, 'Local Government in Southern Nigeria: The Direction of Change', *The African Review*, 4, 4 (1974).
7 Oyeleye Oyediran, 'Council Manager Plan: The Experience of Western Nigeria', *Philippine Journal of Administration* XXI (forthcoming).
8 Oyeleye Oyediran, 'Participation in the Nigerian 1976 Local Government Election', *The Nigerian Journal of Economic and Social Studies*, 19, 1, (March 1977).
9 *Quarterly Journal of Administration*, X, 2 (Special Issue on Federalism and State Administration, January 1976).
10 C. S. Whitaker Jr, *The Politics of Tradition: Continuity and Change in Northern Nigeria, 1946-1966* (Princeton: Princeton University Press, 1970).

11 Ronald Wraith, *Local Administration in West Africa* (London: George Allen and Unwin, 1972).

12 Ali Yahaya, 'Enhancing Local Government Performance: Udoji Recipe', *Journal of Public Affairs*, vol. v (May/October 1975).

Foreign policy

1 S. O. Adebo, 'The Foreign Policy of Nigeria: A Professional Diplomat's View', *Nigerian Opinion*, 4, 2 and 3 (February and March 1968).

2 R. A. Akindele, 'Nigeria's Foreign Relations: Elite Attitudes and Government Policy', *International Problems* vol. 12 (June 1973).

3 R. A. Akindele, 'The Conduct of Nigeria's Foreign Relations', *International Problems*, vol. 12 (October 1973).

4 A. B. Akinyemi, 'The Military Foreign Policy – One Step Forward, Two Steps Backwards', *Nigerian Opinion*, 8, 6-8 (June-August 1972).

5 A. B. Akinyemi, *Foreign Policy and Federalism: The Nigerian Experience* (Ibadan: University of Ibadan Press, 1974).

6 Olajide Aluko, 'Civil War and Nigerian Foreign Policy', *Political Quarterly*, vol. 42 (April 1971).

7 Olajide Aluko, 'Israel and Nigeria: Continuity and Change in their Relationship', *The African Review*, 4, 1 (1974).

8 Ibrahim Gambari, 'The Domestic Politics of Major Foreign Policy Issues in Nigeria'. Unpublished Ph.D. thesis, Columbia University (1974).

9 Gordan Idang, *Nigeria: Internal Politics and Foreign Policy 1960-1966* (Ibadan: University of Ibadan Press, 1973).

10 J. E. Okolo and E. W. Langley, 'The Changing Nigerian Foreign Policy', *World Affairs*, vol. 135 (Spring 1973).

11 Okon Udokang, 'Economic Community of West African States: Theoretical and Practical Problems of Integration', *Nigerian Journal of International Studies*, 2, 1 (April 1978).

Appendix
Constitution of the Federal Republic of Nigeria

Section 4

Second schedule

Legislative Powers

Part I Exclusive legislative list

Item

1 Accounts of the Government of the Federation, and of offices, courts and authorities thereof, including audit of those accounts.

2 Aviation, including airports, safety of aircraft and carriage of passengers and goods by air.

3 Arms, ammunition and explosives.

4 Bankruptcy and insolvency.

5 Banks, banking, bills of exchange and promissory notes.

6 Borrowing of moneys within or outside Nigeria for the purposes of the Federation or of any State.

7 Census, including the establishment and maintenance of machinery for continuous and universal registration of births and deaths throughout Nigeria.

8 Construction, alteration and maintenance of such roads as may be declared by the National Assembly to be Federal trunk roads.

9 Citizenship, naturalisation and aliens.

10 Commercial and industrial monopolies, combines and trusts.

11 Control of capital issues.

12 Copyright.

13 Currency, coinage and legal tender.

14 Customs and excise duties.

15 Defence.

16 Deportation of persons who are not citizens of Nigeria.

17 Diplomatic, consular and trade representation.

18 Drugs and poisons.

19 Designation of securities in which trust funds may be invested.

20 Election to the offices of President and Vice-President or Governor and Deputy Governor and any other office to which a person may be elected under this Constitution, excluding election to a local government council or any office in such council.

21 Export duties.

22 Evidence.

23 Exchange control.

24 External affairs.

25 Extradition.

26 Fingerprints, identification and criminal records.

27 Fishing and fisheries other than fishing and fisheries in rivers, lakes, waterways, ponds and other inland waters within Nigeria.

28 Immigration into and emigration from Nigeria.

29 Implementation of treaties relating to matters on this List.

30 Incorporation, regulation and winding up of bodies corporate, other than co-operative societies, local government councils and bodies corporate established directly by any Law enacted by a House of Assembly of a State.

31 Insurance.

32 Labour, including trade unions, industrial relations; conditions, safety and welfare of labour; industrial disputes; prescribing a national minimum wage for the Federation or any part thereof; and industrial artibtrations.

33 Legal proceedings between Governments of States or between the Government of the Federation and Government of any State or any other authority or person.

34 Maritime shipping and navigation, including—

(a) shipping and navigation on tidal waters;

(b) shipping and navigation on the River Niger and its affluents and on any such other inland waterways as may be designated by the National Assembly to be an international waterway or to be an inter-State waterway;

(c) lighthouses, lightships, beacons and other provisions for the safety of shipping and navigation;

(d) such ports as may be declared by the National Assembly to be Federal ports (including the constitution and powers of port authorities for Federal ports).

35 Meterology.

36 Mines and minerals, including oil fields, oil mining, geological surveys and natural gas.

37 National parks being such areas in a State as may with the consent of the Government of that State be designated by the National Assembly as national parks.

38 Naval, military and air forces including any other branch of the armed forces of the Federation.

39 Nuclear energy.

40 Passports and visas.

41 Patents, trade marks, trade or business names, industrial designs and merchandise marks.

42 Pensions, gratuities and other like benefits payable out of the Consolidated Revenue Fund or any other public funds of the Federation.

43 Police.

44 Posts, telegraphs and telephones.

45 Powers of the National Assembly, and the privileges and immunities of its members.

46 Prisons.

47 Professional occupations as may be designated by the National Assembly.

48 Public debt of the Federation.

49 Public relations of the Federation.

50 Public service of the Federation including the settlement of disputes between the Federation and officers of such service.

51 Quarantine.

52 Railways.

53 Regulation of political parties.

54 Service and execution in a State of the civil and criminal processes, judgments, decrees, orders and other decisions of any court of law outside Nigeria or any court of law in Nigeria other than a court of law established by the House of Assembly of that State.

55 Stamp duties.

56 Taxation of incomes, profits and captial gains, except as otherwise prescribed by this Constitution.

57 The establishment and regulation of authorities for the Federation or any part thereof–

(a) to promote and enforce the observance of the fundamental objectives and directive principles contained in this Constitution;

(b) to identify, collect, preserve or generally look after ancient and historical monuments and records and archaeological sites and remains declared by the National Assembly to be of national significance or national importance;

(c) to administer museums and libraries other than museums and libraries established by the Government of a State;

(d) to regulate tourist traffic; and

(e) to prescribe minimum standards of education at all levels.

58 The formation, annulment and dissolution of marriages other than marriages under Islamic law and customary law including matrimonial causes relating thereto.

59 Trade and commerce, and in particular–

(a) trade and commerce between Nigeria and other countries including import of commodities into and export of commodities from Nigeria, and trade and commerce between the States;

(b) establishment of a purchasing authority with power to acquire for export or sale in world markets such agricultural produce as may be designated by the National Assembly;

(c) inspection of produce to be exported from Nigeria and the enforcement of grades and standards of quality in respect of produce so inspected;

(d) establishment of a body to prescribe and enforce standards of goods and commodities offered for sale;

(e) control of the prices of goods and commodities designated by the National Assembly as essential goods or commodities; and

(f) registration of business names.

60 Traffice on Federal trunk roads.

61 Trigonometrical, cadastral and topographical surveys.

62 Water from such sources as may be declared by the National Assembly to be sources affecting more than one State.

63 Weights and measures.

64 Wireless, broadcasting and television other than broadcasting and television provided by the Government of a State; allocation of wave-lengths for wireless, broadcasting and television transmission.

65 Any other matter with respect to which the National Assembly has power to make laws in accordance with the provisions of this Constitution.

66 Any matter incidental or supplementary to any matter mentioned elsewhere in this list.

Section 4

Part II Concurrent legislative list

Item	*Extent of Federal and State Legislative Powers*
A—Allocation of revenue, etc.	1 Subject to the provisions of this Constitution, the National Assembly may by an Act make provisions for— (a) the division of public revenue— (i) between the Federation and the States, (ii) among the States of the Federation, (iii) between the States and local government councils, (iv) among the local government councils in the States; and (b) grants or loans from and the imposition of charges upon the Consolidated Revenue Fund or any other public funds of the Federation or for the imposition of charges upon the revenue and assets of the Federation for any purpose notwithstanding that it relates to a matter with respect to which the National Assembly is empowered to make laws.
	2 Subject to the provisions of this Constitution, any House of Assembly may make provisions for grants or loans from and the imposition of charges upon any of the public funds of that State or the imposition of charges upon the revenue and assets of that State for any purpose notwithstanding that it relates to a matter with respect to which the National Assembly is empowered to make laws.
B—Antiquities and monuments.	3 The National Assembly may make laws for the Federation or any part thereof with respect to such antiquities

and monuments as may, with the consent of the State in which such antiquities and monuments are located, be designated by the National Assembly as National Antiquities or National Monuments, but nothing in this paragraph shall preclude a House of Assembly from making Laws for the State or any part thereof with respect to antiquities and monuments not so designated in accordance with the foregoing provisions.

C–Archives.

4 The National Assembly may make laws for the Federation or any part thereof with respect to the archives and public records of the Federation.

5 A House of Assembly may, subject to paragraph 4 hereof, make Laws for that State or any part thereof with respect to archives and public records of the Government of the State.

6 Nothing in paragraphs 4 and 5 hereof shall be construed as enabling any laws to be made which do not preserve the archives and records which are in existence at the date of commencement of this Constitution, and which are kept by authorities empowered to do so in part of the Federation.

D–Collection of taxes.

7 In the exercise of its powers to impose any tax or duty on–

(a) capital gains, incomes or profits of persons other than companies; and

(b) documents or transactions by way of stamp duties,

the National Assembly may, subject to such conditions as it may prescribe provide that the collection of any such tax or duty or the administration of the law imposing it shall be carried out by the Government of a State or other authority of a State.

8 Where an Act of the National Assembly provides for the collection of tax or duty on capital gains, incomes or profit or the administration of any law by an authority of a State in accordance with paragraph 7 hereof, it shall regulate the liability of persons to such tax or duty in such manner as to ensure that such tax or duty is not levied on the same person by more than one State.

9 A House of Assembly may, subject to such conditions as it may prescribe, make provisions for the collection of any tax, fee or rate or for the administration of the Law providing for such collection by a local government council.

10 Where a Law of a House of Assembly provides for the collection of tax, fee or rate or for the administration of such Law by a local government council in accordance

with the Provisions hereof it shall regulate the liability of persons to the tax, fee or rate in such manner as to ensure that such tax, fee or rate is not levied on the same person in respect of the same liability by more than one local government council.

E—Electoral law.

11 The National Assembly may make laws for the Federation with respect to the registration of voters and the procedure regulating elections to a local government council.

12 Nothing in paragraph 11 hereof shall preclude a House of Assembly from making Laws with respect to elections to a local government council in addition to but not inconsistent with any law made by the National Assembly.

F—Electric power.

13 The National Assembly may make laws for the Federation or any part thereof with respect to—

(a) electricity and the establishment of electrical power stations;

(b) the generation and transmission of electricity in or to any part of the Federation and from one State to another State;

(c) the regulation of the right of any person or authority to dam up or otherwise interfere with the flow of water from sources in any part of the Federation;

(d) the participation of the Federation in any arrangement with another country for the generation, transmission and distribution of electricity for any area partly outside the Federation; and

(e) the promotion and the establishment of a national grid system.

14 A House of Assembly may make Laws for the State with respect to—

(a) electricity and the establishment in that State of electric power stations;

(b) the generation, transmission and distribution of electricity within that State;

(c) the regulation of the right of any person or authority (other than the Government of the Federation or its agency) to use, work or operate any plant, apparatus, equipment or work designed for the supply or use of electrical energy;

(d) the establishment within that State of any authority for the promotion and management of electric power stations established by the State; and

(e) the participation by that State in any arrangement with one or more States of the Federation to set up an agency to direct the operation of a combined transmission or distribution system for any area over which those States have power to make Laws.

15 In the foregoing provisions of this item, unless the context otherwise requires, the following expressions have the meanings respectively assigned to them—

'distribution' means the supply of electricity from a sub-station to the ultimate consumer;

'management' includes maintenance, repairs or replacement;

'power station' means an assembly of plant or equipment for the creation or generation of electrical energy; and

'transmission' means the supply of electricity from a power station to a sub-station or from one sub-station to another sub-station, and the reference to a 'sub-station' herein is a reference to an assembly of plant, machinery or equipment for distribution of electricity.

G—Exhibition of cinematograph films.

16 The National Assembly may make laws for the establishment of an authority with power to carry out censorship of cinematograph films and to prohibit or restrict the exhibition of such films; and nothing herein shall—

(a) preclude a House of Assembly from making provision for a similar authority for that State; or

(b) authorise the exhibition of a cinematograph film in a State without the sanction of the authority established by the Law of that State for the censorship of such films.

H—Industrial, commercial or agricultural development.

17 The National Assembly may make laws for the Federation or any part thereof with respect to—

(a) the health, safety and welfare of persons employed to work in factories, offices or other premises or in inter-State transportation and commerce including the training, supervision and qualification of such persons;

(b) the regulation of ownership and control of business enterprises throughout the Federation for the purpose of promoting, encouraging or facilitating such ownership and control by citizens of Nigeria;

(c) the establishment of research centres for agricultural studies; and

(d) the establishment of institutions and bodies for the promotion or financing of industrial commercial or agricultural projects.

18 Subject to the provisions of this Constitution a House of Assembly may make Laws for that State with respect to industrial, commercial or agricultural development of the State.

19 Nothing in the foregoing paragraphs of this item shall be

construed as precluding a House of Assembly from making Laws with respect to any of the matters referred to in the foregoing paragaphs.

20 For the purposes of the foregoing paragraphs of this item, the word 'agricultural' includes fishery.

I—Scientific and technological research.

21 The National Assembly may make laws to regulate or co-ordinate scientific and technological research throughout the Federation.

22 Nothing herein shall preclude a House of Assembly from establishing or making provisions for an institution or other arrangement for the purpose of scientific and technological research.

J—Statistics.

23 The National Assembly may make laws for the Federation or any part thereof with respect to statistics so far as the subject matter relates to—

(a) any matter upon which the National Assembly has power to make laws; and

(b) the organisation of a co-ordinated scheme of statistics for the Federation or any part thereof on any matter whether or not it has power to make laws with respect thereto.

24 A House of Assembly may make Laws for the State with respect to statistics and on any matter other than that referred to in paragraph 23 (a) of this item.

K—University, technological and post-primary education.

25 The National Assembly shall have power to make laws for the Federation or any part thereof with respect to university education, technological education or such professional education as may from time to time be designated by the National Assembly.

26 The power conferred on the National Assembly under paragraph 25 of this item shall include power to establish an institution for the purposes of university, post-primary, technological or professional education.

27 Subject as herein provided a House of Assembly shall have power to make Laws for the State with respect to the establishment of an institution for purposes of university, professional or technological education.

28 Nothing in the foregoing paragraphs of this item shall be construed so as to limit the powers of a House of Assembly to make Laws for the State with respect to technical, vocational, post-primary, primary or other forms of education, including the establishment of institutions for the pursuit of such education.

Part III Supplemental and interpretation

1 Where by this Schedule the National Assembly is required to designate any matter or thing or to make any declaration, it may do so either by an Act of the National Assembly or by a resolution passed by both Houses of the National Assembly.

2 In this Schedule, references to incidental and supplementary matters include, without prejudice to their generality, references to—

(a) offences;

(b) the jurisdiction, powers, practice and procedure of courts of law; and

(c) the acquisition and tenure of land.